Advance Praise for *Writ*

"Barbato and Furlich are superb—a dynamic development duo! They have finally managed to demystify the purpose and process of development writing. Newcomers and seasoned professionals alike can benefit from their candor and the behind-the-scenes insights found in *Writing for a Good Cause*."

—Betty J. Marmon, Director of Development, Philadelphia Museum of Art

"How do you convince an individual or organization not only to feel comfortable or good donating to your cause—but eager to do it? *Writing for a Good Cause* shows you the essential communication and human steps that lead to this goal."

—Allan Luks, Executive Director, Big Brothers/Big Sisters of New York City

"A rare find—filled with winning strategies, practical ideas and clear examples. I am recommending it to my entire staff."

—Peggy Dean Glenn, Associate Dean for External Affairs, Nicholas School of the Environment, Duke University

"This book is packed with gems about what's at the heart of fundraising—sincerity, humor, perseverance. It should be required reading for anyone entering this field."

—Eric Graham, President and CEO, Children's Express Worldwide

"Told from the trenches in a very entertaining style, *Writing for a Good Cause* is a terrific resource for fundraising veterans and newcomers. I laughed out loud reading it! For those of us who spend every day working to make the world a better place, this guide will help make your proposals stand out."

—Sheila Dennis, Director of Development, Union of Concerned Scientists

[illegible] for [illegible] for a Good Cause

[illegible]

WRITING FOR A GOOD CAUSE

The Complete Guide to Crafting Proposals and Other Persuasive Pieces for Nonprofits

Joseph Barbato
and Danielle S. Furlich

A Fireside Book
Published by Simon & Schuster
New York London Toronto Sydney

FIRESIDE
Rockefeller Center
1230 Avenue of the Americas
New York, NY 10020

Designed by William P. Ruoto

Manufactured in the United States of America

10

Library of Congress Cataloging-in-Publication Data
Barbato, Joseph.
Writing for a good cause: the complete guide to crafting proposals and other persuasive pieces for nonprofits / Joseph Barbato and Danielle S. Furlich.
p. cm.
"A Fireside book."
1. Proposal writing in human services—United States. I. Furlich, Danielle S. (Danielle Shirley). II. Title.

HV41.9.U5B37 2000
658.15'224—dc21

00-025248

ISBN-13: 978-0-684-85740-4 (trade pbk.)
ISBN-10: 0-684-85740-5 (trade pbk.)

ACKNOWLEDGMENTS

We are grateful for the assistance and resources of the National Society of Fund Raising Executives (NSFRE), the Foundation Center, and the Council for the Advancement and Support of Education (CASE). In particular, we thank Rita Keener and Samantha Phillips at the NSFRE Resource Center, who made us feel right at home even as we ransacked their shelves.

Friends and former colleagues at The Nature Conservancy have helped, inspired, and even read the book in manuscript. They include Tracey Bedford, Beth Duris, Connie Gelb, Lisa Horak, and Patty Housman. Others who generously took time to read parts or all of the work in progress were Louise Barbato, Sheila Dennis, and Carma Fauntleroy.

We are indebted to the myriad foundation executives, development officers, and writers who took time to talk with us and send us their comments about proposals and the craft of writing.

Joe would like to thank his wife, Dusty, for her love and encouragement. He also expresses gratitude to two wise men: Fred English, who taught him to maintain high editorial standards, and Paul Eckhardt, who taught him to maintain his sense of humor. Both knew what matters in fund-raising writing.

Danielle would like to thank her parents, James Shirley and Beatrice Zanger, who never balked at launching yet another English major into the world. She gratefully acknowledges the many fund raisers and writers who showed her the ropes, especially Sally Wells, who taught her to get to the point.

We are both indebted to our agent, Deborah Grosvenor, and to our editor, Marah Stets, for their enthusiasm and support. Without them, we could not have had all this fun playing Butch Cassidy and the Sundance Kid. Cheers!

We would like to acknowledge the following individuals and organizations that allowed us to share portions of their fund-raising and writing materials, including:

D.S. Pensley, chief executive officer of Borealis Community Land Trust and echoing green Public Service Fellow
Kim Coleman, president of Expanding Horizons
Public School Forum of North Carolina
Hill and Vale Affordable Housing
Dartmouth Life and Julie Sloane
The Nature Conservancy
Yale University
Diane Ullius
American Farmland Trust
The Virginia Engineering Foundation at the University of Virginia

For my children, Louise and Joey
—JOSEPH BARBATO

For my husband, Brandon, with thanks for his support—
moral, technical, and otherwise.
—DANIELLE S. FURLICH

It is always the writer's duty to make the world better.

—SAMUEL JOHNSON

CONTENTS

INTRODUCTION

Both of us stumbled into fund-raising writing. Danielle had done virtually no proposal writing before taking her job at The Nature Conservancy in 1994. When she sat down to write her first piece, she was terrified.

Joe wrote his first proposal years ago at New York University. He had little idea what a development office was until he joined the staff there. His boss, a Harvard graduate and friend of James Baldwin and W. H. Auden, was a gifted writer who had learned his craft in fund-raising offices at Princeton and Cornell.

Together we will use our different vantages in *Writing for a Good Cause* to help you produce more persuasive fund-raising pieces.

Most of the time, we will speak in one voice. And the first thing we want to say is this: There is no such thing as proposal writing. There are proposals, and there is writing. The same is true of case statements, brochures, and newsletters. They are all fund-raising material in different formats, and they all require solid craftsmanlike writing.

To write proposals successfully, you must know two things: what to put into a proposal and how to write well. This book addresses both matters, with the emphasis on the latter.

Why? Because you can find lots of advice elsewhere on how to determine which funders are interested in your cause, how to plan and develop a proposal for a particular program, how to work up a budget, etc. What you won't find anywhere else is how to take all that information and shape it into a knockout, beguiling, exciting, can't-put-it-down, and surely can't-turn-it-down fund-raising proposal.

Are we exaggerating? Of course. That is one of the early lessons we will teach you. Controlled hyperbole is a high art. But then we assume that, like our book, your program is worth shouting about from the rooftops. If you don't believe in it, if you don't call attention to it, why should anyone else notice or care?

But wait. Before we go any further, let's deal with an assumption that pervades most fund-raising offices. It is this: *Anyone can write.* The gobbledygook we all encounter in office memos every day gives the lie to those three words. Yet the notion that anyone can write, and presumably write well, persists. The personal computer, which allows us to move words, paragraphs, and sections any which way and to remove and add words with great ease, has given even more power to the idea that we are all writers.

Interestingly, it is an assumption made only outside the world of professional writing: Editors of newspapers and magazines and at book publishing houses are well aware that not everyone can write. Indeed, they spend each day trying to improve the writing of people who actually *can* write. Writing is their product, and they cannot publish material written by just anyone who thinks he or she can write.

Now, of course you can write. You do it all the time, and you give about as much thought to it as you do to other things you do all the time: breathing, eating, walking, watching television, driving to work. The only problem is, most of your writing is for people who know you or care greatly about what you are writing about. Your Aunt Sally is terribly interested in your family, so a run-on sentence or two or a boring paragraph won't keep her from reading your letter. And your boss really does want to know what happened during your call on an important prospect, so he or she will take the time to puzzle out your trip report.

You pay a lot more attention to your conversation when you are with someone you don't know well that you want to impress, don't you? You should. The same goes for writing that is intended to woo.

Or perhaps you know people at the Ford Foundation who care about you and your work to the same degree that Aunt Sally does. If so, congratulations! You don't need this book.

Well, you get the point. Stringing words together with an occasional period is not writing no matter how pretty it looks when it comes out of a laser printer. The people working at *Time* magazine know this; if they published the prose turned out in the typical American office, they would soon be out of business.

All of this is compounded in fund-raising offices because those doing the writing of persuasive pieces are generally neophyte writers or experienced fund raisers harried by a thousand concerns other than writing the proposal at hand. In fact, the *writing* of the proposal is deemed a necessary evil, a chore, an unfortunate task that is often put off and put off until finally the foundation deadline is upon us and— Well, let's get the thing written and out. Thank God for FedEx!

The result is delivered by ten o'clock the next morning to funding officers around the country, and it ain't pretty. Often, it is illogical, unreadable, and boring. And the typos— Well, at least they break up the tedium of stirring the mud with the eyeballs.

On the other hand, we know that some of you considered crawling under your desks as you read the above because you *know* you can't write. You just spent an hour looking at a blank computer screen. You reworked the same opening sentence 68 times. You highlighted your outline in three different colors but don't have a scrap of writing to show for it.

Worse, your colleagues have been slowly piecing together how unqualified you really are, and when they get this first draft, they'll know for sure: You are a hoax. You can't write to save your life. You are doomed.

Believe us, we've been there. And we hereby guarantee that you will not only survive but you will conquer.

What is to be done? It is time to think about how to write for a good cause. Let's take the writing itself as seriously as we hope funders will take our proposals. Let's take a deep breath and begin.

In his classes on proposal writing, Joe has found that most men and women realize they must spend more time thinking about the *writing* in proposal writing. Most have a fairly strong idea of the information that must go into a proposal. It is the *writing* that concerns them, for they are not writers.

They wonder:

- Can you give us an outline for a basic proposal? (Yes.)
- How long should my proposal be? (Long enough to secure funding.)
- How do I find time to write? (You don't find time to write. You make time to write.)
- Does my proposal have to look fancy? (Depends on who's reading it.)
- Isn't there an easy way to do this? (No.)
- What's the best advice you have? (Simplify. Simplify. Simplify.)
- What's the second-best advice you have? (Read everything you can get your hands on.)

We're going to address all of that and more in *Writing for a Good Cause*. We're going to offer the best advice we have about the experience of writing in the context of fund raising. And we are going to offer thoughts related to fund-raising writing from a wide range of people and places.

We collared colleagues—fund raisers and writers—and persuaded them to tell the stories of their work at disparate nonprofits: from the Consumer Federation of America to the Wilderness Society; from the Clarke School for the Deaf in Northampton, Massachusetts to the University of California at Davis; from Borealis Community Land Trust in Alaska to WETA, a public television and radio station serving Washington, D.C. We surveyed program officers at the 100 top foundations; we demanded hot tips from photo, design, printing, and Web site gurus; and we nearly ransacked libraries at the National Society of Fund Raising Executives and other national groups.

We also garnered advice from writers, both living and dead, ranging from Chekhov ("Take out adjectives and adverbs wherever you can") to the Pulitzer Prize–winning columnist Jonathan Yardley, who has been writing persuasively for many years and who reminded us about the string that must run from the beginning of a piece to the end: "If the string breaks, you lose the reader, " he says.

"Put the seat of the pants to the seat of the chair," Rex Stout used to say when asked how he got his writing done. He was writing Nero Wolfe mystery novels. How does that relate to your work? Plenty. *Nothing* ever got written without putting seat to seat. (Hemingway was the exception; he'd often write while standing, with his pad on the top of a refrigerator; when we become Hemingway, we will do that, too.)

We found some of our advice in unlikely places. Zen masters like Thich Nhat Hanh have much to tell us about writing. When doing the dishes, do the dishes, they tell us. When eating, eat. When writing, write!

We're looking forward to spending some time with you aimed at strengthening your writing for the finest causes in this country. We're going to learn a thing or two ourselves as we move ahead. Despite our harsh words about much that gets written, we both remain humble and a bit insecure when it comes to writing well. Writing is hard work; never let anyone tell you otherwise. The more you grow as a writer, the more you will be grateful for those moments when you get the words right.

We're going to toss in a bit of poetry now and again. We're going to show you how accomplished writers lure readers by using plain English for complex subjects. And we're going to describe at least ten wonderful things that enrich our lives every day that would not have existed if someone hadn't written a fund-raising proposal.

We will do our best to be empowering, realistic, down-to-earth, lucid, motivating, sympathetic, and amusing.

In *Writing for a Good Cause*, we'll show you how to use words well to win the support of funders.

PART 1

THE WACKY WORLD OF FUND RAISING

You don't have to know much about the nonprofit sector and the practice of fund raising to be able to write fund-raising materials. But background always helps, and it's interesting to see the wacky things people will do for a good cause. Here's an overview of the exploding world of nonprofits, the work of fund raisers, and the role of the writer.

Chapter 1

What Is Fund Raising, Anyway?

The ABCs of the Nonprofit World

Once, it was called begging. In 1641 a group of clergymen representing Harvard College went to England in search of funds. That was the beginning of fund raising in America.

Small wonder that fund raising still bears a stigma.

"Is there a seamy side to fund raising?" asked *The New York Times Magazine* in a 1997 interview with Vartan Gregorian, noted for his fund-raising successes as head of the New York Public Library and Brown University.

"Not for a good cause," said Gregorian.

The fact is, many people think it unseemly to ask other people for money—no matter what the cause. Gregorian himself noted that he has found it hard having "to please a donor by suppressing your own views," as well he might.

Fund raising is about pleasing donors. A pleased donor gives money. A displeased one does not.

The donor is always right.

If all of this is so, why do people become fund raisers and fund-raising writers? It lies in the satisfaction of having helped bring money to a good cause.

Fund raising has given us literacy, open-heart surgery, Ronald McDonald House, churches to go to on Sunday, public-radio programming, and a restored Statue of Liberty and Ellis Island. It has saved lives, built monuments, cured diseases, fostered artistic careers, nurtured children, advanced scholarship, discovered planets, conserved natural areas, and encouraged social change.

The Council on Foundations once listed the foundation-funded projects that ultimately touched the lives of most Americans. They found that foundation money jump-started Emergency 911, public libraries, the Pap smear, Sesame Street, vaccines against yellow fever and polio, the invention of rocketry, the hospice movement, and the white lines on the shoulders of highways.

Because people have been begging on its behalf since 1641, Harvard is now one of the preeminent universities in the nation and the world. Did money make it so? Yep. If Harvard had much less money, would it make a difference? Yep.

Here is the rule of thumb: Money attracts excellence, and excellence attracts excellence. At universities, this means money attracts an excellent faculty, who in turn attract excellent students. With a 1998 endowment of about $13 billion, Harvard can afford excellence. Period.

And they are still begging! Harvard employs 271 men and women on its fund-raising staff for its current $2.1 billion fund-raising campaign. Why so many? After all, you might think that as some have said, "Any fool can raise money for Harvard, and many do." Yet even a cash cow has to be milked.

AMERICAN GIVING

Each year, Americans give about $150 billion to good causes, that is, charitable organizations. Where does the money go? Let's look at the three biggest gifts of 1998.

According to the 1998 Slate 60, which lists the year's largest donations, James and Virginia Stowers came in first with a gift of $327 million to create a medical-research facility in their hometown of Kansas City, Missouri. The Stowers, both cancer survivors, own a major family of no-load mutual funds, American Century Cos. They plan to bequeath most of their other assets to the institute.

In the same year, Martha Ingram, chairman of Ingram Industries, gave $300 million to Vanderbilt University, putting her right up there with founding father Cornelius Vanderbilt. The funds will go into athletics, health care, research, teaching, and other programs at the school, which is the alma mater of Mrs. Ingram's ex-husband and three of her kids.

Coming in third, David and Cheryl Duffield, who made their fortune in software, pledged $200 million toward finding a home for every stray or abandoned dog and cat in America. The Duffields want to end the euthanasia of homeless animals. They were inspired to make the gift by their affection for Maddie, a miniature schnauzer.

Fund raisers prompt gifts like these. They do so by communicating the good that an organization does, cultivating prospective donors who indicate an interest in the cause, and finally, asking the prospect for a donation.

There are all kinds of ways to do these things.

On a mass scale involving modest sums, Girl Scouts sell cookies door-to-door every year, and the Salvation Army places bell-ringing Santas at every shopping mall each holiday season. Similarly, direct mail is used to pitch everything from Easter seals to improved programming at the local PBS station. They may attract small gifts, but these are significant fund-raising programs: The famous March of Dimes, which literally invited Americans to send in dimes, underwrote the development of the Salk vaccine against polio. Girl Scout cookies bring in several hundred million dollars each year.

Alas, you cannot go door-to-door looking for million-dollar gifts. Few people can afford to make such major contributions. And once you know who *can* afford to give $1 million or more, you have to know whether they care about your cause, you have to establish contact with them, you have to cultivate them over time, and you have to convince them that making a gift to your good cause will satisfy their needs.

Golden Oldies

They didn't have PCs, scanners, and laser printers, but Americans have been writing fund-raising copy for generations.

The first fund-raising piece, "New England's First Fruits," was written at the request of the three clergymen who went to England in 1641 to raise money for Harvard. The threesome—Hugh Peter of Salem, Thomas Weld of Roxbury, and William Hibbens of Boston—needed "literature" describing the "selling points" of New England.

Talk about making the case for a college:

After God had carried us safe to New England, and had builded our houses, provided necessaries for our livelihood, reared convenient places for God's worship, and settled the civil government: one of the next things we longed for, and looked after was to advance learning and perpetuate it to posterity; dreading to leave an illiterate ministry to the churches when our present ministers shall lie in the dust.

In 1853 another classic fund-raising missive was written by Ann Pamela Cunningham after her mother made a trip down the Potomac River and found Mount Vernon—the beloved Virginia estate of George Washington—in ruins, with its roof collapsing, its portico propped up by unsightly supports, and its grounds overgrown.

Moved to act, she wrote a letter urging the "Ladies of the South" to raise enough money "to secure and retain the home and grave" of Washington "as a sacred spot for all coming time!" As published in the *Charleston Mercury* and other newspapers, the letter began:

A descendant of Virginia, and now a daughter of Carolina, moved by feelings of reverence for departed greatness and goodness, by patriotism and a sense of national, and above all, of

Southern honor, ventures to appeal to you in behalf of the "home and grave" of Washington.

Ladies of the South, of a region of warm, generous, enthusiastic hearts, where there still lingers some unselfish love of country and country's honor, some chivalric feelings yet untouched by that "national spirit," so rapidly overshading the moral of our beloved land—a moral blight, fatal to man's noblest attributes, and which love of money and speculation alone seems to survive—to you we turn, you, who retain some reverence for the noble dead, some admiration and remembrance of exalted worth and service even where they are no more! Of you we ask: Will you, can you, look on passively and behold the home and grave of the matchless patriot, who is so completely identified with your land, sold as a possession to speculative machinists, without such a feeling of indignation firing your souls as shall cause you to rush with one heart and spirit to the rescue?

To seek such major gifts (the phrase generally refers to donations of $100,000 or more, although in smaller organizations $10,000 may be deemed major), nonprofit organizations maintain fund-raising offices. Only the offices are rarely called "fund raising." Rather, fund raisers have come up with a bevy of other names for the fund-raising office. Chief among them:

Development Office
Office of Institutional Advancement
Office of Resource Development
Resources Office

Sounds like something that should be based in Langley, Virginia, and involve covert activity, huh? Not really. "Development" is just a bit less direct than "fund raising." Even so, it may not be indirect enough. In her book *Effective Fund-Raising Management*, Kathleen

S. Kelley identifies several euphemistic development job titles: public-support associate for the Louisiana Capital Area Chapter of the American Red Cross, scientific-resources manager for the Missouri Botanical Garden, and donor-acquisition officer for the Lesbian & Gay Community Services Center in New York City.

We've seen people given the title "deputy director" of a program rather than "director of development" just to soften the sell.

LOOKING BACK BRIEFLY

The history of fund raising in America is filled with wonderful stories about idealists, religious zealots, marketers, businessmen, and charlatans. We won't tell any here. (See Scott M. Cutlip's one-of-a-kind history, *Fund Raising in the United States*, if you want the full scoop.)

What we will tell you is that not much has changed over the years. Oh, the *techniques* differ. Until the 20th century, most fund raising was done by personal solicitation, by passing the church plate, by staging church suppers or bazaars, and by writing "begging letters." Now we're a bit better organized, thanks to computers and other technology, but don't we still solicit personally, stage events, and write letters?

Ben Franklin, who said something about everything, told fund raisers: "In the first place I advise you to apply to all those whom you know will give something; next, to those whom you are uncertain whether they will give anything or not, and show them the list of those who have given; and lastly, do not neglect those whom you are sure will give nothing, for in some of them you may be mistaken."

In others words, keep A, B, and C lists of prospects. Thanks for the tip, Ben.

The organized fund drive has its roots in the early 1900s when two pioneers, Charles Sumner Ward and Lyman L. Pierce, began raising large amounts of money for Young Men's Christian Association (YMCA) buildings. Both Y officials, they laid the groundwork for short, intensive campaigns. Soon others engaged in massive organized solicitations of the public to fund hospitals, churches, and colleges as well as civic, health, and welfare associations.

By the end of World War I, a number of for-profit fund-raising firms had emerged. This was the beginning of fund raising as we know it today. Arnaud Marts and George Lundy created the fund-raising firm Marts & Lundy; John Price Jones, a former *Washington Post* reporter, set up what is now Brakeley, John Price Jones Inc. In 1919 the Ketchum brothers set up Ketchum, Inc., in Pittsburgh. These and other pros were brought in to manage fund-raising campaigns for good causes. By the 1950s, major nonprofits began hiring internal fund raisers of their own.

How many fund raisers are there in the country today? Nobody knows. The U.S. Department of Labor batches fund raisers with other kinds of workers, so they are not much help. Kathleen S. Kelley offers what is probably the best estimate. Kelley's "informed guess" is that 80,000 people are employed as full-time fund raisers, either as staff members or consultants to nonprofits. They work for about 150,000 nonprofits. The leading employers: educational and health organizations.

In 1992 the National Society of Fund Raising Executives (NSFRE) surveyed members to find out where fund raisers work. The survey showed the main employers of fund raisers, in declining order, were education (25.3 percent); health, hospitals, and medical centers (19.4); human services (13.5); arts, culture, and humanities (7.7); youth (6.6); religion (4.2); environment and conservation (1.7); and retirement communities (1.6). The remaining members were consultants (4.6), not employed (.4), or not classified (15).

THE NONPROFIT WORLD TODAY

On a Tuesday in mid-April 1997 the grand poo-bahs of America's good causes gathered in Cambridge, Massachusetts, to signal the arrival of the nonprofit sector. They included leaders from the Ford and MacArthur foundations, the Urban Institute and Save the

Children Federation, and scores of other institutions. The occasion was the opening of Harvard University's Hauser Center for Nonprofit Organizations, itself the result of an act of philanthropy—a $10 million gift—from two New Yorkers, Rita and Gustave Hauser.

"Nonprofits used to be a synonym for groups that had neither money nor power," Sara L. Engelhardt, president of the Foundation Center, told a reporter from the *New York Times*. "Increasingly this sector has both. If Harvard is opening a center on this scale, the nonprofit sector has clearly arrived."

The nonprofit sector goes by many names—the "nonprofit," "nongovernmental," "independent," "voluntary," "social," or "third" sector. Call it what you will, it is the part of our society that acts voluntarily to help solve important social problems. It is not the private sector, in which commercial companies sell things to make a profit. It is not government, which provides services paid for by taxes.

The nonprofit sector is the rest: churches, hospitals, schools and colleges, museums, youth groups, civic leagues, community-development organizations, dance companies, philanthropic foundations, public-policy think tanks, small literary publishers, day-care centers, and advocacy organizations, among many others. All are recognized by the Internal Revenue Service as charitable institutions. All rely on fund raising to do their work.

The nonprofit sector has been important since America's colonial period, but never as much so as today. As the crème de la crème of the nonprofit world gathered in Cambridge that spring day, good causes had become the fastest-growing sector in our society, with 1.4 million nonprofit organizations. Harvard, with its popelike blessing, had now joined more than 30 colleges, with schools, departments, or programs of teaching and research dedicated to nonprofits.

As the country enters a new century, nonprofits are growing faster than either government or business. According to the Independent Sector, a group devoted to the field, in 1994 some 16.4 million people worked in, or volunteered for, some 1.4 million nonprofit groups, as opposed to 101.3 million people working at some 23 million businesses and 25 million people employed by 87,000 governmental organizations. The figures—the latest available—show a remarkable one-third growth in the nonprofit sector since 1982. This is opposed to a 25 percent growth in the numbers for government and business.

THE GROWTH OF PHILANTHROPY

The strong economy of the 1990s made the richest 20 percent of Americans richer. Suddenly, wealthy people found themselves with extraordinary new wealth. Following their own instincts—altruism, egotism, tax write-offism, or maybe old-fashioned Andrew Carnegie-ism ("He who dies rich dies thus disgraced")—the rich began giving as never before.

Ted Turner, vice chairman of Time Warner, stunned guests at a black-tie UN Association dinner in New York and pledged to donate $1 billion—$100 million a year for ten years—to a new foundation benefiting the United Nations. Bill Gates, founder of Microsoft, and his wife, Melinda, took more than $17 billion and created a private foundation—the wealthiest in the country—devoted to diverse causes.

This was new money—from booms in technology, entertainment, and the stock market—and alongside the fortunes of aging benefactors like Paul Mellon and Walter Annenberg, it spelled an enormous boost in philanthropic dollars. By the end of the century, there were 94 billionaires in the United States and about 60,000 households with annual incomes of $1 million or more.

At the same time, there began an enormous transfer of wealth; baby boomers would inherit an estimated $5.6 trillion from their parents over the next several decades, two Cornell University economists reported in the early 1990s. In their planned giving departments, many nonprofits had tax-advantageous ways to help structure estates so that transfers occurred in ways that benefited everyone.

The growth of philanthropy (the word comes from the Greek for "love of humankind") in the period spurred action everywhere. Foundations and other organizations began holding workshops and field trips aimed at helping the wealthy—especially "the really extremely wealthy," as one provider remarked—learn how to give their money away.

More than 75 graduate schools—about five times more than in 1990—offered advanced degrees in philanthropy for students interested in managing nonprofits or raising money for them. Not surprisingly, nonprofits expanded their development operations to go after the new wealth.

In the late 1970s, Joe worked as senior development writer on a capital campaign at New York University whose goal was $111 million. That was a major dollar goal at the time. By the 1990s leading universities were launching campaigns of more than $1 billion.

Even public universities, increasingly forced to rely on private funding, entered the big-dollar fray. The University of Michigan, for instance, involved 100 staffers in its development office plus another 100 in individual schools and institutes in a successful $1 billion campaign. Other public institutions conducting campaigns—each for $1 billion—included the University of Virginia, the University of California at Berkeley, and the University of North Carolina at Chapel Hill. By then, Harvard had raised the bar with a $2-billion-plus campaign.

In 1999, facing tight post–cold war defense budgeting, the U.S. Military Academy at West Point weighed in with a $175 million Bicentennial Campaign, the first major private fund-raising effort in the history of the service academies.

From storefront social-action agencies with no paid staff to multimillion-dollar institutions like New York's Museum of Natural History, nonprofits are on a roll. They seem destined to stay there well into the 2000s.

Chapter 2

Today's Development Office

Who Does What and Why

The longer you work in fund raising, the more you realize that there is no such thing as a typical development office. Joe has done a lot of writing for development offices in New York and found vast differences in how Polytechnic University, Montefiore Hospital, and Boys Clubs of America were organized for fund raising.

Sure, those are three different kinds of organizations, with diverse constituencies, so you might expect them to staff up differently in fund raising. But even among clients in the same field—NYU, say, and Fordham and Columbia—Joe found fund-raising people arranged in all kinds of configurations. In nonprofits in towns and cities around the country, the men and women with development responsibilities can wear any number of hats.

Indeed, many proposal writers don't work in development offices at all. They are volunteers or administrative staffers with tiny nonprofits. Or they are program folks. Or they are teachers, lawyers, social workers, artists, doctors, activists—you name it—trying to raise big bucks for a favorite cause.

Not long ago, Joe spent an afternoon with an early president of The Nature Conservancy. The Conservancy ranks among the country's major nonprofits; it is an international conservation group, with an annual budget of several hundred million dollars and a staff of more than 2,000 working at about 250 places. But the group was quite small when Dick Goodwin, a Harvard-trained biologist and land conservationist, became its unpaid president in the early 1950s.

According to Goodwin, the Conservancy was based in the Washington, D.C., home of an underpaid executive director. As president, Goodwin was able to travel to help establish state chapters because the Connecticut college where he taught was willing to pick up his expenses.

It wasn't long before a grant from the Ford Foundation enabled the conservation group to hire a paid president, according to Goodwin.

In his day, Goodwin and other volunteers wrote their own fund-raising materials. Today the Conservancy has a development staff that numbers about 40 at headquarters—including four writers—and many more in its more than 50 field offices.

For our purposes, it really doesn't matter whether you work in a development office or not. A good proposal is a good proposal is a good proposal, whether you are a volunteer writing about a neighborhood sports program or an experienced staff writer at the Cleveland Zoological Society or the Kennedy Center. But it helps to know a bit about how development offices work. When they work properly, they are powerful staging grounds for fund-raising proposals.

WHO *ARE* ALL THESE PEOPLE?

Although development offices vary greatly in size and structure, they all reflect the key stages of the fund-raising process. So whether you are working at a hospice, a college, or a social-welfare agency, you are likely to find fund-raising people involved in the same kinds of stuff. In smaller offices, a staff member may work in many aspects of the process. Large development offices, on the other hand, tend to be highly specialized.

One other thing: Few of the people you'll meet in a development office had special training for their jobs. Most learned by doing. Many began as volunteers for their organization or as workers in other departments. Some just stumbled into their jobs. Joe, for example, had worked as a journalist and a college publicist. Having just lost a public-information job at the City University of New York, he was offered a writing job in the development office at New York University.

Joe had never heard of a development office before. He had never seen a proposal or a case statement, much less written either one. But his prospective boss said a good writer could pick development writing up.

In the years since, Joe has found many people in development who "pick it up": researchers who are former newspapermen or lawyers; giving officers who have worked in sales, teaching, marketing, and public relations; and so on. Despite all the college courses on fund raising, most people going into the business still learn on the job.

LET'S MAKE UP A FUND-RAISING OFFICE

Since development shops vary so much in size and structure, we're going to make one up. If you've worked in development a long time, you can skip this section. If you have not, read on. No matter how your organization is staffed to raise major gifts, it accomplishes the same tasks performed by our fictitious staffers.

Let's imagine the development office at the Good Things Society.

Located in a pleasant suburb of a medium-sized city, Good Things has been providing classes, counseling, and other programs in good things for nearly 20 years. Its president used to head the local community college. Its 200-member staff includes teachers, high-tech experts, and varied specialists—among them, five people in fund raising.

Okay, it's Monday morning in development, and in walks Sara, the receptionist/file clerk/office librarian. She's studying for a master's degree in fine arts at night and is just passing through when it comes to fund raising. She puts on the coffee, takes out her bagel, and starts reading and clipping the morning daily newspaper. She is collecting notices about job promotions, business earnings, noteworthy marriages—stuff involving the money in town, which is what her boss cares about.

When she is not busy steering phone calls to the right people and greeting visitors, Sara keeps information flowing. The library she maintains includes most major national publications about money and the monied: *Business Week*, *Forbes*, *Fortune*, *Town and Country*, the *Chronicle of Philanthropy*, and others. There are also annual reports and foundation directories.

It was Sara who was once heard to remark upon joining the staff, "Who *are* all these people?" in reference to her colleagues. Well, they are an odd group. They all seem to have come from some other line of work.

Fund Raiser-in-Chief

First, let's remember that your organization's chief fund raiser does not work in the development office. That's right. He or she is the president, or whatever you call the top honcho at your nonprofit.

She goes out the door, schmoozes with prospective donors, and sooner or later asks for money. If your proposal is the well-crafted weapon it should be, she is the commander who knows how and when to deploy it for maximum effect.

As a proposal writer, you must get to know your fund raiser-in-chief or at least know as much as you can about his or her style.

Is your president demanding? Does she want depth and concrete examples in the organization's fund-raising copy? Great! You do, too. Is she a nut? Does she change her mind all the time, nitpick, rewrite capriciously, act on whims? You poor thing! We'd say grin and bear it, but you are doing that already, aren't you?

Fortunately, most heads of nonprofits come out in between somewhere. They are savvy enough to want strong proposals, but it *does* matter what they had for breakfast that morning. Your best bet is to try to understand your president—even from a distance or through several layers of bureaucracy, as may be the case—and act accordingly.

And by the way—listen. Your president spends a lot of time with donors. Maybe she's actually picked up a thing or two about what they respond to in proposals. So do listen. Better yet, arrange to accompany her on a call or two. Meet some donors. They are your readers.

The Researcher

There's Sam, who handles research. Sam is a guy in his 20s with an MBA and a few years of experience in corporate marketing. He gets in early each day—he's in his cubicle now—and goes on-line right away to databases on wealthy people. Sam spends much of his time writing briefings on potential donors. The information he gathers—biographical, giving history, relationship to Good Things, and so on—gives the president and others insight into the prospects with whom they must meet.

Sam is a cynical type who enjoys shouting out remarks about the nouveau riche he often writes about. He reads Dilbert, and his boss doesn't

Researchers provide the grist for the development mill: information. They spend their time working with:

- **Newspapers and magazines**
- **Databases**
- **Foundation and corporate directories**
- **Program staff**

and produce:

- **Donor briefings**
- **Project descriptions**
- **Board nominee bios**
- **New prospects**

think he takes his job seriously enough.

The Major Gifts Officers

Peggy and Sally handle major gifts. That is, each manages a group of prospective donors, and each has an annual fund-raising goal. Peggy is mid-30ish, driven, outgoing, attractive, and bright. She works mainly on corporate givers. Sally, 27, who used to work at a small community foundation, handles mostly foundation prospects, which makes sense, since she knows something about that world. Sally is also an extrovert and does amusing stuff at the office holiday party.

Both Peggy and Sally are quite sharp. Peggy comes from money and really doesn't have to work. She started out as a Good Things volunteer, helping to arrange board meetings and such, and gradually segued into her staff job in development. She looks like money, too, which doesn't hurt around donors. Drives a BMW.

As major gifts officers, Peggy and Sally manage the cultivation of prospective donors. Each has a list of prospects, which starts with Good Things' own board members and fans out into the larger world of monied people with an interest in Good Things. With information and

Major gifts officers talk with donors and ask them for money. Sometimes they lay the groundwork for the fund raiser-in-chief to step in and make the ask. Major gifts officers:

- **Choose prospective donors**
- **Cultivate prospects**
- **Strategize approaches**
- **Assign/write proposals**
- **Ask for the money (or help a volunteer do it)**

advice from Sam in Research, Peggy and Sally work with knowledgeable staff and volunteers to strategize ways to relieve prospects of money. They meet regularly to go over prospects lists, to rank donors—A, B, or C list—in terms of how ripe they are for an "ask," and to figure out ways to approach new prospects whom the president of Good Things is forever suggesting to them.

Just the other day, he said, "Now, why can't we get a commitment out of the Local Trust Company?" where, alas, Good Things has no contact, as Peggy and Sally tried to explain.

At the moment, the office is conducting the Campaign for Good Things, a $10 million fund-raising effort, and Peggy and Sally are matching prospects and their interests with the needs of the campaign. It took the staff and board more than a year to put the campaign together, and even now there are disagreements over how Good Things should be pitching itself. Is it a community resource or a regional one? And how about the couple of programs with national potential?

Writers produce the written materials needed to raise funds. They write or edit:

- **Proposals**
- **Concept papers**
- **Case statements**
- **Articles and newsletters**
- **Brochures**
- **Web sites**
- **Letters**
- **Presentations**

The Writer

Jake, the writer, is the person Peggy and Sally rely on to give voice to the campaign and articulate the strengths of Good Things. Jake is in his 20s, bearded, and takes classes in fiction writing. He used to be a reporter for a small-town daily and got tired of covering city-council meetings and zoning hearings. He saw a job ad and thought, Sure, I'd like to write about Good Things all day. Now he does.

Jake won't be in until about 10:00 A.M., but he often stays till 7:00 P.M. or so at night. He writes proposals, edits the quarterly newsletter, and prepares thank-you letters and reports for donors on how their money has been used. He also takes on speech, brochure, and fact-sheet writing, as needed and available, for the president's office and the public-relations office. Mostly, he writes fund-raising material. He reports to Peggy, which is kind of tricky, since he also writes for Sally, the development director, the vice president for external relations, and the president. (Aha! Lots of bosses. More on this in chapter 15.)

Development directors work with top managers and board members to raise money. They:

- **Strategize regularly with the president and campaign leaders**
- **Maintain close contact with board members**
- **Direct the fund-raising campaign**
- **Call on major donors**
- **Supervise development managers**

The Director of Development

Marnie is not in the office this Monday morning. She and the president are in New York City, where they have been meeting with board members and others over the weekend. Marnie is a no-nonsense 40 who wears tasteful suits and scarves, sensible heels, and a constant smile. She grew up in horse country, did some private-school teaching, and then worked her way up through a series of fund-raising spots with colleges and an opera company.

Marnie works under great pressure. She is responsible for raising the $10 million. Sometimes Jake the writer and others wonder at the contradictory signals coming from Marnie's office. One day she says the campaign case copy "lacks punch"; the next day she refers to it in a meeting as "brilliant." Which is it? Peggy and Sally like the copy. It works well, and they are sick of looking at it.

Marnie is quick, well organized, a decision-maker. She is the top fund-raising guru at Good Things. She loves "her board," as she calls them. The chairman has become a good friend. Marnie likes her staff a lot, too. She's already planning next spring's retreat. On the flight back from New York tonight, she will take a look at Jake's latest draft and make sure it sings.

Volunteers and Others

Several volunteers, interns, and part-time administrative assistants also work in the development office

Volunteers range from people who help stuff envelopes to members of the board of trustees. The best development volunteers not only help out with the work; they also share their insights into who is ready to part with their money and how best to approach them. Volunteers can:

- **File**
- **Answer the phones**
- **Maintain the library**
- **Review prospect lists**
- **Introduce the organization to new prospects**
- **Go on fund-raising calls**

at Good Things. Volunteers, in particular, help energize the office. Many have themselves benefited from Good Things' services. Now they want to give back and help others. In time, some will probably join the regular development staff. Others, if they're well connected, will probably end up on the board of trustees. And why not? They are among the group's staunchest advocates.

THE TEAM GETS A GIFT

In recent years, Good Things has earned something of a reputation for training absolutely nontechnical people—single mothers, high school dropouts, and older folks looking for a change—to become successful software programmers and computer-networking engineers. One of the campaign goals is to raise $3 million to completely revamp the technology training center, buy new equipment, and create an endowment for teachers' salaries and equipment upgrades in the future.

Last March, when the board of trustees approved the campaign, shy old Mrs. Wolfinger sidled up to Marnie and began making pleasant chitchat. It was a little unusual. Mrs. Wolfinger always gives generously, but she hates asking other people for money and usually avoids Marnie, lest Marnie ask her to solicit somebody. So it was a surprise when Mrs. Wolfinger mentioned that she believed the son of one of her college roommates was now the chairman of a surburban high-tech company. Which company? Oh, she didn't know. It was probably nothing. But she would check and get back to Marnie. Marnie tactfully inquired about the roommate's name, but Mrs. Wolfinger just patted her hand and said, "Don't worry, dear. I will let you know."

And then Marnie heard nothing. Of course, she talked to Sam the following Monday, but all he could tell her was that Mrs. Wolfinger graduated from Vassar in 1940. Who knew what year the roommate graduated? Besides, Marnie had given Sam a list of hundreds of prospects to research; he would get to this little mystery when he could.

At the next board meeting, in June, Marnie inquired again but got the same response. "I'll let you know, dear."

Six months went by before Marnie finally got a Christmas card in the mail. "Mrs. Constance Vonner and I roomed together in 1938 at Vassar," Wolfinger wrote. "Her son, Carl, is the head of Sky High Electronics. Charles and I could host a reception if you like. Do call me when you get a moment."

Moment, schmoment. Marnie was on the phone in a heartbeat.

Later that afternoon, she called Peggy and Sam into her office. Could Sam give her everything he could find about the Vonner family, Carl Vonner, and Sky High Electronics? As for Peggy, could she organize a cocktail party at the Wolfinger house? Mrs. Wolfinger said her patio could accommodate 50 or 60 people.

On a lovely May evening, 60 VIPs from the local business community show up for an intimate garden party at the Wolfinger house. Good Things' president makes a brief slide presentation about the many ways in which Good Things has promoted the local economy. He highlights the plans for the technology training center and its potential to promote the region's high-tech sector. The rest of the evening, he, Marnie, Peggy, and Sally mingle, press the flesh, and figure out who's ripe for more cultivation.

Carl Vonner, who grudgingly agreed to accompany his aging mother to this affair, hits it off with the Good Things president right away. Thanks to Sam's research, the president knows Vonner is an avid sailor, as he is himself. And wouldn't you know, they both sailed with Mervin Taylor, the old coot—the president as an undergrad and Vonner as a member of an amateur racing team. Eventually the president does inquire about Sky High Electronics and its standing in this competitive market. Vonner is thinking about selling the company. He's done quite well, but it's hard to convince customers that a company outside Silicon Valley knows what it's doing. Most of his growth has come from customers in the state.

The following Monday, the president's news about the potential sale of Sky High puts a crimp in Marnie's plan to ask for a multiyear donation. But if a sale is in the works, then perhaps a planned gift would work. Clearly, more cultivation is in order.

Marnie asks Jake to write a letter, on the president's behalf, asking Vonner to lunch. "Open with how much he enjoyed meeting Vonner and say he was intrigued by his comments about the difficulties of competing against Silicon Valley companies. Say he'd like Vonner's insights into our technology center . . . you know, something about our vision for promoting technology outside California."

Well, that's a new take on the technology center. Jake doesn't know much about all this not-California stuff, but he hops on the Web to search the local newspaper's business articles about technology in the area. None of the material actually makes it into the letter; it just puts Jake into the right frame of mind to write the thing.

Jake doesn't hear a word about the letter for another two months, until Peggy calls him into her office one day and starts talking a mile a minute about a proposal to Vonner. "Did they meet?" he asks. "Oh, yes. I'm sorry, Jake, I never told you . . ." and Peggy spends the next ten minutes filling him in. The lunch went very well, and Vonner said he decided to stick it out with his company. Sam says the company got a major contract from a firm in Oklahoma and seems to be doing well. Anyway, Vonner is totally on board with the idea of making the city a regional technology hub, and he's open to the idea of helping with the technology center.

"What we really need is a menu of options just to get him thinking about what he could do," says Peggy. Peggy and Jake brainstorm a few options together—fund the new auditorium, make a gift of equipment or create an endowment—and Peggy asks Jake to write them up as a memo to Marnie for review. Two days later, Marnie calls Jake and tells him to revise the memo so she can take it in to the president for review—tomorrow. Jake takes lunch at his desk, cranks out the new memo, and hands it to Marnie before she leaves that day. He wants to take a three-week vacation in August, so it doesn't hurt to make Marnie smile before he asks for some last-minute vacation time.

The next day, Marnie stops by Jake's desk to tell him the president likes their ideas. Go ahead and write a concept paper and a cover letter for the president to send.

Jake takes the next three days to write up the concept paper. It sounded easy at first, but once he gets into it, he has to think about what might make each of these options appealing to Vonner. The cover letter, also, takes some thought because he wants to pitch these ideas but not sound too overbearing. After all, the president and Vonner are buddies now.

Jake hands his draft to Marnie, who again makes a few suggestions and asks for a new draft for the president. Two days later, he hears that the president likes the concept paper but hates the cover letter; he crossed out almost every sentence and wrote his own version in the margin. It takes an hour for Peggy and Jake to decipher the microscopic scrawl.

Finally, the concept paper goes out. Two weeks later, Jake hears that the president is having another lunch with Vonner in about a month. Great. In the meantime, Jake is off to Maine for three weeks.

Like clockwork, a month later, Jake, Sam, and Peggy are back in Marnie's office, talking about a full proposal. Vonner's mother is quite ill, and he is more interested in making a personal gift in her name than making one through his corporation. Sam brings his file on the Vonner family. After much discussion Marnie decides they should ask for an endowment of $100,000 and offer to name the technology-center foyer after Mrs. Vonner. Marnie needs a draft quickly—God forbid that Mrs. Vonner die before they get the proposal off to her son.

Jake goes into emergency mode again, spending the next day and a half writing in a white heat. Marnie reads the draft as it comes off the printer and hands pages back with edits so he can make the changes immediately. At the end of the day she takes the revised draft home with her. The next morning, a marked-up copy is on his chair. She wants a bit more emphasis on the vision for the technology center and why that is a fitting tribute to the Vonner family. Marnie hopes he can have a finished revision to her by noon. Jake fires up the coffee pot and gets to work. The draft is ready for her at noon exactly.

Thank heavens the president likes what he sees that afternoon.

He drafts a personal note for the cover letter and sends the whole thing back to Jake. Jake and Peggy finalize the copy and send it out the next morning.

Two weeks later, Marnie sends an E-mail to the entire development office. "Looks like we have a Vonner foyer for the technology center." That afternoon, Sara sets out a couple of bottles of cheap wine and a block of cheddar. A year and a half after Mrs. Wolfinger talked to Marnie, they have their first endowment gift for the technology center. Marnie wants to toast the team.

If you are new to development, you may be surprised by all the twists and turns of our story. Or maybe you are relieved to realize that the nutty stuff that goes on in your office is par for the course! Trust us; it is.

Much of the time, fund raisers have to play it by ear. They have to go with the hunches and situations of the moment. As we shall see, this places special pressures on the writer, who must flourish amid ambiguities and whose words are never in and of themselves the end product but always an important *means* to an end—raising money for the cause.

Chapter 3

The Role of the Writer

Using Words for a Cause

His name was Bill McCarthy, and he was a wise-cracking, prematurely white-haired, 40ish guy who was one of the office pros at NYU. Some days, he would appear at Joe's office door with a smart-ass smile on his face and moving both hands back and forth as if shaking two frying pans on a stove.

"Hey, Joe, can you handle a little short-order action?" he would ask. And Joe, always game, would respond, "Whaddayagot?"

McCarthy handled corporate giving, so the need was generally for a quick proposal to a Fortune 500 firm with an interest in the university.

Quickies are a stock-in-trade for proposal writers. Like breaking news, the sudden need for a proposal can be unpredictable. Maybe the president has decided he wants to get a proposal to the Hearst Foundation. Maybe someone's just realized Hearst's deadline for proposals is next week. Maybe—it doesn't matter. Putting out fires is one of the main jobs of a development writer.

One day at NYU word came down from the vice president for development that the assistant chancellor in charge of the humanities needed a major proposal for a foundation in two days. Joe remembers because he worked at home that night until 2:00 A.M. at a desk next to his baby daughter's crib. The draft he was given to revise read like an academic treatise. Joe recast it into a proposal and won his first multimillion-dollar grant.

On another occasion, Danielle was asked to summarize every gift made by a prominent corporation to every office of her organization over the last ten years—literally scores of gifts, large and small. Of course, the piece was needed in two days. She and another writer spent those two days with heads permanently tilted, holding telephones against their shoulders as they typed like the wind and listened to staffers piece together what happened with some grant back in 1989.

USING WORDS EVERY WHICH WAY

Think of yourself as a writer on call. The nameplate on your desk reads "Words R Us," as far as the rest of the staff is concerned. Sometimes people will come looking for a quickie. At other times, they need polished prose meant to last—a building inscription, an award citation, a tailor-made book for a donor.

A book? Sure. Joe has prepared several for donors. One was produced for a university in the process of cultivating a wealthy businessman. It was a retrospective of his previous gifts and their impact on teaching and research. Brief, just-so copy; photographs; lovely binding. On another occasion, Joe worked with a Washington, D.C., maker of handcrafted books to create a piece for a woman who was a tireless advocate for an issue-oriented group.

A development writer may be called on to write anything: an advertisement; a multimedia presentation; a video script. Sometimes you can farm an assignment out to a specialist. Most times, limits on time and money do not allow that.

So what does a fund-raising writer do?

— He provides the written tools of fund raising.

Without a doubt, people give to people; a well-written proposal sent to someone you don't know is just a waste of time. But no matter how adept you are at talking a good game with a prospect, you must be able to describe your program in writing. The well-tailored written proposal closes the deal. It is the document left behind so that the prospective donor and his colleagues—fellow staff, lawyers, siblings, whomever—can read, feel good about what they are about to do, and act.

Sure, your president can sell a new program with a couple of notes made on a napkin at lunch. But the written piece spells it all out: how many new hospital beds are needed and why; how many new kids will be reached by the museum and to what end; how a new kitchen will make a difference for all members of the church congregation.

Your colleagues can talk from one end of the week to the next about some program need. It may sound great. But only when the idea is committed to paper, with all the details and reasons and measures of success filled in, will it be ready for sale. Now the idea is not only talkable enough to excite a donor; you've actually marshaled your argument, buttressed it with facts, and shown logically why your donor must do this thing.

A fund-raising writer takes information and assembles it to do a job, whether in a proposal, a case statement, a brochure, a newsletter, or other piece. The job is to sell the organization. Sometimes the written piece is sent ahead. Sometimes it is left behind. Sometimes a proposal is in your president's pocket, in two forms, with two different dollar amounts, so that he can pull out either one (or neither), depending on how the meeting with a prospect is going.

— He creates themes and messages.

For example, the name of your fund-raising campaign. Let's say you work for a land-conservation group. You are raising millions of dollars to conserve natural areas. What should you call your campaign?

a. The Land Conservation Campaign
b. Lands and Waters Forever Campaign
c. The Campaign for Last Great Places

You get our point. Memorable and exciting campaign names can make a real difference. Fund-raising writers are in a good position to come up with key words and phrases that resonate with donors. They also know which themes matter most to their audience.

Do your donors care most about how you leverage their gifts? Or are they more interested in how much you promote the programs they are supporting to the larger community? As a writer who knows his audience, you are in the best position to come up with words and images that speak to your prospects' needs.

— He does quality control.

"Words R Us" means that anybody in the office can turn to the writer for a quick edit or proofread. People come in with worried looks; the writer thinks, Oh, no, not another proposal, but instead he gets hit with a request to look at somebody's résumé (and keep it to himself, if he doesn't mind).

When Danielle got promoted to writer and editor, it seemed as if everyone in the department suddenly took to stopping by her desk to ask about grammar. How am I supposed to know how to punctuate "however"? she wondered. So she'd look it up after explaining one more time, Yes, we follow Chicago style, but the membership magazine follows Associated Press style and the president's office sort of follows Chicago but also makes up rules of its own. And see here—the punctuation for however depends on its use in the sentence.

The writer is the person obligated to inform his colleagues that a comma before "and" in a series is optional, depending on the style you use—never mind what your fourth-grade teacher told you. The writer is the person with a shelf filled with dictionaries, style guides, grammar books, and usage manuals. The writer is the person who will read anything anyone brings him just to make sure the organization doesn't make a gaffe in print.

— He goes with the flow.

Now what does that mean? It means what it says: A fund-raising writer meets the needs presented to him. More often than not, he or she *responds* to demands. Short-order cooks take orders, they don't give them. Once given the assignment, the writer may initiate any number of responses. After all, "Words R Us." We don't use them until someone needs something cooked up.

WHOLE-CLOTH CITY

Oh, and sometimes—not often—a fund-raising writer works out of whole cloth. That is, he or she gets highly creative.

One day, a university president came back from lunch with a multimillionaire businessman. The businessman, retired and aging, had been considering how he might help the university. He wanted to do something to advance his key interests. He had always had a secret longing to be associated with the humanities, he said. Moreover, the businessman's wife was an alcoholic. Wasn't there something to be done related to that?

Wags in the university's development office figured, Simple, let's meet both of the man's interests: Get him to endow a chair for an alcoholic poet. Then they got serious and created a new lecture series in the humanities at the medical school. They worked with whole cloth and got the money.

At another institution of higher learning, the development office was asked one day to create an institute of war and peace. It had not been looking to fund such an institute. Indeed, it had never heard of such an institute until the university president sent out for it, in much the same way that you might send out for a pastrami on rye.

Together with a young assistant professor of politics, a development writer created the institute. You may rest assured that no other entity known to man was ever better designed to improve

East-West relations. The institute's purpose, its programs and conferences and publications—everything was created in an afternoon.

Whole-cloth city.

No one wants to talk about them, but these things do happen, given human frailty and the financial needs of nonprofits. What it amounts to is making a suit for the emperor who has no clothes (i.e., the head of your organization). It is always amusing in retrospect but difficult as hell to bring off at the time. It involves frantically inventing a program, writing at breakneck speed, and not knowing whether to laugh or cry when you're done.

So don't say no one ever warned you. And be grateful that on most occasions your colleagues will have real information on real programs about which you must write. Your job is to ferret out the information through research and interviews. (See chapter 5 for more on that.)

JOYS AND SORROWS

Fund-raising writing offers many satisfactions. You have the global satisfactions: Being associated with a noble cause. Knowing that the words you put on paper motivate others to altruistic action. Helping to make the world a better place. As one former salesman working as a fund raiser told Danielle, selling this stuff is a heck of a lot better than selling sump pumps.

You have the local satisfactions of helping people where you work. You don't see your colleagues clamoring for the opportunity to do the writing themselves, do you? No indeed. When you write something well, when you write it quickly, when you help the development officer put just the right spin on a tricky letter, you really help people get the job done. Hopefully they tell you that themselves. But if for some reason they don't, try being out sick for a week. They'll remember how great you are pretty darn quickly.

Then there are the personal satisfactions of writing itself. Writing consists of thinking on paper, and putting the old noggin to use is pretty rewarding. Even if the process doesn't delight you every minute, it sure feels good to hit print, stretch, and pat yourself on the back for being *done*. And that's another bonus. How many of your colleagues have such a definite beginning, middle, and end to their projects? At least as a writer you know eventually, somehow, that the piece will be finished and you will move on to something else.

Sure, there are drawbacks. They are the usual ones associated with writing in a corporate setting, such as writing by committee, indecision, and lack of control. And even these can be dealt with, as we'll show you in the pages that follow.

"You have to learn to stand up for what you've written," says Maura Deering, former director of development communications at the University of California at Davis. "You have to have specific, rational reasons for what you have written, not just that you like your own writing. Otherwise, if you let people change your sentences, you can lose the clarity of your writing. So you have to do battle—in a polite way."

In the end, most development writers take pride in their role at good causes.

"Helping program people actually do their work is tremendously rewarding," says Tracey Bedford, who joined her interests in writing and the environment at The Nature Conservancy. "That—and knowing something is well-written—is what development writing is all about."

Perhaps the only sorrow that can't be overcome is boredom. If you have written the same things over and over month upon month and there is no end in sight, then it's time to look for something new. But the rest of the stuff that gets in your way—Well, that's just there to make your life more interesting.

FINDING OTHER PEOPLE TO WRITE FOR YOU

There comes a time in a writer's life when he simply cannot do it all. Depending on the situation, he may turn for help from many different sources.

- In some cases—what we like to call the all-hands-on-deck cases—others in your department can lend a hand. Danielle once wrote a technology-related proposal to the Kresge Foundation (notorious for its stringent and voluminous proposal guidelines), with the help of all four people on the project she was talking about. She wrote some, the development officer wrote some, the development coordinator crunched numbers and put together the budget, even the director of information systems wrote an overview of the project. Finding this kind of help is simply a matter of saying, "Hey, I need help!" to whomever is in charge of the fund-raising effort.
- If you work for a large organization, try a bit of bartering. Joe used to hit up the magazine staff at The Nature Conservancy for help when he was in a big-time crunch. It usually worked because they used to hit *him* up on occasion as well. A little tit for tat makes the world go round.
- For cash-strapped nonprofits, there's always the intern/volunteer option. The kid looks bright enough. Why not ask him to write the thank-you letter? You might end up having to edit it, but that can be done over a TV dinner at home—much better than having to write it yourself. This option may not work so well for larger and more complex projects, however.
- And then there's the freelance option. Perhaps in your dealings with partner organizations you've met writers in the same field. They may be available for a little moonlighting. You can certainly ask around the development office for the names of freelancers or ask colleagues at other institutions. Most cities have writers centers that offer job postings; an advertisement there may turn up the help you need.

If you do decide to hire a freelance writer, here are some tips before you commit:

Look at writing samples! Ask for samples of similar kinds of work and make sure the person can deliver the goods. A fabulous business writer does not necessarily know how to write fund-raising proposals.

Interview the writer in person. Get a sense of the writer's personality. Will he require a lot of guidance and hand-holding? Will you need to set up interviews for him or will he do that himself? When can you expect a first draft?

Ask for references. As with all vendors, you want to know how other people have felt about this person's services. Does he meet his deadlines? Is he tactful with senior staff and donors? Does he understand the issues at stake? Does he make himself available when you need him?

Discuss finances up front. Most professional freelancers charge on a project basis: They estimate how long they think the project will take them and give you a single figure for the whole job. If the job takes significantly longer, you agree upon an hourly rate thereafter. Ask the writer how many revisions the project fee includes. (It is reasonable to expect at least one revision for your money.)

Discuss firm deadlines. Especially if you don't know the writer well, set actual dates when you will see copy. If the writer gives you a general estimate, like "in a week or two," just look at the calendar and choose a date around then. "Could you get me a draft by the 20th?"

Sign a contract. For obvious reasons, lawyers want you to sign a contract before you part with any money. Freelance writers tend to be a casual lot, however, and many won't have a standard contract for you to sign. They could make one up if you insist, but are you sure you want to bother? If there is no contract involved, then tell the freelancer you will pay him upon delivery of the finished piece.

PART 2

Writing the Perfect Proposal

Here we examine the most important written piece in fund raising: the proposal. Like a heat-seeking missile, it must be crafted exquisitely to strike the target every time. You won't miss with these basics.

Chapter 4

The Marriage Proposal

Asking from Strength

Maybe you're married; maybe not. It doesn't matter (well, not for our purposes). Let's suppose you have just met Mr. or Ms. Right and you are going to pop the big question. You want to form a lifelong partnership. And you are determined to get just one answer when you make your proposal: Yes!

What do you do? Well, let's consider the things you will *not* do if you want a positive answer to your proposal:

You will not announce that there is a bench warrant out for your arrest.

You will not discuss your three previous failed marriages.

You will not bring up your family predisposition to terrible diseases.

Well, what *do* you want to do?

ACCENTUATE THE POSITIVE

Yes, you are going to be winning, upbeat, ambitious, can-do, and above all, strong and getting stronger. You are going to make yourself very, very attractive to Mr. or Ms. Right.

You will announce how wonderful everyone thinks you are.

You will discuss your successes—in business, in friendships, in all aspects of life.

You will tout your charming parents and siblings.

You will dress neatly and arrive on time.

"*Fuggedaboudit!*"

We know you work for a charity, but please, when you write about your nonprofit:

— Never appear "needy."

Sure, we've heard of needy charities. Yours ain't one of them. Needy means missed payrolls. Needy means run-down, ragtag. Needy is a guy with a cup on the corner. Ask Rory O'Connor, whose independent film and TV company, Globalvision, was turned down by a wealthy individual who visited the firm's poverty-stricken offices. "He just doesn't think anything of quality can be produced in such a slumlike setting," O'Connor heard later from an insider. "Maybe you guys should consider moving to midtown."

— Never discuss your failures.

Everybody likes to hear about lessons learned, but please, let them be lessons that let you grow and realize your potential. Save the lessons indicating that your museum is sinking into a black hole for Friday-afternoon bull sessions in your office—with the door shut.

— Never appear too smart, too rich, or too good.

Whether reading your copy or sitting across the table, donors want to look into a mirror. They want to feel comfortable. They want self-assured, stable, bright, positive, and all that other good stuff. The mirror must reflect who they are, with maybe a touch of who they want to be. Hold up something reassuring.

— Never say never.

Yeah, this is our cop-out. You know your donors; we don't. Maybe a hole in your shoe, a secret in your attic, or an unpleasantness in your financial office will turn a donor on. Not likely, but when someone is really a member of the family, you might let your hair down. Even then, do it over a drink, please, not in writing.

Make a complete inventory of your strengths. If you are going to be a successful suitor and get your prospect to say yes, you had better get your pitch together. What's special about your institution? Is it the biggest of its kind? The oldest and most experienced? The most successful? If so, in what way? Does it improve the quality of life? How? Have you figured out how much better the community is because you exist? Is air pollution down by half? Are people better fed, educated, or healthier? Is there less crime? Facts and figures, please!

Maybe you are a new organization or the project you want to fund is new. Have others given a grant already? Has your board committed significant resources to this new effort? Can you demonstrate that the entire community is behind your new effort? All of these things show the strength of your organization and your resolve to get the job done.

Tailor your strengths to your audience. Are you approaching a corporation? Well, put yourself in their place. Chances are, they will appreciate an efficient, effective, businesslike approach to whatever it is you do. So unless your business office is well known for its reckless ways, make a point of how well managed you are. Did your board and staff work for a year on your thoughtful new strategic plan? Say so! Better yet, let a respected member of the community do it for you. Quote from a glowing newspaper editorial, cite your high ranking by a respected civic group, get a solid testimonial from a distinguished corporate leader. There's nothing like an outside seal of approval.

You say you can't find your strengths? Sometimes your strengths are not obvious. Many years ago, in his first job as a junior writer at New York University, Joe was put to work in the records room of the alumni office. He spent several weeks going through file cards on thousands of graduates, looking to see which alumni from the dental, law, and medical schools resided in New York City. The result? A simple, powerful line of copy in university materials noting that half the dentists and a quarter of the lawyers practicing in the city were graduates of NYU. Not bad for an institution that calls itself "a private university in the public service."

What are the facts that back up the progress you've made toward *your* mission?

- Duke University tells donors that six of its humanities programs have been ranked among the top five in their fields by the National Research Council.
- The Chamber Music Society of Lincoln Center quoted *Time* magazine on its role in sparking a renaissance of chamber music in America.
- Special Olympics International cites a 30th anniversary *New York Times* editorial praising the group for its global success in creating opportunities for athletes.
- The University of Chicago says its faculty, alumni, and researchers have collectively earned 58 Nobel Prizes.

Dig into your records and sift through others' research. It should not take you too long to figure out how many of last year's new AIDS patients were served by your agency, how much museum attendance has risen in the past decade, or the correlation between your group's sex-education efforts and the drop in teenage pregnancies.

Sometimes your organization's impact is not so easily measured. "Our mission is to bring children's voices to adults, to decision-makers," says Judy Moak, chief operating officer for Children's Express, a nonprofit news service produced by kids reporting on the issues that affect their lives. "I can't quantify how many policy decisions we affect with these stories or how many adults reconsider their attitudes toward children as a result of our work. I can tell you that we're developing leaders and helping kids shape the future, but that's still pretty squishy."

Yet even in these cases you can find numbers to talk about: the number of hits on your Web site or the number of subscriptions to your newsletter, for example.

THE RISE OF INVESTOR DONORS

Boston consultant H. Peter Karoff, an adviser to the wealthy, calls the new wave of philanthropists "investor donors." They treat charity like a business, demanding accountability and efficiency, he told *Business Week*.

A product of the wealth boom of the 1980s and 1990s, these new donors are impatient, restless, and activist, says Karoff. And you had best be mindful in writing for them. They are looking for something other than charity as usual.

Here's what several players told *Business Week*:

- "It's my money. It's my time. I want to see an impact," said Richard S. Fuld Jr., chief executive of Lehman Brothers Inc.
- "We want to discover what's working and not reinvent what's not," said Jeffrey D. Jacobs, president of Oprah Winfrey's Harpo Entertainment Group. "When you write the checks, you get the power to change things."
- "We don't talk very much about charity anymore," said Bruce L. Newman, executive director of the Chicago Community Trust. "We talk about entrepreneurialism and the ability to make change."

One Wall Street trader, Paul Midor Jones II, won't make a gift through his Robin Hood Foundation until grant seekers pass a tough exam of their managerial skills and financial health. Try some fluff in your proposals to him!

MATCHMAKING, OR WHY ON EARTH SHOULD I MARRY YOU?

Doesn't everybody have one friend who believes that if he tries his best pickup line on every woman in the bar, someone is bound to say yes? This same guy goes to his friends' weddings and wonders, Why not me? We all know why: One-size-fits-all pickup lines don't work. The same goes for fund raising. "Don't just ask everybody in the Foundation Directory," advises Betsy Hamilton, grants administrator at the J. Bulow Campbell Foundation. "Do your homework."

What is your homework? Any happy couple can tell you it is to ask selectively, go on some dates, and take your time figuring out if this is love. Ditto for fund raising: Talk to funders, look for mutual interests, and try to get the timing right.

Get out there and meet people. You cannot send a proposal to the five richest people in town and expect them to give you money. Why should they? They don't know you. You could be some crackpot in an attic with a laser printer. Who's to say?

You may think that foundations and corporate giving committees are different. After all, they exist only to give away money. Just read the guidelines, send the proposal on time, and you're in. Wrong again. You have to get out there and date. Pick up the phone, set up a meeting. Visit. Talk. Listen.

"It simply is not enough to read a foundation's guidelines and annual report," says Craig Impink, director of foundation and government relations at WETA, a Washington, D.C.–area public-radio-and-television station. "When we wanted to fund a special series about campaign-finance reform, I met with many foundations that were interested in the issue. But not one of them cared about reform efforts in the nation's capital; they only cared about what was happening in the states. If I had read only the guidelines, I would have written the completely wrong proposal."

Guidelines and annual reports will, however, give you a sense of the general universe in which the institution operates. You will quickly see that the foundation only supports conservative political causes. You will notice certain buzzwords used over and over. You will find that the foundation consistently mentions the results of outside evaluations of its grants. Okay, then. Frame your argument in terms of conservative values. Drop in a buzzword or two. Suggest an outside evaluation of your project. But don't go a step further until you talk to a member of the foundation staff.

A simple conversation will reveal that the foundation only uses outside evaluations for grants of a certain size. It will also reveal that the board chairman died recently and the younger members are chucking the whole conservative agenda. Aha! With this information, you can tailor your proposal for success.

Finding mutual interests. By "tailor" we do not mean discard your old program and create a new one the prospect will like. We mean look at your programs from the donor's perspective and highlight the aspects that will appeal most.

"Each donor is going to have his or her own reason for being interested in what you are doing," says Candace Kuhta, a development officer and former freelance proposal writer. "One person might be interested in your program because she cares about the people you are serving. A foundation might be interested because of the new method you are using, while a corporation could be interested because of the contribution you are making to a larger body of work."

Unfortunately, every nonprofit tries at least once to twist itself into knots and somehow appear to meet guidelines it clearly does not. As if the reader will be lulled into funding the cause because you worked so hard to turn an apple into an orange. "Proposals that do not adhere to our program guidelines are *not* considered for funding," says Carr Agyapong of the Burroughs Wellcome Fund. "Most foundations are not willing to make exceptions to their mission, goals, and interests."

When you do find those areas of mutual interest, the results can be magic. Just like true love, the right proposal for the right funder *feels* right. Children's Express once submitted a concept paper to a major foundation that happened to be creating a new program in the area of children, diversity, and the media. "That's our mission, right there," says Judy Moak. "We never even got to the proposal stage; they gave us a multimillion-dollar grant based on our nine-page concept paper."

WRITER BEWARE! Even the best-written and most persuasive proposals routinely get turned down for reasons that have nothing to do with the writing. Usually it's because the proposal doesn't meet the funder's guidelines.

Building relationships with foundations. "If you're going to get anywhere, you have to build relationships with these people," says Sally Wells, veteran fund raiser for public television and now a development director at the Wilderness Society.

It is that simple. If a funder feels she knows you and your organization well, you are more likely to get a yes.

A personal meeting can save you even when your proposal *deserves* to be turned down. "One time I got a proposal that was so bad, so lengthy, that I was ready to go to my board and say, Let's just forget it," recalls Joan Kennan of the Washington, D.C.–based Arcana Foundation. "But I ended up meeting with the organization's director and she was wonderful—very capable and devoted to her cause. She sure couldn't convey that on paper, but we did give her a grant."

So how do you build personal relationships? There are dozens of books on the subject, but they all come down to a simple fact: You pick up the phone and make an appointment to meet. Some people send a letter of inquiry first and follow up with a phone call. Others call first and follow up with written materials. Either way, you bite the bullet, make the call, and go to the meeting. (For more on how to write a letter of inquiry, see chapter 6.)

Get the timing right. When you make personal contact with your prospects, try to get a sense of whether the time is right for a proposal. Perhaps one of your board members is about to exercise company stock options—in which case there's no time like the present to talk about the tax benefits of a stock gift. Or you may learn that a rival school just got a huge grant from the foundation you wanted to approach. Oh, well. Introduce yourself now, build bridges, and make your request in a year or two.

Sometimes world events can wreak havoc on your fund-raising plans. One development officer told us he tried for a year to raise money for a program dealing with defense issues. The only problem was that this was 1992, and every foundation he met told him, Sorry, the cold war is over. One officer, in charge of a major foundation's nuclear-nonproliferation program, met with him in an office stacked with packing boxes; the foundation was shutting the whole program down. Needless to say, no money was raised.

If you are not the person meeting with the prospect, be sure to ask your colleagues about the timing before you write. If the election is just six months away, you can honestly say that a gift for leaflets and radio ads will have a critical impact.

THE RULES

You've courted, talked, and listened. You are ready to make a proposal. Here again, rules abound regarding how to behave. We surveyed funders around the country to discover the rules they wish had been written down somewhere—permanently.

1. *Thou Shalt Give the People What They Want*

When writing to a foundation, follow their guidelines religiously. Do not skip questions, do not omit any single piece of information that has been requested. "Sometimes people forget their financial statements or the budget or the list of their board of directors," says Joan Kennan of the Arcana Foundation. "It is annoying. People should know better."

One writer told us that when she is finished writing, she puts her draft side by side with the guidelines and for each question asks herself, Have I answered this as completely and succinctly as possible?

"If you do the right research, find the right project at the right time, and follow directions, you can't fail," says Nancy Enzler, whose development career has included work for the Red Cross, National Trust for Historic Preservation, and American Farmland Trust. "I have seen other people's grant applications and I often think, What question were you answering? I see the question here, and I see your answer, but I don't see the connection between them."

"In my cover letter I make sure the donors know I understood what they asked for," says Sally Wells. "I might even write, 'I know you told us to apply for $10,000, but the total budget for this project is $15,000. We will be just delighted with a $10,000 grant, but we are asking you to consider $15,000.' "

2. *Thou Shalt Not Go On and On*

Be brief. Or as Mark Twain suggested, eschew surplusage. "Often we'll see the same point made three, four, five times, just using different words," says Kennan.

"So many people wander all over kingdom come," says Wells. "Obfuscation doesn't help anyone. You have to get the essence without going on for 14 pages."

"Long proposals with expansive hyperbole lose my interest," says Meyer Memorial Trust's Alice McCartor.

Nancy Register, who both writes and reviews proposals for the Consumer Federation of America, says that it was one good writer who brought this point home for her. "I used to argue with her and say we needed to get this or that certain idea across. She would point to one sentence and say, 'This sentence does it. It's all you need.' "

3. *Thou Shalt Organize Thy Thoughts*

Writing forces you to think. How will you order your information? "When you have a lot of information, you have to make choices at every point down the road," says Beth Duris, a writer at The Nature Conservancy. "You have to decide what to include and where."

"The reader is searching for factual information to determine whether or not the proposal should be funded," says Whitaker Foundation president Miles J. Gibbons Jr. "It is the writer's responsibility to gather the facts and present them in an orderly manner."

4. Thou Shalt Not Pluck the Heartstrings Too Vigorously

An executive of the Turner Foundation once told a group of development officers that rhetoric made his teeth hurt. The Arcana Foundation isn't a big fan of rhetoric, either. "The chairman of my board always says, 'I wish they wouldn't include all this poetry. I don't want to read poetry,' " says Kennan.

That doesn't mean you have to edit out all the human-interest stories and quotes and examples. Just use them appropriately. "Don't start with a tear-jerking summary of a child or an adult horribly disadvantaged who finally overcomes," says Mary Bellor of the Philip L. Graham Fund. "Those anecdotes fall flat. I like clean, concise descriptions of what people are doing. I like proposals that sound like real people wrote them. They carry the conviction and passion of the organization they represent."

"I don't do the spin thing," says Moak. "I don't think, I'll put these quotes in here to really pull on their heartstrings. I make the case. Then the kids' voices reinforce what I say."

5. Thou Shalt Not Speak in Tongues

A good proposal speaks in plain English. Do not use jargon. If you must use a technical term, define it when you first use it. The same goes for acronyms. If you are writing about the WAWP, make sure you include (Words Are Wonderful Program) after the first mention.

Choose a short word over a long one. Trust us on this. "Use" is better than "utilize." "Will act" is better than "would be able to perform." Write your proposal so that both your mother and the guy who fixes her car will understand it.

Or you could simply post the following list next to your computer. It is the Champlin Foundation's executive director's list of biggest complaints about proposals: "Use of jargon; use of acronyms; saying the same self-serving stuff over and over; not getting to the point; using ten words when one will do."

6. Thou Shalt Keep at Least a Pinkie Toe on the Ground

Be realistic. Don't let your desire to land a big gift cloud your judgment when you're writing down your objectives. Remember, you and everyone on your staff have to live with these promises once they are made.

"If you send me an incredible agenda that will be staffed by one and a half people and you're only asking for $5,000, it makes no sense," says Register.

"Novice proposal writers seem not to realize that many foundation program officers are former academics or charity administrators," says Dr. Susan M. Fitzpatrick, program director at the James S. McDonnell Foundation. "We used to *write* proposals, so let's be more honest."

7. Thou Shalt Take a Positive Approach

You know the adage about rats aboard a sinking ship? Well, if you want the rats to jump on rather than off, try to look as if you're a seaworthy vessel.

"Sometimes I feel like I'm reading about an organization as a victim," says Register. "We don't have enough money, all our computers were stolen, there's too much going on, we need some help . . . Organizations should emphasize what they can do. I say happily occupy your niche and exploit it."

That goes for your attitude toward other organizations as well. Do not bad-mouth the competition. If you want to convey how much better you are than the agency down the street, then just keep hitting on your strengths, the unique aspects of your program, the qualifications of your staff. Do not mention the other guys at all.

8. Thou Shalt Ask for the Money

You've gone to all this work to write a knockout proposal, so don't blow it by forgetting to ask for some money. No pussyfooting around or getting shy about this, either. Ask clearly for a specific amount of money in the conclusion and mention the sum again in the executive summary and the cover letter.

"It's hard to believe, but a lot of people forget to ask," says Register. "I read a proposal with all this great language about a wonderful project, and then I think, Well, that's nice. But there's no ask."

Another no-no is to ask for "whatever you can spare." Ask for a specific amount. Choosing the right amount is always a guessing game, but it is better to overshoot a bit than to ask for too little. One development officer told us she sent a proposal to a foundation officer who was known to ask tough questions. His question for her was "Why didn't you ask for more money?" She had a revised proposal on his desk the next day.

9. Thou Shalt Not Employ a Cookie Cutter

"Any foundation officer can't help but feel a twinge of dismay when you read, 'We are grateful to the Public Welfare Foundation,' even though the proposal is being sent to the Graham Fund," says Bellor. "But that happens so often."

Every fund-raising guru will tell you to speak to each donor's individual interests. Yet the temptation to write one proposal and send it to 80 foundations remains. All we can tell you is that the cookie-cutter approach usually doesn't work. Moreover, it takes all the intellectual stimulation out of writing.

"Every proposal is different, even if you're writing about the same thing for the same amount of money," says Kim Coleman, president of Expanding Horizons in Washington, D.C. "You have to write each one for the person who will read it. And foundations are just people. You get to know what the program officers like and don't like."

Where's the line? Here's our opinion: To cut and paste key sections is okay. To merely change the name and address and send the same proposal is not.

10. *Thou Shalt Proofread Carefully*

At best, typos and inconsistencies reflect poorly on your organization. At worst, they are cause for the proposal to be turned down immediately. "Proposals with typos and mistakes happen all the time," says Kennan. "It leaves me thinking, Isn't this organization careful enough to review its proposal? Didn't the staff even proof this?"

Yes, mistakes happen all the time, in all kinds of development communications. One development professional told us she printed up a very expensive membership package, only to find a glaring misspelling right on the front of it. The solution? Every time she sent a package out, she used cream-colored whiteout to cover the mistake and then a special blue pen to write in the correction. She kept her supply of special blue pens in the organization's safe.

When a mistake happens, don't disembowel yourself immediately. Acknowledge what the mistake is telling you: You must spend more time proofreading. Nobody likes to proofread, but it is necessary. It is like eating your spinach. Tastes yucky but gives you strong muscles and bones.

So, now that you know the rules of the road, let's talk about how you're going to get this proposal researched, organized, and written.

Chapter 5

Getting Your Material Together

How to Research and Interview

Your most vital research has almost nothing to do with writing. Rather, it has to do with finding out whom you will ask for money and what you want the money for. If you don't know these things, don't waste your time trying to write a proposal.

But let's assume that you do know whom you are writing to and what you are asking for. Now you need to pull together the pieces that will make up your heat-seeking missile of persuasive prose.

RESEARCH: DIGGING FOR GOLD

When you research your proposal, keep in mind the general categories of information you will need.

First, you need the basic information that will fill out each section of your proposal. (For more on this, see chapter 6, "Parts of a Proposal.")

- Introduction and Problem Statement. What problem do you want to fix? Why do you want to fix it now?

- Program/Project Description. How will you fix the problem? What's your goal? How will you know you succeeded?
- Budget and Time Line. How much will the project cost? What other sources of income do you have? When will the activities take place and in what order?
- Supporting Documents. You may need the list of your trustees and their credentials, biographies of the staff who will lead the project, the executive summary of your strategic plan, media clips, letters of support, audited financial statements, maps, photos, and charts. Whoever has closest contact with your prospect should help you decide which of these items to include. Keep in mind that you want to inform, not overwhelm.

Second, you want to find the concrete details about your program. By concrete details we mean items that you can count, see easily in your mind, and/or describe with one-syllable words. Things like the number of staff you have, the number of kids who use your youth center each week, the games they play and the time they go home each day, and the kind of van your counselors need to take these kids on field trips. Such details make your program real.

Statistics also lend credibility. Tell the reader that only 12 percent of eligible seniors use the state's new medical-insurance program. Opening with that statistic will make your goal of increasing participation to 50 percent sound quite logical. It's a tangible, *understandable* goal.

The same goes for establishing your track record. If you can quantify how many children your nonprofit feeds each month or the percentage of kids whose grades went up as a result of your after-school program, all the better. These facts answer the larger question of why you, and not the scores of other groups out there, should get this gift.

Third, look for special nuggets of information that will make your proposal stand out: moving quotes, outside endorsements, stories of your program in action. These nuggets remind the donor of the human element in your proposal. You aren't just asking for money; you are asking to help people. You aren't the only one saying your organization is wonderful; everyone in the neighborhood is saying so.

Nuggets can also be details or descriptions that arrest the reader. Vivid or memorable facts make terrific nuggets. Consider the following:

> *Several of our trips helped to get our participants thinking about their future goals and careers. For example, after our trip to Howard University, a participant told her parents that she wants to go to college. The parents of this honor student thanked us for positively affecting their daughter as they had been unsuccessful in persuading her to think of college as an option.*
>
> —EXPANDING HORIZONS YOUTH PROGRAMS, INC.

> *Lessons from pre-existing or planned housing co-operatives in the contiguous United States must be filtered through the context of Interior Alaska. The winter's cold, of course, is the most salient characteristic of this region—a cold so cold that it cannot be felt except as breath taken out of one's throat. Car tires sometimes take the flat set of the ground beneath them and roll "square," and the slightest draft in one's house may form a cloud that hovers a foot above the floor.*
>
> —BOREALIS COMMUNITY LAND TRUST

Keep a file of your own nuggets even when you aren't researching for a particular proposal. If a participant in your training program landed her first salaried job, make a note of it and copy her thank-you letter to the director (with her permission). This is priceless stuff!

Where to Find That Gold

In general, you will find the information you need for a proposal in:

- internal written documents
- external written documents

- your very own genius brain
- people inside your organization (staff)
- people outside your organization (everyone else)

In our experience, most concrete details come from either first-hand knowledge, internal written documents, or your colleagues on staff. Usually the most sparkling nuggets come from external sources, such as the people your organization serves, your volunteers, or your local community leaders. These nuggets may be told to you by other staff members, but they usually originate outside.

In general, you will begin your research by looking at written materials. Who wants to talk to people before you have to? Besides, if you read up on your topic first, you'll know what information you need to ask other people for.

What have you and your colleagues written about your organization, this project, and the need it addresses? Check old proposals, donor files, newsletters and magazines. How about last year's annual report? How about that memo the president sent to the board last month? How about the program director's five-year work plan? Collect copies of all these things.

HOT TIP: Collect more background material than you think you need. If you have time, pursue avenues that seem redundant or tangential. You will often find useful bits of information that help to put your activities into context.

Next, check outside written sources. Do a World Wide Web search on your topic. Not only will you find background material on your general topic—very helpful if you're writing about a subject you don't know well—but you may also find that current events are playing into your hand. This happened to Danielle when she was writing a proposal to fund research in three freshwater streams in the Midwest. Just as the foundation was asking for follow-up information, the U.S. Environmental Protection Agency unveiled a new plan to protect freshwater ecosystems under which it was looking for model projects just like the one she had proposed. The national significance of the project figured prominently in her follow-up letter.

Finally, try to experience the program you are writing about. If you are fund raising for new diagnostic equipment in the medical lab, visit the lab and watch the equipment in use. (Hey, if it doesn't hurt, why not have the technicians use the equipment on you?) Go see the historic theater district you are lobbying to protect. Eat dinner in the soup kitchen.

INTERVIEWING: TAPPING INTO PEOPLE POWER

At the very least you should try to interview two key people before you sit down to write: the development person who knows the prospect best and the program person in charge of the project you want to fund. Now, if you are the executive director of a small nonprofit and you are the development person, program person, and proposal writer in one, terrific! The interview ought to be a snap.

But if you are not the superdirector, please prepare for your interview before you go knocking on a colleague's door.

HOT TIP: Check to see what the other fund-raising writer types have on hand before you bother your colleagues. Especially in large organizations, it is all too common for a busy program director to be bombarded with questions from the direct-mail writers and then three days later find you in the doorway asking similar questions for a proposal. We know that proposal writing is not direct mail and vice versa, but they look awfully similar to a non–fund raiser.

The interview: gut-wrenching horror or just plain fun? In his work for *Publishers Weekly* and other magazines, Joe has interviewed scores of authors, from unknowns to Joyce Carol Oates and Stephen King. To him, interviewing is just a matter of doing your research, getting your questions together, and asking.

Danielle, on the other hand, used to take days to work up her courage to talk to anybody she didn't know well. She would prepare and prepare and delay and delay and tell everyone in the vicinity how much she didn't want to do the interview until—finally!—the fear of not getting the interview done outweighed her fear of sounding like an idiot and she was forced to go talk to the person.

Joe's approach is much easier. Be cool.

Regardless of whether you like interviewing, being a good development writer requires that you talk to other people to get information. If you are feeling insecure, consider William Zinsser's advice from *On Writing Well*:

> *Interviewing is one of those skills you can only get better at. You will never again feel so ill at ease as when you try it for the first time . . . but much of the skill is mechanical. The rest is instinct—knowing how to make the other person relax, when to push, when to listen, when to stop. This can all be learned with experience.*

Remember, you will be asking people to talk about something they love—namely, their good cause. The job is even easier when you're talking to your own colleagues on staff, because you are in the noble position of helping the organization get the money it needs.

Do your homework. Preparing for an interview requires two basic steps:

1. Read about the subject at hand.
2. Put together a good list of questions.

"The point of research beforehand is not to impress the interviewee but to talk intelligently on the topics he takes up," says

John Brady in his classic guide *The Craft of Interviewing*. Maybe so, but research does also prevent one from making stupendous gaffes—an added bonus.

After gathering all the written materials you can find, read through them and write down questions that come to mind as you read. When you're done reading, think of other questions you want answers to. John Shepard, associate director of the Sonoran Institute, says he sometimes plays devil's advocate with his colleagues, asking questions that the opposition might ask. (Shepard is quick to tell his colleagues *why* he is asking such provocative questions, however, lest they hang him as a traitor.)

If you feel nervous about the interview, draw up a really long list of questions arranged in order of importance. You won't ask all of them, but they will prevent embarrassing silences and oversights on your part.

Open and closed questions. When interviewing, use a judicious mix of open questions and closed questions. Open questions are the essay questions of the interview. They bring forth lots of information. Open questions often begin with How? Why? and Tell me about (not a question but close enough).

Here are some open questions:

- How will the soup kitchen increase its capacity?
- Why are we asking for two vans?
- Tell me about the new literacy program.

Closed questions bring forth short, one-sentence-or-less, answers. They are the true/false or multiple-choice questions of the interview, helpful for verifying facts and getting specific details. Closed questions often begin with When? Who? and How many?

Here are some closed questions:

- When will the soup kitchen increase its capacity? (Next spring.)
- Who will drive the vans? (Volunteers from Zion Baptist Church.)

- How many people will the literacy program reach this year? (About 200.)

In most cases, you should load your interview with open questions and use them toward the beginning of the interview. Why? Because someone answering an open question is likely to throw in lots of information, including details you wouldn't have known to ask for. Open questions leave room for the golden nuggets of stories, firsthand accounts, and other real-life information that will add depth to your proposal.

When should you load your interview with closed questions? When your interviewee is being hopelessly vague and general. Closed questions help nail down those big talkers. Closed questions also work well at the end of the interview, when you just want to confirm a few last facts.

Clopen Questions

Novice interviewers often ask questions that sound like open questions but really are closed questions. For example: Do you think the plays we are running this season will attract a more diverse audience?

An enthusiastic general manager might say, "Yes, I really do, especially I think the Lopez plays will bring in the Latino community, and we're posting bilingual announcements in the subway . . ." and you are off and running (or scribbling, as the case may be).

But the unenthusiastic general manager might say yes as he shuffles the papers on his desk and frowns at the clock. You would then follow up with a true open question, "Why?" But that takes chutzpah, and you'll already be feeling uncomfortable because the man is being such a pill and you'd think he'd at least stop looking at the clock and now he's answered quite tersely again and . . . it's time for another open question.

Say what? What if you are interviewing a good talker but he doesn't make any sense?

"For my first proposal assignment I interviewed our Southeast program director," recalls John Shepard about his job as a writer for the Wilderness Society. "I didn't understand a thing he said."

Ah, the joys of jargon. There are times when interviewing an expert—even your own expert, your bosom buddy in the next cubicle—can be downright baffling. What is he talking about?

Do not stand on ceremony in these situations. When you find yourself confused by your interviewee, ask again. Ask him to tell you in simpler language or to give an example of what he means. Do not let those indecipherable descriptions just sail by, assuming that everyone—except you—understands. They don't.

"Trust the questions you have, even the dumb ones," says Beth Duris, a development writer who has spent years interviewing biologists, ecologists, and other scientific types. "The questions that come to mind are the ones that others will have, too."

Eventually you will get to know your subject better and face a different problem: getting jargon out of your own vocabulary. For advice on how to do that, turn to chapter 9.

Sometimes you won't understand the interviewee because he speaks in generalities. Some people are like that. It takes two or three questions on the same topic before they get down to a concrete example of how the new program will run or why we are spending all this time helping farmers track their inputs and outputs. (There's some jargon for you.)

Again, keep asking questions. Go back to the person later if you have to. Shepard recalls days when he would go back to a program director's office almost every hour, looking for more information or clarification.

And remember the bright side. Sometimes the interviewee talks nonstop about all the details and accomplishments and future plans he can think of. He digs through his desk to get the most recent program update and draws you a little map so that you understand the goals better. The guy is so articulate that the proposal practically writes itself. Interviews like that are one of the great joys of development writing.

The tape recorder versus the pen. Pens are universal. Everybody uses them. Not so with tape recorders. Some people swear by them, while others despise them. Joe thinks tape recorders are fine; Danielle thinks they are a pain in the butt.

The truth of the matter is that whether or not you use a tape recorder, the pen will always be your best friend. The pen (or pencil) is cheap, easy to use, and enables you to see immediately what was said rather than have to transcribe it first.

Unfortunately, most interviewers can't write as fast as people talk.

Check the B.S. Meter

"If someone's describing a project to you but it's just not clear no matter how many questions you ask, then it's not a real thing," says writer Beth Duris. "All that general talk doesn't translate when it comes time to write it down. You need to get to a point where you can be specific about what the money will do."

Sometimes your colleagues don't give you specifics because they don't *have* specifics. If that is the case, be very wary. Somebody, at some point, must figure out the specifics, and if you don't look out, that somebody might be you. After all, you always said you'd like to write fiction someday, didn't you?

Fiction happens. If you're stuck writing fiction, then write what makes sense to you. If you think there should be a newsletter for this new collaborative team, then write it into your draft. At worst, the people who should be making these decisions will say no, no, no and tell you what they really want to do.

Furious note taking. "It is a fine art to be able to write your notes accurately," says development writer Tracey Bedford. "The interviewee will say one thing, and so you start to write that down very carefully, but then the next thing he says is even better, so you skip ahead, but then you can't remember what you started to write before, and so on."

Instead of writing carefully, develop a system of abbreviations and shorthand so that your pen *usually* can keep up with the person speaking.

For example, you can drop unnecessary words and only half-spell the big ones. "Because" becomes b/c, "before" becomes b4, and "unnecessary" becomes unnec. When Danielle worked at the National Trust for Historic Preservation, "pr" stood for preservation. When she worked at The Nature Conservancy, "bd" meant biodiversity.

HOT TIP: Abbreviations work better if you type up the notes or fill in the gaps right after the interview. You will be amazed at how much you remember, even when your notes only say "res meas–John B., 2001." Of course, the results will be measured in 2001, and John Burns has an old proposal with a description of the methods that will be used for evaluation.

Even if your pen isn't keeping up, you can always ask the person speaking to wait for a moment while you scribble.

It pays to learn how to take fast notes because in many cases you have no other choice. You probably don't have the equipment (or inclination) to record telephone interviews. Sometimes you find the person you've been calling for days sitting next to you at a staff meeting. The pen saves the day.

HOT TIP: Danielle swears by the rollerball-type pens. Those pens can *fly*.

Tape recording has its place. Tape recorders require more work, but they capture everything. If you are in a situation where you must be very precise about the quotations you use—interviewing a corporate tycoon very sensitive about being quoted, for example—a tape recorder ensures that you won't mistakenly forget something or misrepresent what the person said.

When using a tape recorder, be prepared for the worst. For every interview, you should:

- check the batteries and/or replace them
- put in a fresh tape
- bring extra batteries and tapes
- test how close the recorder needs to be to the person speaking
- take notes during the interview, anyway
- keep an eye on the tape recorder to ensure it is still recording

Oh, and don't drop it.

You must keep track of the tape recorder constantly. Just ask any interviewer about what happens when you don't. The war stories abound:

"I got the greatest story!" says journalist to editor. Journalist hits the PLAY button.

Nothing.

Editor shakes his head and walks away.

The problem is that tape recorders often make people ill at ease, and this can be particularly difficult for the novice interviewer to overcome.

"The first time I used a tape recorder in an interview it was a nightmare," says Tracey Bedford, a writer who generally uses pen and paper now. "I was interviewing a donor, and she kept staring at the tape recorder because I was looking at it so often to make sure the little wheelies were turning. At one point the wheels *did* stop turning, so I had to stop her, change the tape, start it up again. It was really uncomfortable."

The solution? Just keep asking questions. The more you practice working with the tape recorder, the easier it will get.

Once the recording is done, transcribe the interview. It is much easier to pick out the best quotes when they are written on paper.

Using the interview in the proposal. Let your interviews rest for a day or so and then go back and read them, strictly to gauge which parts sound the most compelling. Later, you will sift through to find basic information for your proposal, but while you are still fresh, you have a better chance of finding the golden nuggets.

Put a little check mark or sticky note next to passages that look promising. The human stories might work well in your introduction or your description of the problem. The quote from the woman whose kid used your program could fit nicely when you discuss your organzation's strengths.

Judy Moak of Children's Express sometimes quotes what the children themselves say about her program. "Often they say in a sentence what would take me two or three paragraphs to describe," she says.

A good quote or example makes a point forcefully *and* quickly. If you find yourself writing three sentences of explanation to make your one sparkling quote comprehensible, then the quote isn't helping you very much. Likewise, if your example of the program in action takes a page to describe, think again. Is all that text needed to convince the reader? If you're not sure, cut.

Chapter 6

Parts of a Proposal

Making Each Section Sing

⧅

And now we are on to the Great Almighty of fund-raising writing, the proposal. In this chapter we will give you tips on how to write each section of the proposal well. We'll also cover the many variations of a basic proposal and the different audiences you will be talking to. But before we pick the proposal apart, let's look at the big picture.

CLARITY AND COMMON SENSE

Clarity and common sense are your two best friends in writing a proposal. Fancy words won't help you, nor will lengthy descriptions. A clear vision of the problem and what needs to be done will.

Clarity and common sense will make your proposal so immediate to the reader that she will feel as if she would have come up with your idea if you hadn't done so first.

This is what a good proposal feels like to the reader:

You're walking down the street in your neighborhood when you meet a group of children with a pile of lumber next to a large tree.

"We want to build a tree house so all the kids on the block have a place to meet," one says. "Danny's dad says he'll help us build it, and Mr. McDonagh gave us lumber, and Mrs. Smith said we could borrow the tools out of her shed as long as we're careful. All we need is nails, screws, and bolts and we can begin building!"

Will you refuse them the $20 for hardware? Of course not.

You can see the problem clearly, and the solution is so easy, so logical. Plus, these are pretty appealing kids. They have obviously put a lot of work into getting their materials together.

Your proposal will no doubt tackle issues more complex than a tree house. And you may not have as much support already lined up as the kids do. But the clarity and common sense should be there.

THE GREAT ALL-PURPOSE OUTLINE

Following is an outline for a formal foundation proposal. Proposals usually don't get any more detailed than this, but many will be less formal, especially if the donor is an individual or knows your organization well. You can pick and choose sections to meet your proposal needs. Change the order in which they appear. Add or delete at a whim. Or follow it exactly. No problem.

The Great All-Purpose Outline for a Formal Proposal

I. Cover Letter (required)
II. Cover Sheet (optional)
III. Table of Contents (optional)
IV. Executive Summary (required)
V. Introduction (required)
VI. Problem Statement (required)
VII. Program/Project Description
  A. Statement of Goals/Objectives (required)
  B. Methods (required)

C. Evaluation (sometimes optional but worth having)
D. Future Funding (optional)

VIII. Conclusion (required)

IX. Budget (required)

X. Appendices

A. Longer Background Narrative (optional)
B. Credentials of Key Leaders (optional)
C. List of Trustees and Their Affiliations (optional)
D. Strategic Plan, Press Coverage, Letters of Support (optional)
E. 501(c)(3) Tax Exemption Notification (optional)
F. Audited Financial Statements and/or Annual Report (optional)
G. Maps, Photographs, or Charts (optional)

To help you visualize each section we talk about, we've made up our own proposal for a very important good cause: building the Brooklyn Bridge. (If you'd like to learn the real story behind the bridge, we highly recommend David McCullough's book *The Great Bridge* (Simon & Schuster, 1972), from which we have borrowed liberally.)

THE COVER LETTER (REQUIRED)

The cover letter is a one- to two-page letter that accompanies your proposal. A senior-ranking official in your nonprofit signs the letter.

The cover letter tells the reader right away whether the proposal is worth reading. "I always read the cover letter first to see if the proposal responds to a real need," says Mary Bellor, president of the Philip L. Graham Fund in Washington, D.C. "I want to see who you are, what you do, who benefits, and why it matters. It's also nice to encapsulate what's to follow. Give me a preview of what I'm going to find in the proposal."

FOLLOW THE DONOR'S OUTLINE

Although our outline is wonderful (how could it be otherwise?), ignore it if the grantmaker has asked for something different. This is especially important when writing to a foundation. You must check its guidelines before you start anything.

Why?

- Because a 1990 survey by the *National Society of Fund Raising Executives Journal* found that the top complaint by foundation program officers is that grant seekers don't follow foundation guidelines.
- Because our own survey of the top 100 foundations in America revealed the exact same complaint. (For more tips from foundations, see "The Rules" in chapter 4.)
- Because you will certainly be turned down if you do not follow the grantmaker's guidelines.
- Because you will at best annoy, and at worst forever alienate, the grantmaker if you can't follow even the simplest directions—that is, the guidelines.

Follow the guidelines. If you don't understand the guidelines, call the grantmaker and ask questions. And if the grantmaker's guidelines conflict with our advice, then do what the grantmaker says. Always.

The cover letter is also the place to get personal. "The cover letter can be more important than the proposal," says Matthew Schenker, director of foundation relations at Clarke School for the Deaf in Northampton, Massachusetts. "It's a chance to make reference to personal connections and conversations and to highlight things that you and a trustee have understood one another on."

The cover letter presents an opportunity to tie your proposal to current events or put it in the context of what's happening in the community.

For example, you could:

- Thank the grantmaker for the delicious lunch last week and congratulate her on her alma mater's basketball victory.
- Delicately mention that her brother knows your board member and they both suggested you send this proposal.
- Announce that Dr. Emilio Suarez, the renowned infectious-disease expert, has agreed to head your proposed clinic in Ghana.
- Mention that the *Seattle Post-Dispatch* just ran an editorial about the importance of programs like yours. (Of course, a copy appears in the appendix.)
- Describe your cooperative arrangement with the local school district and the city library on this proposed project (especially if you know she is a supporter of the library).
- Discuss how your program actually decreases crime—an especially important outcome given the recent public outcry about crime in your city.

Sample Cover Letter

January 12, 1870

Mr. Roger Winthrop
President
The Brooklyn Foundation
100 Garfield Place
Brooklyn, New York 11215

Dear Roger:

I am pleased to enclose a proposal to the Brooklyn Foundation to begin work on a Great Brooklyn Bridge across the East River between Brooklyn and Manhattan. With a grant of $500,000, we will hire a team of technical personnel and begin construction of the two towers that will suspend the bridge.

As you know, our bridge promises to bring new prosperity to this borough and its people. No longer hampered by the vagaries of weather and ferry schedules, businesses in Brooklyn will easily reach customers and trading partners in Manhattan. With commerce thus improved, the borough will attract more businesses, residents, and cultural institutions, such as universities and theaters. In short, this bridge will put Brooklyn on the map.

Our request covers only the initial phase of the bridge's construction, but the Brooklyn Foundation's participation at this early juncture is critical. With your support, we will build the towers and the caissons that will support them, as well as conduct tests to ensure the integrity of the entire bridge structure. With these highly visible pieces in place, I am sure we will be able to secure full funding and the support of New York and the nation for this great endeavor.

Thank you, Roger, for your long-standing enthusiasm for our bridge and the vision behind it. I will visit your office next Wednesday to ensure that this proposal arrived safely and answer any questions you or the trustees may have.

Sincerely,

John Roebling
Founder, the Bridge Company

WRITER BEWARE! Don't put vital information in the cover letter without also putting it into the proposal. The proposal may be photocopied for several readers without the cover letter attached.

Even if you choose a short and simple letter, make sure you mention the amount of the request, what you will use the money for, and how to get in touch with you. (This latter information presumably will appear on your letterhead.) Also, tell the recipient when you will next be in touch.

THE COVER SHEET (OPTIONAL)

The cover sheet is merely the cover of the proposal. It usually contains the name of the organization to which the proposal is being sent, the title of the project or program, the name of your organization, and the date.

A separate cover sheet lends an air of formality to your proposal. Although it must include the items mentioned above, the cover sheet could contain a lot more. If you are applying to a large foundation, you may want to put the following facts on the cover sheet so that a busy program officer can see immediately that your proposal is appropriate:

- your name and title
- your agency's address and phone number
- the name of the program you are applying to
- the amount you are requesting
- a paragraph describing the program for which you seek support

Sample Cover Sheet

**TO BUILD A GREAT BROOKLYN BRIDGE
ACROSS THE EAST RIVER**

**A Proposal Prepared for
The Brooklyn Foundation**

**by
The Bridge Company**

January 1870

If you are writing to an individual or a corporate donor on the other hand, you may want to place a photo on the cover sheet in hopes of grabbing the reader's interest. Or, for a less formal proposal, you could simply put the title and date at the top of page 1 and begin writing.

Make sure the title reveals the nature of the proposal within. "New Horizons" won't tell the reader a thing about what's inside the cover. "A Compendium on Nonsense, Turgidly Rendered, at Great Length and with Academic Citations Blazing" may be more accurate, but who wants to read on?

A good title builds excitement and frames your argument. "From the Moon to the Stars: The New Program on Interplanetary Travel" sounds interesting and ambitious. Or how about this title: "Finding Common Ground: Community Outreach in Orange County." Sounds like a focused program, right? If outreach and activism are the main activities of your organization, this proposal could support your annual operating budget.

TABLE OF CONTENTS (OPTIONAL)

Include a table of contents if your proposal exceeds seven pages or has lots of appendices.

At most foundations, a program officer writes a summary of your proposal for the trustees and thus finds herself flipping back and forth through your proposal to assemble the basic facts. She will appreciate a table of contents.

HOT TIP: Most word-processing programs have an automatic table-of-contents feature, but make sure you understand how the program works before you start writing. In some cases, you have to put the section titles into a uniform style so that the program can identify which lines belong in the table. Figure out how the table of contents feature works before you start typing or you'll end up going back to redo all your headings.

Sample Contents Page

Contents

WRITER BEWARE! Double-check the table of contents against the actual pages. And don't forget to number your pages! Your proposal is likely to be taken apart so that copies can be made, and when the copy machine messes up–which we all know is practically guaranteed–the unfortunate recipient will have to decipher which page goes where and mess around for minutes at a time getting things back in order. Trust us; such annoyances do not build good karma.

EXECUTIVE SUMMARY (REQUIRED)

The executive summary provides a "cheat sheet" for readers who want to quickly find out what your proposal is about. It should never be more than one page, although it can be much less than that. A short executive summary includes a sentence each on the problem you want to address, your proposed solution, and how much your proposal requests. In a longer executive summary, you might take a paragraph for each item, but generally the amount of money you want and what it will be used for should appear in the first paragraph.

Pay attention to the executive summary. This is where many readers decide to throw your proposal into the garbage pile. The language must be succinct, yet appeal to the donor's interests. If you know she cares about immigration issues, then describe your literacy program as a lifeline for people who want to pursue the American Dream. If she cares more about adult learning, then highlight the innovative ways your program reaches out to working adults.

Sample Executive Summary

Executive Summary

The noted bridge builder John Roebling and his nonprofit Bridge Company seek $500,000 in start-up funding from the Brooklyn Foundation toward construction of a Great Brooklyn Bridge across the East River between Manhattan and Brooklyn.

The Great Bridge will put Brooklyn on the map. It will stimulate the borough's economic growth, raise property values, and provide a much-needed alternative to the ferries.

As the longest suspension bridge in the world, the bridge will also become a symbol of our age and a glorious testament to the genius and enterprise of the people who build it.

The following pages describe the scope and importance of the Great Bridge. Leadership support by the Brooklyn Foundation will help launch a project whose benefits will be felt for generations by the people of Brooklyn, New York City, and the nation. It will also help inspire further support from others.

Many people write the executive summary last (or second to last, before the cover letter) because it is easier then to quickly summarize each section of the proposal. But others, like Judy Moak of Children's Express, write it first: "The executive summary sets up everything else," she says. "It makes the short case for why the reader should support us. If I can't get through it, then I know I'm in trouble."

HOT TIP! If you are going to agonize over just one part of your proposal, this is the one. The executive summary is fraught with peril. You must hit the points that will interest the reader the most, yet you must not get too wordy. Revise; edit; revise some more.

THE INTRODUCTION (REQUIRED)

Some people refer to this section as the "Background" or "Organizational History." After skimming the executive summary, the reader will have a general understanding of what you hope to do. The next logical question is: "Who are you, and how are you qualified to do this work?" The introduction answers these questions in a page or two.

The introduction may briefly mention the problem and then discuss your qualifications in terms of that problem. The introduction often includes the size and scope of your organization: the number of employees, the number of offices, the number of clients, the size of the annual budget. It also cites partnerships with other organizations and makes reference to letters of support, media clips, and other attachments establishing your credibility.

The introduction is where you speak from strength. Rally the statistics that point to success. Your organization has grown from a staff of one to a staff of 25 in the last five years. Attendance at your workshops has doubled in the last three. The city's child-welfare agency has referred more than 2,000 youth to your organization.

Make your organization look as if it has been destined since the beginning of time to address this special challenge at this moment in history. Perhaps your staff are experts in the field, you've done similar work before, or there is no one else around with the facilities and equipment that you have. When the reader gets to your description of the challenge at hand, she should nod her head and think, Of course they're the ones to do the job.

One executive director of a new nonprofit organization told us that she always talks about the qualifications of her staff and the active involvement of her board of directors in the introduction. Doing so builds confidence in a small organization like hers.

If at this point it seems natural to also give a brief history of the project you'll be talking about, by all means do so.

If the grantmaker knows your organization well, then you may focus on why your organization is the best qualified to take on this project. But if there is a chance that others will see the proposal—foundations being a prime example, where the entire board of trustees will see parts of your proposal—it makes sense to keep at least a paragraph of basic organizational information in the introduction.

WRITER BEWARE! Do not ruin your introduction by giving the entire history of your organization or listing all your programs. "Established in 1971, Merrimack Family Services has spent nearly three decades addressing the needs of single-parent families. Our programs include parenting classes, family counseling, a mentoring program that matches new mothers with experienced mothers, and a baby-sitting bartering pool . . ." A list of programs does not illuminate why your organization is qualified to tackle society's problems. If you want to include more information on your organization, put it in an appendix in the back of the proposal.

Sample Introduction

Introduction

For generations, New Yorkers have yearned for a Great Bridge that would span the East River and link the boroughs of Manhattan and Brooklyn. As early as 1800, a carpenter named Thomas Pope proposed to build a wooden bridge that would soar 200 feet over the river like "a rainbow rising on the shore."

His vision of a heroic, monumental East River bridge has persisted. Time and again, bridges have been proposed—chain bridges, wire bridges, bridges of all kinds. "Manhattan and Brooklyn must be united," declared Horace Greeley in the *Tribune* in 1849.

Today, with the populations of Brooklyn and Manhattan growing rapidly, the city's leaders continue to call for a Great Bridge. Such an East River bridge will serve as a much-needed safety valve to alleviate crime and overcrowding in the city. Moreover, it will further hasten the economic growth of Brooklyn, which has already enjoyed prosperity with the introduction of steam ferries.

The time has come to build the Great Bridge. As designed by John Roebling, the leading bridge builder of our time, it will be the largest suspension bridge in the world. It will measure 80 feet wide and 5,862 feet in length from end to end, will bear an unprecedented load of 18,700 tons, and will be suspended by four enormous cables from two Gothic towers rising 268 feet above the riverbed. It will be constructed by a unique method—sinking two timber caissons deep into the riverbed as foundations for the great towers.

Since 1844, when he received his first commission and designed the world's first suspension aqueduct in Pennsylvania, John Roebling has demonstrated his superb ability to succeed in such a project. Often called a "lesser Leonardo," he and his Bridge Company have constructed such outstanding works as the Allegheny River Bridge, connecting Pittsburgh and Allegheny; the Cincinnati Bridge, hailed as a "structural and architectural marvel" and the largest bridge of its kind; and the spectacular International Suspension Bridge over the gorge at Niagara Falls. Each project exemplifies the company's mission to build bridges that bring economic prosperity and civic pride to America's cities.

Indeed, the building of the Great Bridge is a logical and compelling extension of the Bridge Company's earlier achievements. The company consists of six full-time engineers and a network of hundreds of designers, skilled craftsmen, and laborers who work on a contract basis. Together the company's six employees possess more than a century of experience in innovative bridge-building projects such as this one.

THE PROBLEM STATEMENT (REQUIRED)

Also called the "Needs Statement," this one-half-to-one-page section describes the specific problem that you want to address. The problem might more accurately be termed a challenge or an opportunity. No matter what, this section focuses on some need in society you want to address.

Must we even mention that your agency's lack of funding should not be "the problem"? Why should anyone care if you have enough money or not? Just so a few people can stay employed? So you and your buddies can lament society's ills at the water cooler?

"Not so!" you cry. "If we fold, then one of the few recreation programs for disabled kids will be gone forever!" Okay, then. The problem, or opportunity, is to help disabled kids run, dance, jump, and play. Focus on what makes your organization worthwhile.

If the proposal is for your general operating budget, frame your request in terms of your organization's mission. If your mission is to reform tax laws, then a grant to your general budget is a grant toward helping all Americans get a better tax system.

Sample Problem Statement

Linking Brooklyn to the New Prosperity

With Manhattan's population expanding rapidly, there will soon be few decent places for people to make a home in the city. Across the East River, however, there is such a place: Brooklyn.

"Brooklyn happens to be one of those things that can expand," the editors of the *Brooklyn Monthly* wrote recently. "The more you put into it, the more it will hold."

Clearly, Brooklyn and Manhattan will benefit enormously from a Great Bridge that connects the two boroughs. Experts predict the Great Bridge will lead to a doubling of the present rate of prosperity as new customers from Manhattan enter the borough and as Brooklyn's manufacturers and brewers move their wares across the river more efficiently. (Please see the city report on the economic impact of the bridge in Appendix A.)

Such well-known Brooklyn residents as the poet Walt Whitman and James S. T. Stranahan, the man behind Brooklyn's new Prospect Park, have said they look forward to the day when such a bridge will make Manhattan and Brooklyn "emphatically one." Such a permanent linkage augurs well at a time when the new Union Pacific Railroad is casting the city in the role of "commercial emporium of the world."

Apart from these immediate practical benefits, the bridge will also be a symbol of our age, a great connecting work like the Atlantic cable, the Suez Canal, and the transcontinental railroad. The bridge's great towers will serve as landmarks to the adjoining boroughs and will win a place as national monuments. As a work of art as well as of advanced bridge engineering, the bridge will forever testify to the energy and enterprise of the city and people who build it.

Whatever the problem, discuss it in terms that will interest your donor. If the foundation wants to integrate kids with disabilities into community life, then your proposal should talk about the need to give these kids the confidence, strength, and motor skills to participate in public-school activities just like other kids. If the prospect is more interested in innovative teaching methods, discuss how physical recreation teaches key skills in a way that is both enjoyable and immediately beneficial.

Has your group researched this problem? Say so. Cite facts and statistics. (And if you are tackling a local problem, cite local facts and statistics.) Use a story. Quote people who are experiencing the problem directly. Do not go overboard, however. Just lay out enough facts to demonstrate that your organization understands the issues fully and that the problem can be tackled effectively.

WRITER BEWARE! Avoid circular reasoning in which you say the problem is the lack of your solution. For example, you might say the problem is that the library lacks a computer center and your solution is to build one. A better problem statement would describe how many people come to your library to conduct research that would be better serviced through the Internet.

How important is the problem statement?

"Personally, I think needs statements are a dime a dozen," says Mary Liepold of the Child Welfare League of America. "Many of the foundation officers I work with are former social workers, and they really know the field. You should put much more time into describing the tasks you will perform to address the problem."

Joan Kennan, executive director of the Arcana Foundation, agrees. "I see so much written about low-income neighborhoods and unwed mothers and drug abuse. The needs statements go on and on, as if I had never heard of these problems before."

Take a tip from the pros and keep your problem statement relatively short, especially for readers who know the issues as well as you do.

PROGRAM/PROJECT DESCRIPTION

The program description is the meat of the proposal; in it you tell the reader what you plan to do to address the problem or opportunity stated above. This section includes four basic parts: goals and objectives, methods, evaluation, and future funding.

Don't worry too much about distinguishing between goals and objectives and methods. We want you to write a proposal that makes sense, not nitpick about precise definitions. As fund-raising consultant and community organizer Andy Robinson notes in *Grassroots Grants*, "I'm reminded of kids who don't want their peas and mashed potatoes to touch each other on the dinner plate. I've seen people waste a lot of time fretting about these categories."

Your prospect should come away from this section thinking your program is a logical response to the problems you talked about. So logical, in fact, that it would be a sin to let this opportunity pass by.

Goals and Objectives (required)

The goal is often one sentence describing how things will be different if the project is successful and how you plan to get to that successful outcome. The objectives, on the other hand, are specific, measurable benchmarks that together will indicate you reached your goal. Objectives are often listed in a bulleted format.

For example, Hill and Vale Affordable Housing in Schenectady decided that its goal was to provide housing to low- and moderate-income people in the city. Its objectives for one year were as follows:

- Three persons/families of low or moderate income will purchase Community Land Trust (CLT) homes.
- Three persons/families of low or moderate income will enter "Lease-to-Purchase" contracts on CLT homes.

- Two persons/families of low or moderate income will be "successful renters."
- Six homeowners will benefit from our Maintenance Outreach Program by saving at least $200 in home maintenance and repair.

Note that what makes these objectives so concrete is that they use numbers; we know exactly how many families the organization intends to reach. For some projects, however, it is almost impossible to come up with quantifiable objectives. In that case, you might take the approach of the Public School Forum of North Carolina: "To enhance the capacity of elected and appointed officials to make reasoned, research-based decisions concerning school improvement, especially in the areas of mathematics, science, and technology."

Another objective might be to make your program a pilot or a model for others. This can be very appealing to donors, but don't bill yourself as a model if you have no time or resources to share your results. In fact, savvy donors will question how you intend to become a model. The National Science Foundation, for instance, notes in its guidelines that "setting up a Web page about the project is not considered sufficient."

Methods (required)

This section describes the tasks you will complete to achieve your goal and objectives. Tackle this section like a journalistic exercise, answering who, what, when, where, how, and why. If you propose a long or complicated program, consider including a time line or a work plan that outlines the tasks, who will do them, and when they will be completed.

It is not uncommon to be cruising along on your proposal, happily typing away, only to come to a screeching halt at this section, because this is the place where you have to be specific about what you plan to *do*.

Do. It is an action verb. It is not a soft and fuzzy concept. It is quite concrete. What are you going to do? How are you going to do it?

Friends, this is where the rubber hits the road. You have told the reader what you want to achieve; now you need to tell her how you will achieve it. Good research and interviewing really pay off in the methods section. Pursue your program people doggedly and ask what they plan to do with the proposed gift. Get more detail than you need.

HOT TIP: If yours is a relatively new organization, a discussion of staffing and administration in the methods section may help to reassure the reader that you can do this work. Be very specific about who is in charge of what.

For example, if your colleague tells you that the grant will enable your agency to help communities in Green County fight sprawl, you better put her through her paces:

What do you mean by sprawl? How will you help the communities get involved? When you say community, do you mean local citizens, government officials, community groups, or a combination of the three? Why do you want to hold community meetings? What is the desired outcome of those meetings? Who will run them? How will you publicize the meetings? Where will the meetings be held? How many will be held? How will you relay all this information to the planning commission? Are you working with other organizations on this effort? Who specifically? What role will they play?

Just because you have all that detail does not mean you're going to include it. You will not load on the detail like a kid with ketchup, explaining every participant and potential pitfall and piece of equipment and partnership. Rather, you will select the details that make your program easy to visualize. The more concrete your description, the more believable your program becomes.

To decide which details to include, ask yourself, What is really compelling about this program? Which parts will appeal to the donor most? If you can answer these two questions, then you can scrape off some of the unnecessary detail. Be selective. Look for the meat.

"It helps if I think about what the headline would look like in the newspaper," says Judy Moak. "It would say 'Ford Foundation grants $50,000 for . . .' For what?"

Sometimes it also helps to think of your methods as a logical reaction to the problem statement. If you know a certain population in the city doesn't have adequate access to health care, then what are the logical steps to take? Publicize public-health programs; provide transportation to clinics; work with the local churches—you know what makes sense. Just write it down.

When it comes time to revise your methods section, remember the perverse law of proposals: The length of the proposal usually has a direct, inverse relationship to the amount of money you will get.

"The largest grant we've gotten came from a four-page proposal," says Craig Impink of WETA in Washington, D.C. "It was clear. We didn't try to snow the reader with language."

So keep your eyes on the prize: Tell the reader specifically what you will do. If you really feel the donor needs lots of detail, put most of it in an appendix. Better yet, have faith that when you next talk to the prospect, you'll have an opportunity to give her more detail if she wants it.

HOT TIP: Make sure your methods section matches the budget. If you say you will print brochures but forget to include the expense in the budget, the reader will begin to wonder whether you really know how to run your operation.

Evaluation (optional)

The evaluation section describes how you will determine whether your program was successful. Evaluations can be done by your own staff or by an outside agency. In addition, you may choose to evaluate not only whether you achieved your measurable objectives but also the process by which you achieved them.

Foundations in particular love the evaluation section; it helps them ensure that their money creates some good in society. Most nonprofits, on the other hand, hate evaluation sections. They make you think about your rhetoric. After all, you can wax poetic about your objectives and methods, but your poor colleagues (or you yourself) will be held accountable later on. You'll have to report back to the foundation about whether you met those criteria. Hmmm. Those foundation folks aren't so dumb, after all. The evaluation section is a reality check for you and an insurance policy for them.

The evaluation section may simply list questions that you will answer once the project is over or the grant has been spent. Did we get at least 100 community members to attend each meeting? Did we help at least three communities establish a balanced plan for growth? Were we able to involve all segments of the community? If so, what method worked best for getting that input?

The section can also include a discussion of how you will evaluate. If you are running an after-school program, will you track report cards to see if the extra help is improving grades? Or will you ask parents and kids to fill out evaluations of the program's activities?

A surprising number of organizations do not invest much effort in the evaluation section, which means you have an opportunity to make your proposal stand out from the pack. "We get a lot of proposals that merely say, 'We are planning to evaluate,' " says Joan Kennan of the Arcana Foundation. "Or they say they will interview their clients to get their reactions. But that type of evaluation is not very reliable."

So put together a thoughtful, effective evaluation section. Your readers, especially foundations, will notice the effort. "Try to keep track of records," says Kennan. "To be a responsible provider, you must have some idea of what happens to the people you're helping. If your assistance is only short term and then the person is back to drugs or has another baby or commits another crime, you're not having much of an impact."

Nancy Register, who evaluates proposals for a grants program at the Consumer Federation of America, sees the same problem. "What does success look like, and how will you know you got there? Maybe you'll get 50 new members. You don't have to be elaborate, but do include it."

HOT TIP: If you are seeking general operating support, finding evaluation criteria may be tricky. Try looking at your organization's strategic plan, if there is one. If your goal is to expand by 30 percent over the next five years, then perhaps your two-year goal should be to expand by 12 percent.

For especially large or complex projects, you may suggest hiring an outside firm to evaluate your success. If so, explain who will do the evaluation and what they will provide: a final report, interim feedback, survey results, etc. Be sure to include the expense for hiring an outside firm in your project budget.

WRITER BEWARE! Remember, if you decide not to invest much time in an evaluation section, you risk having the funder evaluate you on criteria you didn't prepare for. It is much better to know up front that the donor will look at your program in terms of cost per child rather than in terms of changes in the child's behavior.

Future Funding (optional)

If appropriate, discuss the other sources of funding for this project and how you will meet the needs of the project beyond the period of the grant. Show that you have given serious thought to the program and are committed to making it work for the long term.

Sample Program/Project Description

Toward the Building of the Great Bridge

To help improve the lives and economies of the people of Brooklyn and the city generally, the Bridge Company now intends to construct a Great Bridge across the East River.

The Great Bridge will be the largest suspension bridge in the world. (Please see Appendix B for specifications and statistics on the bridge.) It will be half again the size of Mr. Roebling's bridge over the Ohio at Cincinnati and nearly twice the length of Telford's major suspension bridge over the Menai Strait in Wales.

The bridge will cross the East River in a single span. It will be held aloft by huge cables slung from the tops of two stone towers standing about seven stories tall—taller than most of the buildings in New York. They will occupy most of a city block and be heavy enough to offset the weight of the cables.

The 268-foot-high towers will stand on either side of the river, in the water, with their foundations out of sight below. Each will have two Gothic arches through which the roadways will pass.

As detailed in Mr. Roebling's plans and diagrams in Appendix C, the Great Bridge will measure more than a mile from end to end. It will become a vital new link between the boroughs for the use of carriages, riders on horseback, drays, farm wagons, and other commercial traffic. It will also include tracks for specially built trains that can carry an estimated 40 million passengers annually as well as an elevated boardwalk for pedestrians.

Goals/Objectives

With a start-up grant of $500,000, Mr. Roebling and the Bridge Company will hire technical personnel and build the two towers that will suspend the Great Bridge. As they rise hundreds of feet into the air on either shore, these towers will become a symbol of the coming prosperity and the union of Brooklyn with the rest of the city. They will allow the roadway to make its splendid eventual leap across the river.

METHODS

During the tower-building stage, workmen will assemble the towers' granite upper sections and the limestone lower sections and attach them together. The workmen also will build the immense wooden caissons that will serve as foundations for the towers, then fill them with concrete and sink them into the riverbed as permanent supports for the towers.

A secondary goal of the tower-building stage will be to call widespread attention to the Great Bridge. An obvious point of interest for the public will be the pioneering use of the caissons during construction. Their construction will require heroic effort on the part of engineers and workmen alike and will mark a milestone in bridge engineering.

Specifically, the Bridge Company will hire four supervising engineers and a work crew of 100 men, as outlined in Appendix B. Over a six-year period, these workmen will execute Mr. Roebling's plans for the building of the bridge towers. They are expected to complete the towers by July 1876. Construction of the entire bridge will take an estimated 14 years, with the opening tentatively scheduled for the spring of 1883.

EVALUATION

In evaluating the success of this initial stage, the Bridge Company will seek to answer several basic questions. Did we successfully build the 268-foot towers that will suspend the cables and roadway of the bridge? Was each stage of the tower work carried out in accordance with Mr. Roebling's plans? Are the towers in fact effective as supports for the entire bridge?

The Bridge Company will carefully photograph and make written reports on progress at key stages, including the building of the wooden caissons, the filling and sinking of the caissons, and the building of the two major sections of the towers (limestone below water and granite above).

Future Funding

The Bridge Company has already secured pledges of support toward construction of the Great Bridge from several individuals and foundations. These commitments now total $2 million toward the $8 million required to complete the entire project. It is anticipated that several prospective donors, including two major Brooklyn corporations, will offer support once the tower building begins.

Future funding is particularly important to a foundation. Most major foundations will not support the same program year after year. Eventually you will have to find other sources of support, and the foundation wants to know how you plan to make the transition.

Of course, you can't know how exactly the money will come in. All the donor wants to know is how you plan to tackle the challenge. Perhaps your literacy program will eventually seek funding from local businesses that are hiring your graduates. Or you may initiate fund-raising readathons. Or you may start an annual giving program among your alumni. More likely you plan to do all three. This is what the foundation wants to hear.

If you prefer, you can eliminate this section and include the information in the budget instead.

THE CONCLUSION (REQUIRED)

The conclusion is where you ask clearly for the money and the time period in which you want it. You may also describe recognition of the donor if there is to be any. Then you end with a noble sentence or two about how this project and the grantmaker's involvement will make the world a better place.

When you ask for the money, do just that. No euphemisms, no "whatever you can spare" nonsense. For example: The Words Are Wonderful Program respectfully requests a grant of $2,000 to fund our summer literacy programs in Alexandria, Virginia, in 2001."

The last part of the conclusion tells the donor, "Your gift will make a big difference," but does so with a bit of panache and elegance. The donor wants to feel good about this decision. You've given her all the reasons why and how and wherefore. Now remind her of her higher purpose: to build, to empower, to create, to change the way, to provide new hope for, to ensure the future of. It is a reprise of the larger theme you have been sounding all along: You, dear donor, will help humanity and be remembered for the ages.

Sample Conclusion

Conclusion

The Bridge Company now asks that the Brooklyn Foundation consider making a start-up gift of $500,000 toward construction of the Great Bridge linking Brooklyn and Manhattan. In recognition of such support, the Bridge Company is prepared to prominently emblazon the foundation's name on each of the bridge towers. It will announce the foundation's leadership role in key news publications and will call attention to its support in opening-day ceremonies that will gather city, national, and international leaders.

To offer such fundamental support is to provide strong leadership for a project with the potential to enhance the prosperity of Brooklyn and its residents for generations to come. Such a gift will also help create a great beacon in the night to people the world over proclaiming Brooklyn and New York City as centers of commerce and democracy.

If you are stumped on how to hit that high note, try looking at how others structure their conclusions. One of our favorite approaches is the "not only . . . but also," as in: "The foundation not only will provide immediate assistance to women in this rural province but also will lay the groundwork for an organized, permanent weaving cooperative." Another good one is the "to do this is really to do that" approach, as in: "To establish a weaving cooperative at this time is to invest in the power of these families to improve their lives and build for the future."

Some people prefer to divide the ask from the conclusion. They create a separate section, such as "Request for Support," where they ask for the money. Then the conclusion is devoted to a final, eloquent pitch. A typical request for support simply says the following:

"The Joe and Danielle Agency respectfully requests a one-year grant of $10,000 from the Benificent Foundation. This grant will be used to build a new clubhouse and bar for nonprofit writers in metropolitan Washington, D.C."

Then a separate conclusion expresses the importance of a new clubhouse and bar for the future of writing in the nation's capital.

THE BUDGET (REQUIRED)

Make your budget easy to read and understand—no microscopic numbers piled on top of each other!

The level of detail in your budget depends on the audience. If it is a graduate of your institution who is known for big ideas and a lust for life, she probably just wants the basic rundown on what your project will cost. If you are applying for a three-year grant from a major foundation, however, you will probably want to show a lot more detail and include notes or a budget narrative to explain how you calculated your costs.

Many foundation officers begin reading your proposal on the budget page. Therefore, make sure the budget is very easy to understand. The headings for line items should be self-explanatory, and the format should be pleasing to the eye. Pay attention to the budgets and invoices that you receive in your personal life and note which ones you like. If your bank statement is a breeze to understand, apply some of those formatting tricks to your budget.

WRITER BEWARE! Make sure the text matches the budget. You may have a draft of the proposal ready but find out at the last minute that your colleague budgeted to hire a consultant for the project. You can't just list a consultant in the budget without explaining somewhere in the methods section what the consultant will do. Go back and fill in.

Most proposal budgets have just two columns: the item and how much it will cost. If you are asking for a portion of the money you need, you may want to indicate that the donor is only paying for half of the total cost or whatever portion is appropriate. Usually, it is preferable to avoid specifying exactly which pieces the prospect will pay for. (E.g., the foundation will pay for computer equipment but not the data administrator's time.)

Of course, there are always exceptions. If you are talking to a sophisticated donor who has made it clear she will pay for capital improvements but not operations, then a three-column budget may be the most convincing to her: one column for the item, one for what you want her to pay, and one for the remaining money that you will get from other sources. That third column reinforces that you understand her wishes (her name appears only next to line items that are capital improvements) and demonstrates how much money your organization is devoting from other sources (or from its own coffers) to cover the operations. Or, if you are applying for a matching grant, you may decide to devote the third column to listing what you have already raised toward the match.

What items go in the budget? Again, this is a matter of discretion, but here are some of the items to consider.

- Personnel. If you are hiring a new person for this project, try to get a good estimate of what the salary will be. If an existing staff person will devote 50 percent of her time to the project, then list half of her salary as a project expense. If the grant will span more than one year, calculate salary increases and cost-of-living adjustments for future years.
- Benefits. Some budgets break out benefits as a separate line item from salaries. Usually grantmakers will allow you to calculate the entire benefits package as a percentage of payroll. (I.e., the Words Are Wonderful Program pays 30 percent of payroll in benefits.) Unless specifically requested, do not torture yourself by listing every benefit and its cost (health insurance, disability insurance, social security, vacation, etc.).
- Consultants and Contract Service. Get an estimate from the consultant for how much services will cost.

HOT TIP: If you have a volunteer providing free services, you may be able to count the value of those services as part of your match for a matching grant. (Obviously, check with the donor's guidelines before you do that.) Even if you're not working toward a matching grant, valuable volunteer service is a sign of external support for your project.

- General Overhead/Operating Costs. This category includes things like rent, utilities, telephone service, postage, copying costs, insurance, office supplies, bookkeeping, janitorial service, and landscaping. Again, use your best judgment. If your project includes several mailings to the community, then perhaps you will list copying, office supplies, and postage as separate line items and forget the rest of the overhead. If the proposed grant is for a project that will occupy your entire organization for the next six months, however, it may be appropriate to list half of your annual operating expenses as an item in the budget. Before you try this latter strategy, *please* check the prospect's guidelines.

- Equipment. If you will be buying new equipment for the project, find out what it will cost. You may also want to include money for installation, service, and future upgrades. (This is especially true for computer equipment.)
- Travel. Will someone be flying to Asia on a regular basis for this project? If so, you'd better estimate how much money will be needed for airline tickets, lodging, meals, and tips. (And as any international traveler will tell you, define "tips" pretty loosely.) If the project director will be driving a lot, don't forget to include money for mileage reimbursements.
- Indirect Costs. Indirect costs are a lot like operating costs; they are the expenses associated with housing a project at your institution. You may create a new hotline center at your medical clinic, and those hotline operators will sit in a room to which you provide heat and electricity. The hotline operators may also make use of your receptionist and medical library. In that case, charging a small percentage of the costs of having a heated and well-lit building, a receptionist, and a library may be appropriate. Again, check with your prospect before putting this in your budget.

Who writes the budget? Whoever has the time and knowledge, that's who. It may well be you, the writer. If someone else does the budget, read it carefully to ensure that the line items match your text and the format matches the rest of the proposal.

HOT TIP: If you are the person calculating all the numbers for the budget, make sure that you save your worksheets and notes on figures. They will help you write the final report and save your skin if someone suddenly insists she told you the computers would cost $40,000, not $10,000.

Sample Budget

The Great Brooklyn Bridge
Phase I Budget

Item	Year 1	Year 2	Year 3	Year 4	Year 5	Year 6
Personnel	$ 0	50,000	52,000	54,000	56,000	58,000
Equipment	$15,000	45,000	10,000	10,000	10,000	10,000
Services	$40,000	15,000	15,000	15,000	15,000	20,000
Travel	$ 2,000	2,000	2,000	2,000	1,000	1,000
Total	57,000	112,000	79,000	81,000	82,000	89,000

Grand Total: $500,000

Notes:

- During the first year of the project, we will hire an engineering firm and bridge consultants to model the caissons and towers, test the models for integrity, and document construction and implementation methods.
- In year two, we will hire a team of 100 technical engineers and construction professionals to begin building the caissons and towers. At this time, we will also secure the bulk of the machinery and materials needed. The consultant team will be reduced to all but a few managers to oversee the technical aspects of the construction process.
- In year six, we will reengage the engineering consultants to assist with the placement of the caissons and the erection of the towers.

For an example of how to create a budget for a massive project, we highly recommend Judith Mirich Gooch's book *Writing Winning Proposals* (published by the Council for Advancement and Support of Education). Her chapter on creating a budget for a multidisciplinary program at a university is eye-poppingly thorough. Those of you in similar situations have our condolences.

HOT TIP: Do the math. Do it again. At least half the development writers and officers we interviewed for this book had a story about sending in a proposal with a budget that either didn't add up or didn't match the text. Promise yourself that you will *always* check the math before the budget goes out the door. Don't trust the computer. Grab your calculator and take five minutes to check everything. In fact, take a lesson from Mary Liepold. She prints out her text, her time line, and her budget and compares them side by side.

APPENDICES (OPTIONAL)

Thank heavens for the appendix. Here is where you put everything that you wanted to put in the proposal but the little angel on your left shoulder convinced you to have mercy on the reader. Now that we're here, don't let the little devil on your right shoulder go wild.

Don't add background material just to make yourself feel secure. Do it because you are reasonably sure the reader will want to know more about your organization. Include a list of your board members if it will bolster your credibility. Leave it out if the donor doesn't care. Include newspaper clips if the stories further illuminate a point made in your proposal. Leave them out if they talk about a totally different program for which you do not need funding.

What might appear in an appendix?

- more background information on your group's history and mission
- short biographies of your leaders or the people who will lead this particular project
- a list of your board members and their business/philanthropic affiliations
- the executive summary of your five-year strategic plan
- the work plan for the scientific study you will be conducting

TIPS FROM TOP FOUNDATION FUNDERS

What do the major foundations think of the proposals they receive each day? Are they well written? Persuasive? A mess?

More than a dozen of the country's leading foundations—those with the most assets—responded to our survey asking what advice they have for proposal writers. Many had nice things to say about the fund-raising writing they encounter: "The quality of proposals received by our foundation is excellent overall," says Paul B. Mott Jr., executive director of the F. M. Kirby Foundation. "There is no substitute for good writing skills, and the improvement over the years has been enormous."

And yet.

Says Carr Agyapong, senior program/communications officers at the Burroughs Wellcome Fund: "Our biggest complaint about proposals is the writers' inability to communicate clearly what they want, who they are, and why our organization should provide them with a grant."

At the James S. McDonnell Foundation, program director Susan M. Fitzpatrick says she is put off by the "rhetoric" of canned pitch letters. She seeks "clarity, conciseness, and a match between guidelines and project." She adds: "Do your homework—read and research. Get advice! The first person critiquing your proposal should not be a program officer."

Many funders urge you to marshal the facts—and make sense.

Says Alice McCartor, program officer at the Meyer Memorial Trust. "Ask someone outside your field to read your proposal and tell you what he/she thinks it says."

"I most appreciate brevity, clarity, and some sense of passion," says David Bergholz, executive director of the George Gund Foundation. "Read what you have written several times and see if it would sell you on the idea you are attempting to put forward."

"Too many proposals are not well thought out—they're too vague or broad," says Herbert D. Doan, president of the Herbert H. and Grace A. Dow Foundation. "Make sure you've thought out the total budget for your project with details on how funds will be acquired and expensed. Also, what provisions have been made for future financial self sufficiency?"

Again, facts, please!

"The reader is not going to be swayed by superlatives," says Miles J. Gibbons Jr., president of the Whitaker Foundation. "He most appreciates factual information pertinent to the proposal."

And then we heard a mantra: Guidelines! Guidelines! Guidelines!

"Some organizations don't do their research as to what our foundation funds," says John W. Cook, president of the Henry Luce Foundation Inc. "Even if they see our name listed in a newspaper or other source, they should obtain our own guidelines to establish if they fit our criterion." He adds: "Do your homework on the organization that will receive your proposal. You waste time and money doing a blanket mailing to every organization on some list."

So, our respondents keep saying, write a concise, fact-filled proposal, send it to the right place, and you've got a shot at funding.

"Make it succinct and easy to read," says E. Ray Cope, president of the Kate B. Reynolds Charitable Trust. "Believe in your project and present it clearly," says Yvonne Engel, program and network administrator at the Lynde and Harry Bradley Foundation. "If you're too emotional or not specific enough in describing the need," says grants administrator Betsy Hamilton at the J. Bulow Campbell Foundation, "there's very little likelihood a foundation will respond."

- two or three newspaper clippings about your nonprofit or the issue you seek to address
- letters of support from government agencies or cooperating organizations
- your 501(c)(3) Tax-Exemption Notification
- your audited financial statements for the last fiscal year
- maps of the area you're working in
- charts showing recent trends and increases you hope to achieve in the next three years
- photographs of last year's summer program
- architectural drawings of the new building

VARIATIONS ON THE ALL-PURPOSE PROPOSAL

Sometimes the situation doesn't call for a full-blown proposal. If not, there are five common subspecies of the proposal that you might use.

The Letter Proposal

The letter proposal opens like a cover letter but after a paragraph or two becomes a proposal. At the end of the proposal section, you revert back to a letter with a personal paragraph saying how you hope the recipient will give this request careful consideration. Many nonprofits use letter proposals for individuals who know the institution well. In such cases, the letter proposal might open this way:

> Dear Bob:
>
> I hope this letter finds you recovering well from the holiday rush. As we discussed in December, the Lung Organization will soon launch a ten-city education program highlighting the relationship between transportation choices, air quality, and health. This is a groundbreaking initiative that will require a great deal of coordination among our chapters, public agencies, and health providers in each city. Our goal is to increase the use of and support for public transportation in these areas as well as to increase awareness of resources for people concerned

> about respiratory ailments. I hope you will consider helping us launch this effort with a gift of $500,000 over two years.
>
> **SMOG IN AMERICA'S CITIES**
>
> A recent study by the U.S. Environmental Protection Agency states that the ten largest cities in America also experience the worst smog levels, and this takes a direct toll on residents' health . . .

Then your letter proposal launches into the problem statement, the goals and objectives, the methods, evaluation, and a summary of your budget and future funding situation. The letter proposal closes with paragraphs that address the donor's own interests in this area. For example:

> Bob, your support for the Lung Organization over the years has been instrumental in our success. As you yourself have noted, however, our future success depends on our ability to work closely with the people and institutions that affect respiratory health—government agencies, environmental organizations, and health providers. The program outlined above will not only help people make informed choices about how to improve their own health but also enable us to forge strong relationships with the agencies, institutions, and medical practitioners critical to our future.
>
> I hope you will consider making a gift of $500,000 to support this effort. I will be in Detroit next week and will call you to discuss this proposal. Again, thank you for your consideration and dedication to our mission.
>
> Best regards,
>
> Regina Mickelson

The Concept Paper

The concept paper is really a preproposal. Think back to when you were in high school and you wanted to borrow a car to go to the movies. You had a couple of options. You could make a formal proposal to your mother: "Gee, Mom, if you let me borrow your car on Saturday, I will use it to achieve our mutual goal of providing America's youth with happy and fulfilling lives. Specifically, I will take my friends to the movies, and afterwards I will drive them all home in the most careful manner possible and deliver the vehicle safely back to you by midnight at the latest. Could I please borrow the car, please?"

But in high school the direct approach was not always the best one. Sometimes it was better to float the general concept of borrowing the car just to see your mother's initial reaction: "Gee, if somebody loaned me a car on a weekend night, I could use it to provide America's youth with happy and fulfilling lives. In fact, I have been thinking about taking some of my friends to the movies using a borrowed car and then afterward driving them all home in a very safe manner and bringing the car back to the rightful owner by midnight at the latest. You've always encouraged me to pursue interests outside of school—what do you think of this idea?"

We call the latter approach the concept paper. The concept paper opens a dialogue with the prospective grantmaker. It does not actually ask for funds.

A concept paper still includes the basics of a proposal: the introduction, the problem statement, the goals, the methods. But you skip evaluation and future funding. You do not specifically name an amount of money you want or from whom you hope to get the money. In your conclusion you simply describe the wonderful impact this program would have and your eagerness to discuss the idea further. In most cases, you do not include a budget unless it's a rough tally of the estimated costs.

The Letter of Inquiry

When you first approach a foundation, you should send a letter of inquiry to find out if the foundation would be interested in your idea. The letter itself looks and acts like an executive summary. It enables the reader to find out what you want and decide if she cares to learn more.

From your perspective, the purpose of the inquiry letter is to give the foundation the basic outline of your proposal and convince the reader to set up a meeting or to invite you to send a full proposal. From the foundation's perspective, the purpose of the inquiry letter is to nip unwanted proposals in the bud. A foundation officer uses the inquiry letter to decide whether you fit within the foundation's current priorities, and if so, whether you deserve a tiny sliver of her already overburdened schedule.

What goes in the inquiry letter? "Provide enough information to convince the grantmaker that you have a full command of the situation and the field, without overloading her with details," advises Susan L. Golden in her book *Successful Grantsmanship: A Guerilla Guide to Raising Money.* Golden recommends writing the inquiry letter in a tone that is businesslike but a bit warmer than that of a formal proposal.

A letter of inquiry should never be more than three pages long. Any longer and you're straying into proposal land. It should cover the following topics in the order that makes the most sense to you:

— Hello, this is why I am writing (one paragraph)

In the opening of your letter, tell the foundation what your project is about and that you are writing to inquire about its interest in such a project. For example: "In 2001, Sister Cares will expand its downtown clinic to provide gynecological services to low- and moderate-income women. We would very much like to meet with you to discuss the program described below."

With a large foundation, you might tell the reader which program you are applying to: "In 2001, Sister Cares will break ground on a new wing at our downtown clinic. This expanded facility will enable us to provide mammograms and menopause-related health services to 1,200 women each year, filling a critical gap that I believe will be of interest to the Glory Foundation's Women and Health Program."

— Introduction/organizational background (one or two paragraphs)

Give a brief explanation of who you are (one sentence; two tops) and your special credentials to handle this project. What makes your organization different?

— Problem statement (one paragraph)

What need are you seeking to address? A quick statistic or two will be helpful.

— Your proposed solution (no more than three paragraphs)

This is your project description, including your goals, objectives, and methods.

— Budget narrative (one paragraph)

Summarize the total budget and the kinds of expenses you anticipate. (All the money is for personnel, or maybe one half is for equipment and the other half is for personnel, etc.)

— Next steps and closing (one paragraph)

This is the most important part. Tell the reader what you want next—a meeting, a further discussion, an invitation to submit a full proposal—but keep the ball in your court. Tell her when you will call to arrange the next step. In the meantime, make sure she knows who to contact at your organization if she just can't wait to speak with you.

HOT TIP: It is perfectly appropriate to indicate that you would like the foundation's feedback regarding your project. In fact, the Fundraising School at Indiana University's Center on Philanthropy suggests that you write a cover letter to the foundation and request the reader's assessment of the attached summary–the summary being essentially a letter of inquiry without the Dear Ms. Smith part.

The Menu Proposal

When Mrs. Beedlemeyer made a five-year $500,000 pledge to your capital campaign, she asked if she could choose a different program to support each year. But of course! So each year you cook up a menu proposal suggesting three options for her $100,000 pledge payment. In this case, you still write the problem statement, goals, methods, and evaluations, but you summarize this information briefly for each of the three options.

HOT TIP: In your introduction or cover letter, describe why you are choosing these particular options. What is the theme that ties them together? Perhaps they all relate to Mrs. B's interest in the arts, or maybe each one represents an opportunity to ensure the long-term excellence of programs at the university she so loves. (I.e., each one involves an endowment.)

Another variation on this theme is the menu concept paper. Think of it as an even-more-conceptual concept paper. You want the prospect to get a sense of the range of programs that she could support, in theory, if she were interested. In this case you follow the concept-paper approach—introduction, problem, goals, and methods—but summarize these elements for each option in the menu. Skip the budget, evaluation, and future funding questions altogether. Provide just enough information to get a conversation going about the donor's interests.

The Two-Pager

Sometimes you need a condensed version of a concept paper to hand to people as an introduction to a program or giving opportunity. For example, maybe your organization just received a challenge grant from the National Endowment for the Humanities (NEH). Now your development officers are hitting the road to tell potential donors about the opportunity to leverage their gifts by matching the NEH grant. You want to hand these people a quick summary of the NEH challenge itself and the program it supports.

This scenario calls for an even shorter version of the concept paper. You will include the introduction, problem statement, goals, and methods. The conclusion is short and to the point—maybe just one sentence. In the NEH example above, the two-pager conclusion might simply say that potential donors have the opportunity to leverage their gift by joining a highly successful public/private partnership to create this exciting new program.

TAILORING PROPOSALS TO INDIVIDUALS

Writing a proposal to a specific individual can be a wonderful treat, because you often know the person well enough that you can hit that person's interests with laser precision. You know that Joan's brother died of cancer as a child and all Joan cares about is helping kids with cancer. You are going to write with gusto about your hospital's special programs for kids and their parents.

Unlike foundation officers, however, individuals are not paid to read your proposal. They can toss that proposal in the garbage anytime they feel like it. So grab Joan's interest with a story and get to the point quickly.

"We usually write two- to three-page letters to our top individual donors," says John Shepard of the Sonoran Institute. "I think individuals are more keen on the stories than they are on the mechanics of the program. They may or may not even want a budget."

In fact, a letter proposal seems to be the communication vehicle of choice for individuals. Most of the proposal writers we talked to said they used short letters—no more than four or five pages and even shorter if possible—to solicit their major individual donors.

A letter proposal to an individual is like any other letter proposal except that it is a tad shorter, focuses on human stories, and does not use formal subheadings like "Introduction," "Program Description," and so on. Throughout the letter proposal, keep your thoughts on that donor and her particular interests.

"You have to answer what's in it for me," says Nancy Register of the Consumer Federation of America. "Never underestimate the exchange that takes place. What do they get for this money? It might be a sense of helping people, of being part of a larger effort. It might be a status thing. Altruism is alive and well, yes, but there is an exchange."

Foundations Are People, Too

Although we are stressing the differences between writing for individuals and writing for foundations, don't forget that there is a specific person at the foundation who will open your envelope, pull out your proposal, and start reading. That person, most likely a program officer, will in turn send your proposal to other people—experts in the field, other readers, board members.

"You have to remember that foundation board members are usually all volunteers or family members," says Kim Coleman, president of the Washington, D.C.-based Expanding Horizons. "They want to feel good about what they're doing, just like everyone else."

WRITING FOR CORPORATIONS

Boy, if you thought individuals have a short attention span, try busy corporate executives. The trend in corporate proposals is to make them short—really short—and lead off immediately with the benefits to the corporation.

You will have to make a judgment call as to how to express these benefits. Some people put them right on page 1 under the heading "Benefits to General Motors." Others write the proposal in the usual order but in every section hammer away at the benefits to the company.

For example, the Words Are Wonderful Literacy Program might solicit a local restaurant chain for a gift. When it introduces the problem of illiteracy, it will talk about how qualified immigrants—the restaurant's potential employees—are kept out of the workforce because they can't read English. When it describes the program, it will talk about how these people go on to get better jobs, like the ones at the restaurant, and eventually improve their incomes enough to spend more at local businesses, like the restaurant. It will offer to recognize the restaurant chain in its newsletter. You get the message: Helping Words Are Wonderful will ultimately help the restaurant.

Nonprofits don't always ask corporations for money. Some corporations prefer to donate goods and services. Still others are more interested in cause-related marketing, or CRM, whereby they pay a fee or percentage of sales in exchange for using a good cause's name and logo in marketing materials. CRM is not a charitable transaction. Your organization's logo and reputation have value, and the company is merely paying for the use of those commodities.

Even if you are asking for a CRM gift, you still should treat the proposal like any other; just make sure you hit the benefits to the corporation prominently. Some organizations have great success pitching a two-part gift: One portion is strictly charitable; the other is part of a CRM arrangement.

WRITING FOR THE GOVERNMENT

Applying for government grants is like writing for a foundation with a vengeance. Guidelines are the name of the game. Depending on whether you apply for a local, state, or federal grant, there could be entire manuals out there dictating allowable costs, reporting guidelines, eligibility, and more.

We are not government-grant experts, but we do know that it is a whole different ball game. If you enter the world of government-grant writing, more power to you. There is a lot of money to be had, but never kid yourself that the process will be similar to writing for the private sector.

"Development people write proposals like a college paper," says Mark Longo, director of development services at the National Trust for Historic Preservation and an experienced writer of government grants. "Trust me—government application readers don't want flowery language. They want things as simple as possible. Fill in each space in the application exactly. Don't make them search for anything."

To succeed at getting federal grants, you must know such things as the requirements for matching grants and cost-share arrangements; the difference between a grant, a cooperative agreement, and a contract; and where to find information in the Catalog of Federal Domestic Assistance, which in its book form literally stands six inches thick. (Thankfully, it is also on the World Wide Web.) Longo recommends that you take a course in government-grant seeking, buy a book on the subject, or look on the Web for assistance.

One thing that government-grant seeking has in common with private fund raising: You should talk to the donor. "I highly recommend calling the agency you're planning to solicit and pitching your idea on the phone," says Longo. "Often the person will tell you which areas to emphasize in your application or even invite you to send a draft early for comments and feedback."

PROOFREADING, PACKAGING, AND PLEASING THE DONOR

When the Grantsmanship Center in Los Angeles drew up its "Program Planning and Proposal Writing Guide," it offered the following point as its first (first, mind you) basic principle:

"The proposal should be neat, clean, and easy to read!"

Neat, clean, and easy to read. This comes ahead of things like write in English, keep it brief, and be positive. What do we mean by neat, clean, and easy to read?

Neat: no typos, no mistakes in the budget, no inconsistencies in the format, no alternating between first and third person (e.g., alternating between saying "The Good Hope Agency believes" and "We believe").

Clean: no typos, no coffee stains, no ink streaks from the printer.

Typo Nightmares

Although we both believe strongly in the "no typos" motto, mistakes do happen. Danielle once started a new job and was told on her first day that the chairman of the board was a stickler for typos—and the development department had a pretty bad record in that regard.

Wouldn't you know, her very first assignment was an emergency proposal. She finished it in three days. On the fourth day she followed the proofreading procedures described here and even had other people read the document after it had been proofread aloud. She then sent five copies of the finished piece to the chairman for distribution at a meeting. On the fifth day, Danielle discovered that a sentence on page 4 was missing the word "the." Joe got a phone call that afternoon. The weary voice on the other end said, "Shoot me now."

P.S. Danielle ended up sending a letter of apology and five corrected copies to the chairman. The chairman never mentioned the matter to her or anyone else.

Easy to Read: no typos, lots of white space, margins of at least one inch on all sides, headings to signal the different parts of the proposal, boxed quotes or photos to break up the text.

Did we mention no typos?

Mistakes do count against you. "Deliver me from 'it's' used as the possessive!" says Mary Bellor. "Mistakes break the flow of concentration and call into question the competence of the people sending the proposal."

Proofreading Like a Pro

To avoid typos, one must proofread. If you have time, proofread in several stages.

After you've written your proposal, read it for meaning and the big-picture problems: Do the paragraphs flow? Do the section headings make sense? Are there any long or awkward sentences? Fix any problems you see.

Once the big picture has been addressed, it is time to get to nitty-gritty proofreading. The best proofreading process goes like this:

1. Spell check the document.
2. Print it out.
3. Proofread the document.
4. Make corrections.
5. Spell check again.
6. Print again.
7. Check the corrections.
8. Print the final copy.

The best way to do step three—proofread—is to have two people read the proposal to each other. One reads aloud; the other follows along on paper. Both stop when an error is spotted. Try this just once. You will be amazed at the mistakes and inconsistencies you find.

Tips for Proofreading.

Diane Ullius, president of Word Tamers in Washington, D.C., offers these additional tips for proofreading:

Where Errors Lurk

- Be especially careful with heads, numbers, technical terms, and proper names: read them character by character.
- Watch for beginnings and endings—of words and sentences, lines and paragraphs, pages and sections. Errors are more likely to be missed in those places.
- Errors tend to cluster. If you find one error in a line, reread the entire line to see if there are more. Don't let your guard down.
- Pay close attention to "boilerplate" copy. Don't skip over it, thinking, It's always the same; there can't be anything wrong here. There can be!
- Look for pairs. If you see an opening parenthesis, bracket, or quotation mark, check immediately for the corresponding closing mark; then go back and proofread the copy in between. Do the same with dashes; they don't always need to be paired, but it never hurts to check.

Focus on Accuracy

- Try making an enlarged photocopy or copying the document on colored paper; it may help errors to jump out at you.
- Accurate proofreading requires close attention to detail. Don't try to do it while you are on the phone, in a meeting, or otherwise distracted.
- Go through the document a second time to check formatting. Don't try to do it while you are doing the major proofreading of text.

- Count to verify that any list has the correct number of items and check the sequence of any numbered or lettered list.

Take Advantage of Special Tools

- Use an opaque ruler or a sheet of colored paper to reveal a line at a time.
- Follow along with your finger or with the other end of your pen or pencil.
- Keep a running list of your own spelling demons or things that you tend to miss.
- Mark errors with a highly visible color.

Special Circumstances

- For tables or other nonnarrative material, proofread with a partner.
- Especially with tabular material, turn the copy upside down to check for errors in spacing or alignment.
- Double-check anything that seems peculiar.
- When checking corrected copy, "slug" it by comparing the first word of every line; then proofread the corrected areas or any area where the slugging didn't match.

After the two of you have finished reading to each other, go back and make the changes in your draft. Then print out a new copy and compare the new against the old in every place where you made a change. Check to make sure you didn't accidentally delete a word, cause one line of a paragraph to appear alone at the bottom or top of a page, or make a noun change that now requires a plural verb. Also check to make sure you did indeed make all the corrections you were supposed to make.

On Time

Always get the proposal to the donor on time. Do everything in your power to avoid asking for an extension. Write into the wee hours of the morning; take the proposal home over the weekend or with you on vacation. Joe has written more than a few proposals from a bungalow on the Jersey shore while his family enjoyed the beach outside. You do what you have to do.

Once you have compared the two versions and ensured that all the changes were made correctly, go back and print your final copy. If you did find a couple of problems, fix them, use spell checker again, and print again to be sure everything is in place before you print the final copy.

The second best way to proofread is to ask someone else to read your proposal carefully and mark it up. Choose someone who has not read a draft of the proposal before.

The worst way to proofread is to do it yourself after you're exhausted from writing and sick to death of the topic itself. The danger is that you will read over mistakes unwittingly. For example, you might read

The program will be implemented is three counties by the year 2003.

and think it is just fine because your brain knows you mean "in," not "is."

And yet we all find ourselves in situations where we have no other proofreader to turn to. If that is the case, try your mightiest to take a break before you proofread. Print the blasted thing and let it sit overnight. Give your brain a break.

When you do sit down to proof, read the document twice. The first time, look at the big picture again—flow, style, logic. Does it all make sense? Is it easy to read?

Then go back a second time and check the small picture. Look at spelling. Look at consistency. Try reading backwards, word by word. Try reading aloud to yourself.

Packaging to Please

Appearances count big time when asking someone for money. In addition to weeding out mistakes, you must arrange your proposal so that it looks like an inviting read.

Think about the impression that you want the proposal to make. If your organization feeds the homeless, do not send a proposal printed on slick paper filled with color photos. A proposal printed on plain white paper, formatted neatly, says that you are putting your resources where they are needed most—in the kitchen.

If you are raising endowment funds at a university, on the other hand, by all means print your proposal on bond paper and use the embossed cover with the university logo. Your proposal's appearance says it all: We are one of the foremost institutions of higher learning, and we are here to stay.

How you bind your proposal also depends on the recipient. Foundation staff usually photocopy your proposal, so make it easy for them to take apart. Most foundations appreciate just one staple in the corner or even an extra, paper-clipped version for photocopying use. Individuals and corporate readers, on the other hand, may appreciate a plastic binding that holds the proposal together neatly and can bear repeated page turning.

How each page appears also affects how closely your reader looks at your text. White space is your friend. Try any variety of ways to introduce white space into your proposal:

- Use double spacing.
- Create a wide left margin so the text appears to be a column.
- Use boxes or call-out quotes for key facts; these items help to break up the text.
- Include photos and charts.
- Divide long paragraphs into two.
- Include subheadings to break up long sections.
- Use bullets for lists.

Such gimmicks may seem trivial, but they can make the difference between an interested reader and a person who tosses the document aside.

To Photo or Not to Photo?

A good photo not only breaks up text but also shows the reader what your program looks like in action. As of this writing, the world of desktop computing is totally changing how we include images in our documents. Joe well remembers a time when he pasted actual three-by-five photos into empty spaces he left in his proposal texts. He had 50 copies of a single photo made at a time so he would have enough on hand for any occasion—paste away!

Now, people scan photographs and electronically paste these images into their documents. But are photos worth the time and expense? It depends.

"Lots of people say using photos is really easy, and others say it's really hard," says Polly Stamatopoulos, a staff assistant at the National Trust for Historic Preservation who has formatted proposals for many good causes. "The truth is somewhere in the middle."

Although technology changes all the time, the following process illustrates the challenges she faced when adding photos to a document in 1999:

- Stamatopoulos selected slides from the photo archive that showed people enjoying historical sites and had good colors. From that group she weeded out photos that would be too difficult to explain in a short caption.
- Stamatopoulos tried to scan the slides using the organization's two scanners, but neither one was working. The next day, a colleague brought in her own scanner, and they scanned the slides with no problem.
- Using Photo Deluxe software, Stamatopoulos adjusted the colors in the scans. (Some were too dark; others were too green.) When finished, she saved the files to disk.

- In Wordperfect, she created a custom box for each photo and used the cut-and-paste feature to insert the image in each one. She assigned a border around the photo (just a thin black line) and then checked to make sure the photos had not caused any weird page breaks.
- Stamatopoulos then went back to the custom-box option, pressed the button for captions, and typed in a short sentence for each photo.
- Everything looked good until Stamatopoulos printed and realized she scanned the photos thinking they would be a larger size. Now reduced, they looked terrible. She rescanned all the photos for a smaller size.
- She printed out again, this time to find that the paper the laser printer used was too thin. She could see photos on the following page through the paper. She bought heavier paper, printed again, and declared success.

"Now people go ga-ga over this concept paper," she says. "We customize it for different people. I add a paragraph here, take one out there—whatever we need for the situation. The process is pretty easy if you aren't afraid of the technology."

Chapter 7

After the Proposal

Thank-You Letters and Reports

In the fall of 1998, Danielle decided that she couldn't abide walking by panhandlers on her way to work each day without giving something. But rather than give to the individuals, she sent a $500 check to a soup kitchen in Washington, D.C.

She felt good about herself. For a little while.

But then a month went by, and no thank-you letter came from the soup kitchen. She began wondering if she had chosen some ramshackle operation that couldn't even write a letter. After six weeks, she wondered if they had gotten the money at all.

Finally, two months later, the thank you arrived—a one-page, computer-generated form letter. However, it had been signed by a live human being, in blue felt-tip pen. And whoever signed it had underscored "very" in the closing line, "Thank you very much."

All was forgiven.

Stupid, right? Someone underlines one word in a letter, and Danielle decides the organization deserves her support, after all? Even though she knows some volunteer probably forged the director's signature and underscored "very" as an afterthought?

You bet. Call it narcissism, call it egotism, call it what you want. Even the most jaded among us relish a personal thank you. For Danielle, that $500 was a big gift. She needed the thank-you letter to make her feel as if she had done the right thing, to reassure her that she had chosen a good organization. She so much wanted to believe she had chosen wisely that the smallest amount of personalization and sincerity was enough to satisfy her.

The experience was a textbook case of what fund-raising expert Bill Sturtevant proclaims in his seminars: The best donor cultivation is a good giving experience. We would add that a good giving experience begins with a thank-you letter.

THANK YOUR HEART OUT

It is almost impossible to thank a donor too much. One development professional told us that she sends a thank-you letter to her foundation donors for meeting with her, then thanks them when they call to say she got the grant, thanks again when the official grant letter arrives and again if the check comes separately.

Who gets thanked? The donor and everyone else who helped you get this gift. If your donor is a foundation, thank both the program officer and the president and any foundation trustees that you know personally. If it is a corporation, thank the chair of the corporate-contributions committee, the employee who presented your request, and the president of the company. (The president may not even know that his company gave you a gift. All the better that you inform him in this pleasant way.)

Thank your volunteers. They tend to get lots of verbal thanks, but an occasional letter from the president will make them feel that much more appreciated.

Thank your staff, especially if they are donors, too.

Thank the people who say no. Even if a prospect turned your proposal down, he did take time to consider your request and deserves to be thanked for the effort. Besides, your gracious attitude may pave the way for a successful request later on.

In some cases, it may even be appropriate to thank the people your organization serves. If a school asked your organization to make a presentation about conflict resolution, thank the principal and teachers who invited you.

I'll take mine warm and fuzzy, please. According to Emily Post's *Etiquette*, the most important qualifications of a thank-you letter are that it sounds sincere and that it be written promptly.

Ideally, you will send a thank-you letter within one week of receiving the gift. If this idea makes you laugh and shake your head, we understand. Writing a thank-you letter always takes longer than you think it will—potentially a few hours a day when the money is rolling in. (We should all be so lucky!) Some large organizations hire full-time thank-you letter writers to cope with the flow.

There's nothing we can do to help you with the timeliness challenge, but we can help you make the letter sound more personal even if you don't know the recipient very well.

- Use the person's name in the body of your letter and refer to your organization in the first person. For example: "John, your gift means a great deal to all of us at the college." Or, "Mr. Chung, all of us at the museum thank you for your dedication to this institution and your confidence in our mission."
- Even if you are writing a form letter for lots of people, picture just one donor in your mind as you write it. Write the letter from one person (you) to one other.
- Personalize the form letter. Underline a word or sentence. Cross out "Mr. Heilbrund" and handwrite "Herb" above it. Or handwrite a P.S. at the bottom of the letter.
- Spell the person's name correctly. (Rocket science, this is.)

Writing three letters for the price of one. The best thank-you letter not only makes your donor feel good; it educates him and prepares him for the next gift.

WHAT SHOULD I CALL YOU?

Should your president's thank-you letter say Dear Mrs. Jackson or Dear Beatrice or Dear BeeBee? It should say whatever the president would say in person. If you don't know what the president would say in person, ask him. If he doesn't know, check Mrs. Jackson's file and see if she has written any letters to the president. If so, check the salutation and her own signature. If she is addressing him as Mr. Andrade and signing Beatrice Jackson, go with Mrs. Jackson. If she writes to Diego and signs BeeBee, then follow suit.

What if the president just had a meeting with Mrs. Jackson for the first time and even he isn't sure how to address her? In that case, play it safe and go with the more formal title.

One last thing: Make sure the president's signature matches his salutation in formality. In most cases, it is not appropriate to open with Dear Beebee if you plan to sign as Mr. Andrade.

Always begin your letter with an expression of appreciation. Put that thank you right up front. If you like, close the letter with another expression of thanks. Use the body of the letter to give your donor a sense of the daily business of your office or your current initiatives. For example:

"I have just returned from a very productive meeting with the mayor's office, and I think he is giving serious consideration to our youth-corps proposal."

Or:

"I am delighted to tell you that just last week we closed on four acres that adjoin the boys camp on Lake Rose."

After you talk about current doings, slip in a sentence or two about what lies ahead. Consider these follow-on sentences to the ones above:

"Our communications director is working on a pamphlet that will explain the youth-corps concept and urge parents to voice their support."

"Now that the purchase is final, we will begin plans for two new bunkhouses and an advanced ropes course." Aha! Your donor is primed for the next ask.

Legal obligations. It used to be that the Internal Revenue Service would accept a cancelled check as proof that you had made a tax-deductible donation, but that is no longer the case. Thanks to regulations enacted in 1993, donors making gifts of $250 or more must receive a written acknowledgement from the charitable organization or else the gift is not tax-deductible. The acknowledgment must include:

- the amount of cash (or a description of the property donated)
- a statement of whether the charity provided goods and services in exchange for some or all of the gift
- an estimate of the value of the goods and services provided

These new regulations also say that low-cost trinkets and some items with logos on them don't count as goods and services. The value of everything else you give your donors has to be subtracted from the deductible total.

You can imagine the confusion all this caused at first. How do you calculate the value of giving your top donors early access to tickets to your theater?

The lawyers have had a few years to sort all this out, and you will be able to find answers to your specific questions if you search fund-raising magazines and journals or talk to your own legal counsel. (We researched this question at the National Society of Fund Raising Executives Resource Center in Alexandria, Virginia, which contains journals on laws concerning charitable giving and solicitation.) The writer's challenge is to smoothly insert that mumbo-jumbo into the thank-you letter. If you have not provided goods and services for the gift, the necessary language goes something like this:

> "*Internal Revenue Service regulations require us to advise you that since the value of benefits received through your donation is negligible, the full amount of your donation is tax-deductible.*"

But where to put that beautiful verbiage? We've seen many different approaches:

- That one sentence appears as its own paragraph in the body of the letter.
- A footnote at the bottom of the letter says the same thing, but in small type.
- A separate receipt included with the thank-you letter contains the mumbo-jumbo.
- An invitation to join an arts organization tells the prospect right up front how much of his gift will be tax-deductible. For example, Friend—$50 ($45 tax deductible); Benefactor—$100 ($95 tax deductible).
- Two thank-you letters go out. One from the president to thank profusely; the second from the director of development to spell out how much of the gift is tax deductible and to thank again.

Formatting thank-you letters. In general, follow the format of a traditional business letter, with the date at the top, an inside address, and notations for enclosures and carbon copies. (*The Gregg Reference Manual* by William A. Sabin is an invaluable book with information on business letters, alphabetization, and more.)

Use white space generously to make the letter look inviting to read. Write short paragraphs and make sure the transitions between paragraphs make sense. Some other formatting tips:

- If the letter goes on to a second page, use a header on the second page citing the recipient's name, the date, and the page number.
- If the closing consists of two words, only capitalize the first one. E.g., Sincerely yours, Best regards, etc.
- Do not leave single lines of paragraphs dangling at the top or bottom of a page (known as widows and orphans). Make sure you have at least two lines together.

INNOVATIVE THANK YOUS

Thank-you letters are so time-consuming that many organizations just barely keep up with sending one thank you per gift and leaving it at that. Yet all the fund-raising consultants chirp away about thanking the donor again and again, as if you had all the time and staff in the world.

If you want to keep thanking your donors after the official letter has gone out, consider some of these ideas we've come across:

- An environmental organization takes out a full-page ad in major state newspapers to thank its corporate donors.
- Each member of a dance company on tour sends one postcard to a donor who helped make the tour possible.
- Each student at an inner-city private academy sends a handwritten thank-you note to the foundation that gave the school its biggest grant ever.

And don't forget the old standbys: List donors in your annual report and newsletters, put their names on a wall, and send them certificates of appreciation.

REPORTING ON THE GRANT

In civilized society, one does not take the money and run. At some point—at the end of the grant period or 11 months after your donor's last annual gift—you must report on how you used the money. There is nothing more rude than to take a major gift, spend it, and then ask for more money without ever telling the donor what you did with the first gift. Indeed, if you do that to a foundation, it will most likely refuse to work with you again.

Reports can be as formal or informal as you like. Just make the donor feel good about what he or his organization has done. Be specific. Tell how many people attended the conference. Include anecdotes about the activists from Maine and Alaska who found they were confronting the same problems and spent all night sharing ideas. Send the conference program packet and a list of the papers that were submitted.

Once you're done with the specifics, state the obvious: None of this could have happened without your support. Thank you.

If the gift was made in response to a specific proposal, then go back and look at your goals, objectives, and evaluation criteria from that proposal. Address those items in your report point by point. The important thing here is to have something to say. One foundation officer told us that most of the reports she gets don't say much of anything except that it was another great year at the ______. Fill in the blank. Reports like that don't inspire a great deal of loyalty.

On the other hand, another foundation officer told us that a shelter for homeless men sent her a photograph of the three washing machines her foundation helped them buy—all of them running and filled with clothes and suds. Her board loved it.

What if your program flopped? Should you tell the truth in your report?

Every foundation officer we spoke to said yes. Of course they did. Who would want to be lied to? But their comments reveal an important point: Acknowledge your failures but spend most of your time writing about how you are learning from your mistakes.

"I appreciate candor if an organization tells me they tried something and it didn't work and here is why and now they are trying this other thing," says Joan Kennan of the Arcana Foundation. "I think that is an organization that is learning."

Longtime development professionals agree. "Let's face it—most of the time our efforts don't work," says John Shepard of the Sonoran Institute. "If they did, we would have solved most of the world's problems by now. Even if you failed, your approach was worth testing. You still learn important lessons."

So tell the truth but keep beating the positive drum. If things didn't work, be specific about how you are correcting them and where your organization plans to go from here.

PART 3

The Writer's Craft

Now it's time to think about how to use words to create a concise, lucid, and compelling fund-raising piece. "Aw, c'mon, Joe, the writing doesn't have to be 95 percent," a development director once told us. She's right. The writing has to be 100 percent. It must reflect the excellence of your nonprofit's programs.

Chapter 8

Seat of Pants to Seat of Chair

How to Get Started

Okay, Joe has his Duke baseball cap on, so now we can get started. Like anything ever written, the first draft of this chapter had a long foreground.

It is 8:38 A.M. on a mild Saturday in March. Joe got up at about 7:00, put on coffee, took the family dog, Zeus, out for a walk, came back, and skimmed the morning paper while drinking his first cup of coffee.

He made the coffee extra strong because he wanted to write in a white heat today. Coffee gives him a boost. Then he read this and that as he drank more coffee and thought about what he would write in this chapter. He read the directions for his new exercise bike, then a short essay by the critic Stanley Crouch about a Spike Lee movie, and he glanced at Peggy Noonan's book *On Speaking Well*, wondering why he didn't just tell everyone to read that. Then he could go see the new Clint Eastwood movie instead of worrying about writing this chapter.

He remembered talking to Danielle about the chapter the day before. He'd told her that he had been thinking about what to put in a chapter about writing for more than thirty years and now he wasn't sure and couldn't get started.

"Well, how do you usually start?" she asked.

"I usually put my *Pulp Fiction* or Duke baseball cap on and feel real can-do and start writing," said Joe.

"That sounds ridiculous—a baseball cap!" said Danielle. Her own sophisticated jump-start system for writing consists of keeping a little figure perched over her computer screen: a man holding a pistol in one hand and a rifle in the other. Both weapons are always pointed at her head.

"Well," said Danielle, "if it means putting your baseball cap on, put it *on* and start there!" And so he did, at 8:38 this morning. Joe's hat is on his head. The seat of his pants are on the seat of his chair. He is writing.

REPEAT AFTER US: "WRITING IS NOT EASY"

If writing were easy, getting started would be simple. You would sit down and write. Period. You would do a "brain dump," as some people say. Open up and dump. Next?

Writing is hard. Even for seasoned professionals. Listen:

"There's nothing to writing," said Red Smith. "All you do is sit down and open a vein."

"Every writer I know has trouble writing," said Joseph Heller.

And Jimmy Breslin: "Anything that isn't writing is easy."

The critic Ellen Willis has observed: "Like Joe DiMaggio catching a fly ball, good writers make their craft look easy; but that brilliant paragraph of social analysis that sounds as if it flowed directly from the writer's spontaneous perception to the page has likely taken hours, if not days, of hard work."

What's all the fuss about? you ask. Why not just get the brain dump down on paper? Isn't that the hard part? Well, yes and no. Getting black on white, as Joe likes to say (with a nod to Guy de Maupassant), is crucial. But making sense of that brain dump—whittling, cutting, shaping, honing it—so that it forcefully conveys your meaning—that's writing.

THE TEN BEST WAYS TO PROCRASTINATE

Says Gloria Steinem, "Writers are notorious for using any reason to keep from working: overresearching, retyping, going to meetings, waxing the floors—anything."

You will find your own special ways to delay the inevitable. These Top Ten come from our experience and that of our closest partners in crime. Procrastinate boldly, enjoy it, and then *sit down and write!*

1. Surf the Internet. Check out the weather, news, hobbies. Visit salon.com, amazon.com, and obscurestore.com.
2. Rearrange your desk. Sharpen pencils, create new file folders, go through the mail, put the stapler in the right place, stack the Post-its, check the dial tone on the phone, even the edges of books on the shelf, check the time.
3. Call a friend. E-mail another.
4. Have a glass of wine at a long lunch.
5. Make lists. Work to-do lists. Grocery lists. Errand lists. Upcoming birthday lists. (For added procrastination, make them color-coded.)
6. Succumb to food cravings that take a while to satisfy: microwave popcorn, a pot of loose-leaf tea, those pumpkin cookies from the bakery five blocks away.
7. Balance your checkbook. Pay bills.
8. Go chat with that co-worker who's always willing to chat.
9. Study the directions to your ergonomic chair and workstation. Practice working with perfect posture.
10. Work on nonessential assignments that have been waiting in your in-box for months. What better time to revise that introduction to the new employee handbook?

In the wacky world of fund raising, many people do brain dumps and call them proposals and case statements. Bright, well intentioned, and nothing if not thorough, these folks will read here or elsewhere about the parts of a proposal, gather every bit of information one could conceivably put into each part, and put it in. There: a total superproposal!

Not so.

We are reminded of one writer who produced a four-page, single-spaced outline for a proposal. There were major headings, subheadings, and sub-subheadings. The outline was comprehensive, impressive in its detail, and incomprehensible. We couldn't wait to see the finished proposal.

Are we being unfair? Not if we're all in this game to *get the job done*. And the job, dear reader, is to raise money. Bloated, incomprehensible brain dumps do not raise money. They make foundation officers roll their eyes in their heads and wonder that the organizations sending them are ever able to achieve anything on behalf of the commonweal.

Because writing is not easy, we are not all fighting to sit down at the PC first to write the next proposal. In fact, for many fund raisers, writing is one of the most dreaded tasks in the development office.

Well, put your own can-do cap on and follow us through the minefields of writing. The craft ain't easy. But you can master it, open yourself to advice, and cultivate a new mindfulness about words and their uses.

When doing the dishes, do the dishes, says the Zen master Thich Naht Hanh.

When writing, write.

WHEN IT'S GOING WELL

Is it possible to really get off on writing? You bet. The prolific Isaac Asimov once wrote:

"Thinking is the activity I love best, and writing to me is simply thinking through my fingers. I can write up to 18 hours a day. Typing 90 words a minute, I've done better than 50 pages a day. Nothing interferes with my concentration. You could put on an orgy in my office and I wouldn't look up—well, maybe once."

Not long ago, a University of Chicago psychologist gave a name to that sort of all-consuming activity, or optimal experience. He called it "flow." Flow is a state of concentration so focused that it amounts to absolute absorption in an activity.

Have you ever played tennis, handball, or some other game and lost all track of time and your surroundings? Welcome to flow.

In describing the state in his book *Flow: The Psychology of Optimal Experience*, Mihaly Csikszentmihalyi says: "Concentration is so intense that there is no attention left over to think about anything irrelevant, or to worry about problems. Self-consciousness disappears, and the sense of time becomes distorted."

What are some flow activities? Sex, play, art, pageantry, ritual, and sports, says the author. Writing, too. Like sex, writing can be a total concentration activity.

"For me, writing is a sensual pleasure, really," says Ron Chernow, author of best-selling business biographies, putting his finger on this phenomenon. "There's a kind of sublimated sexuality about it. There's nothing that gives me greater pleasure than stringing words together."

Maybe that's why Isaac Asimov wouldn't notice an orgy in his office while he was writing. He was busy having one of his own!

HEMINGWAY WROTE WHILE STANDING UP. PLEASE SIT DOWN.

Joe owns several Ernest Hemingway T-shirts and about a half-dozen hardcover and paperback copies of *The Sun Also Rises*, so Papa gets mentioned here now and again. Joe was born at the tail end of that era when, if you wanted to be a writer when you grew up, your model was Hemingway.

Whether Hemingway is in or out of fashion now means little. His craft, his use of words, the way he made sentences—these matter. He was a master of the language, a great stylist, and he broke all the rules. Sometimes he wrote while standing up. Joe suspects he could have written perfect sentences while bound, gagged, and lowered into icy waters.

The rest of us would do better to simply sit down.

By all means, go through your prewriting ritual. E. B. White drank a martini. Rita Dove lights two candles. Do whatever *you* have to do, then sit down so we can get started.

HOT TIP: Sit in a comfortable chair. Turn the phone off. Put the lights on. Clear extraneous material from your desktop. Decide that anything you are about to write will be terrible. Know that you can fix that later.

NOW, WHAT DID YOU SAY YOU ARE WRITING ABOUT?

As speechwriter Peggy Noonan says, every piece of writing has a job to do. What's yours? Do you want the reader to feel warm and cuddly about your new campus? Do you want her to take pride in the quality of your museum's landscape-painting collection or in the astonishing speed with which your relief agency can get to disaster sites?

Get focused. Take a deep breath and then another. Close your eyes if you like. Think about what excites you most about the story you have to tell. That is what will captivate a reader. Make a few notes. Just a couple of bulleted points like this:

- Intro—Great Plains as America's heartland
- History and enduring values
- Great biological diversity
- New conservation program
- What your support will accomplish
- Conclusion

That's the initial outline Joe worked up when he was writing a case statement for a twelve-state Great Plains program at The Nature Conservancy. He wrote it after several weeks spent talking to program and development officers, gathering reports and plans, and reading articles and books about the Plains. He had steeped himself in material and now had reduced it all to six bulleted points.

He had an outline.

Not a detailed outline, to be sure. But an outline of main points. If these points were nails, Joe knows he would have to drive them with all his might into the wood. Get those nails in and his argument is made. The moment an outline appears, the battle is half-won.

Once, Joe and a photographer got lost on assignment in Connecticut. They were on their way to visit with a scientist about whom Joe was writing a profile but made one of those wrong turns from hell that tell you the day is over. And they had no map. Needless to say, every service station and dime store they stopped at had no Connecticut road map. Time was passing, the scientist was a crotchety sort, and Joe and the photographer were growing more and more anxious.

Then they found a map. They saw the clear route to the scientist's house. They might get there late, but by God they would get there. It was a great feeling. They knew the route; all they had to do now was drive.

That's how it is with an outline. You've got the lay of the land. You are going from point A to B to C to D and so on. Oh, there will be some fancy turns and asides. But the key landmarks stretch clearly in front of you. They are the linchpins of your journey. You will not want to lose sight of them. Keep them firmly in mind and you will get where you want to. You will *get the job done*.

Is it the same with any piece of writing? Just about. We have done the same kind of outlining for most things we have written, whether Joe's feature piece on publishing or Danielle's ghostwritten speech about historic preservation.

No matter what you are writing—an article, a proposal, a brochure, or any other expository piece—you must first *find the key points you must make to get the job done*.

Sometimes you know what you want to say early on. Your outline is in your head. Great! Get it down in writing, anyway. Make those few notes. Then, depending on what's most comfortable for you, you can group all your research material around those key points.

You might, for example, want to list a few details under each key point in your outline. Or, as Joe sometimes does, you might just want to pile your source material into batches on the floor near your desk. The Great Plains project meant putting anecdotes and quotes evincing Plains history into one folder, notes and reports on plants and species in another, and so on.

Like drivers on the road, each of us has a different way of getting from A to B to C. As long as you make the key points effectively, you are okay. No two people will go from A to B to C in quite the same way. That is the beauty—and individuality—of writing. But good writers *will go* from A to B to C with grace and dispatch. They will pull their readers right along with them.

It all starts with a few words on paper to remind you what you are writing about.

THE MUD PIE YOU ARE NOT GOING TO BAKE

First drafts—God love 'em. We all want to get it just right the first time out. You know, Babe Ruth comes up to the plate, points to centerfield, and then belts one into the bleachers. Home run! It happens. Babe Ruth did it. Once.

What can we tell you about first drafts?

Hemingway said, "The first draft of anything is shit." Please read that sentence again. Do you find it offensive? Good. Then you will remember it. One of the finest American writers who ever lived said that his first attempt to write anything was doo-doo. Okay? So don't go looking for a miracle the first time out.

What you can hope for is to *get it down*. Yes, we are talking about the old black on white. We don't care how you get it down; just get words onto paper. Make believe you are writing a letter to a friend about this great new hospital wing you want to build that is going to save hundreds of lives. What would you tell her?

How Do You Find the Time to Write?

Fund raisers spend most of their time in meetings. They meet with the president, program staffers, volunteers, vendors, prospective donors, consultants, and one another.

Some hire development writers whose sole job is to write. That's one way to tackle the writing hurdle. But what if you are a fund raiser who can't afford staff or freelance writing?

We hate to say it, but you will never find the time to write. You have to *make* the time to write. There's a big difference.

You can steal time in many ways:

- Work at home one afternoon or one whole day each week. You will be amazed at the amount of writing you can get done. Call the office to get information when you need it, but be sure to tell them not to call you.
- Go into the office early. You'll meet some of your most successful colleagues getting tea in the pantry. They know the quality work they can get done before the opening bell.
- Close your office door and put a sign on it that says: "Writing. Please do not disturb. This means you." People will smile and go away.
- Skip the in-flight magazine and bring the laptop. We've often wondered how many fund-raising proposals have been drafted on shuttle flights between cities like New York and Washington, D.C.

"Dear Ellen: I know you will think I am crazy, but the hospital is planning to put up a new wing for chemotherapy patients that is going to be so great. I have met a lot of these patients, including little kids who don't deserve a day of pain. Some of them never make it. The new wing will have an activity center so that they . . ."

In her warm and insightful guide to writing, *Bird by Bird*, Anne Lamott notes, "Very few writers really know what they are doing until they've done it." She goes on:

"The first draft is the child's draft, where you let it all pour out and then let it romp all over the place, knowing that no one is going to see it and that you can shape it later."

If that is so, why do so many of us freeze up and keep reworking the opening sentence again and again and again, determined to get it right the first time? Joe will tell you why. Because you are a perfectionist. You won't accept less than your best work now. You won't play with the mud a bit. You want to bake it right away and see it come out whole and bright and shiny for the world to see.

Be kind to yourself. Give yourself permission to mess around. Draw a funny picture in the margin. Turn your baseball cap around on your head. C'mon, get down! Lighten up, girl. Writing is hard enough without your climbing on the rack in your opening sentence.

WRITER BEWARE! None of this means you shouldn't have an outline. It does mean you should do your jazz improvisation within the confines of your A to B to C route. Let the words knock about, but stay on the map. You'll start, stop, and zigzag, but you'll get it down and even be headed in the right direction.

Once you've got a rough first draft, you are ready to go to work. Now the real writing starts. As a friend of Anne Lamott's says, "The first draft is the down draft; you just get it down. The second draft is the up draft; you fix it up."

So, you've had your brain dump, you've got your pile of doodoo, and now you want to make it into something pretty. Let's see what we can do.

Chapter 9

Second Drafts and Other Saving Graces

Revising, Editing, and Editing Again

There are no rules about writing.
Look at the sentence: Does it work?
—Dave Barry

In a remedial writing class at a New York college, Joe once had a student whose first draft for an autobiographical theme was a 500-word sentence. The sentence never stopped, so technically it wasn't a sentence at all. It was five hundred words written one after the other.

It was offensive.

It was impossible to understand.

It didn't look pretty.

Then the student produced a second draft. He put the periods in. What a difference!

Some of us just don't know when to put certain stuff in. Others don't know when to take certain stuff out. Doing those things is what good writing is all about.

The crime novelist Elmore Leonard likes to say that you should leave out the parts that people don't read. That's one way—a great way—to look at it.

LEAVING OUT THE PARTS BILL GATES DOESN'T WANT TO READ

When Joe and his wife were first married, they went to a butcher every Saturday and bought meat. "Nice and lean," his wife would say. And that's how they got their meat—with very little fat.

We'll bet Bill Gates likes his steak lean, too.

"Simply. Simplify. Simplify," said Thoreau.

"Less is more," retorted Hemingway.

The CEO of the corporation you are asking for money might say, "What's the bottom line?"

All these folks are saying the same thing. Be concise. Be direct. Be clear. And then be gone.

Nobody has time to wallow in words. Your reader wants to know what you've got, what you want, and what's in it for him.

Your readers haven't got time. Let's think about your readers. They are wealthy individuals, foundation officers, or business executives. Chances are most are savvy, well-educated, high-tech, busy folks with a track record for getting things done, considering they are now giving away vast sums of money.

It's doubtful they are kicking back in their offices with mai tais, waiting for your sterling prose to come along and amuse them.

In fact, they are probably buried in the gobbledygook of business and philanthropy all day long. They will be relieved to read something that is simple and elegant and convincing. They actually *want* to find ways to advance their agendas through your good cause. But they have to understand exactly what it is you want to do and want them to do.

Leveraging is the buzzword of our day. Your prospects want to leverage their action and get the greatest possible impact from their giving. They want to be effective and efficient in their philanthropy.

You can do the same thing with words. Just a few can bring you a long way. Drive your point home. Keep it tight and bright. Hone it. Polish. Trim the fat. Less and less and still less is a whole lot more.

THE HEIGHTENING OF REALITY

For many years New York novelist Sidney Offit taught students in his fiction-writing classes about the importance of heightening reality.

Take a look at a scene in a fine novel, Sid would say. Maybe it takes place in a Paris café. A man and a woman are breaking up. In a half page of dialogue we feel the pain and immediacy of the moment. We are deeply moved. Perhaps the lines are memorable.

You prefer movies? Okay. The Nazis are entering Paris. A Brooklyn-born saloon keeper and his beautiful and mysterious girlfriend stand on a café balcony, drinking champagne, wondering about the future. These are their last moments together.

Now, it is quite possible the couple spent two hours in the café. Had the writer turned on a tape recorder, he could have shoveled in all of their conversation so that you could share every single moment of their last time together. Instead, he was *selective*, using only the material needed to distill the essence of the encounter.

Your writing must also heighten reality. You must cut away the chaff of your program and get to the living heart of the grain. Revealing anecdotes about people, achievements, levels of excellence, must be presented as characteristic of the soundness of your effort.

Don't describe three lackluster student internship experiences when you have one gripping story to tell.

Show the effect of your cardiac unit on one aging man's life, and do it in a tightly focused way.

Let us see an inner-city child whose worldview has been transformed in your museum. Go easy on the mind-boggling abstractions behind your community outreach.

Remember: Be selective. Heighten the impact of your message. Don't leave the tape recorder running!

Cut! Cut again! Cut some more! How do you keep your writing bright and tight? To begin with, you put in as little as you can. You favor some words over others. And you cut, cut, cut.

Famous Last Words

Why bother revising? You've listened to your donor, given him everything he could possibly want to know, and you're rather proud of yourself for being so thorough.

In fact, you will probably tell yourself lots of things in the hope you won't have to do any revision on a proposal, concept paper, or other piece.

— "It's all there."

It certainly is. You've answered every question in the guidelines. You've made no distinctions between the significant and insignificant. You have given them more than they could ever want. Once they pry it out of the FedEx box, will you be stopping by to help them make sense of it?

— "Surely they can figure *that* out . . ."

Oh, now the funder is supposed to do the work? If it is not clear how your program will achieve results, you have failed in your job as a writer. Assume the funder doesn't care. Assume he will stop reading when he can no longer figure out what you are saying. Assume he is five years old and rolls toy trucks on the conference-room table all day. Assume anything, but *never* assume they will figure it out.

— "They probably won't notice."

You thought your mother wouldn't notice, too, didn't you? Please: They *always* notice. They notice when a sentence runs on or turns purple. They notice when "i" comes before "e" after "c." They notice fat paragraphs, tangents, dumb headings, misspelled names, exaggerations. Trust us; if you wrote it at breakfast, they will know the kind of Danish pastry you ate. Anything you don't want them to notice they will spot immediately.

— "If we don't send it now, we'll miss their deadline."

If friends asked you to contribute to a community bake sale, you wouldn't send them flour, eggs, sugar, and chocolate, would you? No, you would mix and bake the cake. Why do less when you are asking someone for thousands of dollars? Stay late and finish it up.

— "We can always send that later."

F. Scott Fitzgerald said there are no second acts in American life. But you are going to tell a prospective funder *later* that a famous scientist is heading your biology department or that your hospital has been rated one of the three finest in the region? Always include vital information the first time. There probably will not be a second chance.

— "I thought that was pretty clever."

Watch out! When you become enamored of your own writing, chances are you are being a mite too clever for your own good. Run that marvelous passage by a colleague. If he says it doesn't work, he's probably right.

Hedrik Hertzberg, a *New Yorker* writer, once said the best tabloid newspaper writing is "as direct and riveting as a ransom note." Forget the tabloid part. Imagine whittling your writing down to a point where the reader gives it the attention he would to a note demanding money for his abducted son.

How do you achieve that?

- Use five-cent words. Avoid five-dollar words. It's the difference between "poor" and "impoverished," and between "small" and "diminutive."
- Eliminate adjectives and adverbs. "As to the adjective: When it doubt, strike it out," said Mark Twain. Yet writers insist on piling adjectives up against nouns like so many cars in a chain highway wreck. The reader is left gaping at the accident.

Many writers seem to think that because our language includes adjectives and adverbs, we have to use them. Not so.

Listen to Anton Chekhov in a letter to his friend Maxim Gorky:

Take out adjectives and adverbs wherever you can. . . . You understand what I mean when I say, "The man sat on the grass." You understand because the sentence is clear and there is nothing to distract your attention. Conversely, the brain has trouble understanding me if I say, "A tall, narrow-chested man of medium height with a red beard sat on green grass trampled by passersby, sat mutely, looking about timidly and fearfully." This doesn't get its meaning through to the brain immediately, which is what good writing must do, and fast.

— Don't repeat the same word again and again.

As a *Parade* magazine editor once told Joe, never use the same word twice or more on a page of copy if you want your writing to be fresh and inviting. Avoid using "work" three times in three paragraphs: "We will work to . . . the work accomplished . . . working toward . . ." Use other words—seek, project, effort, or whatever, as appropriate.

— Keep sentences and paragraphs short.

"Jesus wept" is a powerful sentence. In its simplicity it conveys emotion and an image. More words would mar.

If your sentence fills more than three lines on the computer screen, reread it. Does it make sense? Or has it gone on a bit too long for its own good? When in doubt, cut.

— Avoid "tion" words.

Always choose verbs over nouns. Too often a writer turns a verb into a noun by adding the "tion" ending, writing: "Let me give you an explanation . . ." rather than "Let me explain." The "tions" just clog your sentences.

LEAD WITH YOUR BEST SENTENCE

There's no sentence like your first sentence.

Some writers fuss with the lead sentence and get it right before they write anything else. Others just get the first draft down, then go back and worry about the lead. If you have been able to identify your lead in the process of research, if something strikes you as so fascinating that it will sweep the reader into your piece, so much the better.

With any luck Joe's research notes will generally contain a couple of crucial queries to himself: "Lead?" and "Conclusion?" Watch for nuggets every step of the way.

The opening of a proposal, brochure, or article sets the stage. It is a window on the world into which you are inviting the reader. It must grab his attention and hold it.

The only way to learn how to write enticing leads is to watch how accomplished writers do it. Read as much quality writing as you can: the front-page features in the *Wall Street Journal*, the essays and articles in *Harper's* and the *Atlantic Monthly*, and the work of nonfiction masters from A. J. Liebling to John McPhee.

Take a look at these leads:

- "My 18th high school reunion was held in the Okefenokee Swamp, 700 miles from the scene of the crime." (David Quammen, "Swamp Odyssey," *Outside*)
- "At just about the hour when my father died, soon after dawn one February morning when ice coated the windows like cataracts, I banged my thumb with a hammer." (Scott Russell Sanders, "The Inheritance of Tools," *North American Review*)
- "I have gone through the hell of trying to figure out my tenth computer in fifteen years and I am just as baffled and irritated as I'd been that fateful day in 1979 when a KayPro4 landed on my desk in Baltimore and screwed up my life forever." (Andrei Codrescu, "Intelligent Electronics," *The Dog with the Chip in His Neck*)

- "Shopping for men is as dull as white socks." (Clare Ansberry, "Shopping for Men at Christmastime Is So Unrewarding," *Dressing for Dinner in the Naked City and Other Tales from the Wall Street Journal's "Middle Column."*)
- "My mother died the other day." (Molly Ivins, "The Good Mother Who Put a Shoe in the Icebox," *You Got to Dance with Them What Brung You*)
- "There is a mistaken idea, ancient but still with us, that an overdose of anything from fornication to hot chocolate will teach restraint by the very results of its abuse." (M. F. K. Fisher, "Once a Tramp, Always. . . ," *With Bold Knife and Fork*)

They all make you want to read the next sentence and the next, don't they? That's the idea. Do the same thing for readers and you will advance your good cause considerably.

OKAY, LET'S REVISE

Imagine a sculptor working on a block of marble to bring out the statue within. That's you with your first draft. Now you have to look at your copy with a very critical eye.

There's a lot of good stuff in there. Perhaps you've caught the excitement and determination behind your nonprofit's new outreach effort and described it cogently. But your draft contains dreck, too. It gets unwieldy in trying to convey the need for more outreach. It bogs down in the jargon of rehabilitation. And it is kind of light on why you need three new staff members.

Remind yourself that a first draft is never very good. Feel free to cross out and toss out. Better, make believe someone else wrote it. Someone whose feelings you don't care about. Pretend.

Why, the thing is bloated and indecipherable in part, isn't it? The writer has just emptied his notebook. There's no main point. There's no logical sequence in the presentation of facts. Why, the thing jumps hither and yon. There's nothing pleasing or inevitable about the way in which the program unveils itself here. It's a contrivance! A sham! Who the hell wrote this?

For many years, Joe brought his writing home and asked his wife to read it. She didn't know much about the fine arts and alcoholism and other topics Joe was writing about. If she understood the piece, maybe most people would. Maybe you have a friend, spouse, or colleague who's willing to look at your stuff. There's just one rule: They must be frank. They can do nothing better for you than to identify passages that they do not understand.

Ask your reader-friend to identify the holes in your piece. You may need to go back to your program people and get more information to flesh out a section. You may need to rethink the way you present the kernel of the program and work in some anecdotes or quotes to bring abstractions to life.

TIME TO DOUBLE-CHECK

Beyond the broader concerns of logic and structure, there are many smaller points that go into a well-written piece. As you write more and more, these considerations become second nature. Early on, though, you may want to self-consciously examine your work for each of the following:

— Choice of words.

Are you using mainly nouns and verbs? Are the verbs active? Have you avoided jargon and clichés? Do you subtly vary your choice of words to keep the writing fresh?

— Voice.

Are you appropriately serious? Are you talking out of strength? Are you making your case in a tone that exemplifies the way your nonprofit sees itself?

— Accuracy.

Have you got all your facts right? Make sure you use up-to-date figures for enrollment, admissions, or whatever and that you've got correct historical dates. If you can't get the facts straight about your nonprofit, who can?

— Reprise.

This is your ending and then some. At the end of your piece try to sound a lovely note of closure that brings the reader back to the notion expressed at the beginning. Reprises close and satisfy and—maybe—leave a little of your wonderful cause resonating in the donor's mind.

THAT STRANGE LANGUAGE SPECIALISTS SPEAK

It's called jargon, and it's everywhere. Lawyers use it. So do doctors, engineers, educators, curators, and car mechanics. Jargon is specialized language that allows members of the group to communicate clearly, efficiently, and quickly.

The problem is, if you are not a member of the specialized group, jargon fails to communicate at all. Would you know that "fused silicate" means glass, that a "discontinuity" is a crack in a metal support, or that your house burning down is an "involuntary conversion" of property? Of course not.

Here is a sentence from *Data Communications* magazine:

"Networks conforming to IMT-2000 will be packet-switched and designed for bursty data transmission at up to 2Mbit/s."

We think we could use some bursty data transmission, but we're just not sure.

The solution? Write in plain English, please. That's the simple, straightforward language you use when talking to a friend or neighbor who works outside your field. How would you explain your fund-raising needs to your barber or hairdresser? That's the language you should be using.

Oh, you say your prospect is actually a specialist in the field? So you want to really lay on the technical terms about levitation? Do it at your peril! *He* may understand it, but how about the program officers and board of his foundation? Maybe they don't know levitation from hibernation. Like the writers at the *New York Times*, your job is to translate jargon into plain English that everyone can understand.

WRITER BEWARE! Many scientists and others will fight vigorously to clutter your prose with jargon. They will argue that a term is more specific or scientifically accurate. That may be true, but it's also irrelevant. If your prospect doesn't understand what you have written, you've wasted his time–and yours.

SO YOU THINK THAT DRAFT IS IN SHAPE NOW?

Once you are relatively happy with the revisions you have made, you are ready for one of the most important things a writer can do.

Nothing.

Set the piece aside for a few days. This may naturally occur in the review process at your nonprofit, anyway. You probably circulate your draft copy to program people and others as soon as you think it is in decent shape.

Go on to other projects. Clean your desk. Play solitaire. Do anything but give thought to the draft you have just revised.

Within a few days, something strange will happen. You will pull out your draft and look at it with fresh eyes. The lead sentence will seem too long. Blocks of copy will look clogged and bloated. The same words will be repeated time and again within a single paragraph.

When comments come back from your program people, you will notice that some of them have caught the same weaknesses. And you will agree with them. Not on everything, but on a surprising amount.

At this point, too, one or more of your reviewers may start modifying some aspect of the program you are writing about. For the first time, he or she has seen how his vision for levitation looks in print, and he's, well, kind of gone back to the drawing board. Let's say he's spruced it up a bit. Okay. Good for him. Get the kinks out now—*before* the piece goes out the door to a funder.

Chapter 10

Other Key Craft Stuff

How to Get It Crisp, Styled, and Polished

We all learn by imitating. A child learns to walk by following her parents' example. A writer learns to write by reading other writers.

Alas, you can know the difference between that and which, you can use active verbs, check your spelling carefully, and a hundred other things and still not write well.

We are talking here about style, heart, and passion.

We are talking about orchestration.

We are talking about the difference between the adequate and the superb.

Oddly, some people will tell you that merely competent writing is okay for development work. Oh, you writers! Always getting hung up on the words! As if polished writing ever won anybody funding.

Let's reiterate: Polished writing does *not* get projects funded. Rather, it helps ensure that your project gets considered and then, we hope, on its merits, gets funded. Have you ever sat on the receiving end of a flow of written material? Résumés? Manuscripts?

Award entries? It's hard to make choices, isn't it? How do you discriminate between the pieces you receive? If you are going to winnow a pile down, will you eliminate pieces that don't look and read well? Pieces that are boring? Pieces that seem thrown together and lack both substance and style?

How about the proposal or brochure that grabs you by the collar and won't let go. Which pile are you going to put that in?

We are here to say we want all of your proposals and other pieces in the "A" pile, where the thoughtful, convincing, winning stuff goes.

Enough said?

It Ain't Wrong to Do These Things

Drawing on the work of language gurus, lexicographer Bryan A. Garner cites many writing superstitions in his *Dictionary of Modern American Usage* (Oxford, 1998). Here are 11 misconceptions—"arrant nonsense" that the average person has about writing well:

- Never end a sentence with a preposition.
- Never split an infinitive.
- Never split a verb phrase.
- Never begin a sentence with *And* or *But*.
- Never write a one-sentence paragraph.
- Never begin a sentence with *Because*.
- Never use *since* to mean *because*.
- Never use *between* with more than two objects.
- Never use the first-person pronouns *I* and *me*.
- Never use contractions.
- Never use *you* in referring to your reader.

The truth is, it's perfectly okay to do any of these things.

GIVING DISTINCTIVE VOICE TO YOUR NONPROFIT

What's special about your organization? We know you do fine work and help improve the lives of so many people each year, but what's different about your nonprofit? Do you know? Do you want to find out?

Denise Reaman, a reporter at the *Morning Call* in Allentown, Pennsylvania, immersed herself fully in a piece about a murder case. Over a period of months she returned to the victim's grave site for "sensory reporting," she told the *American Journalism Review*. Why? "The best work I do is when I really open up not just my ears but my eyes and my nose and my sense of touch. You have to take the story on a more personal level."

You're probably not writing about a murder, but we'll bet there's some sensory reporting to be done about your nonprofit and its programs. What's it like to take a class with professors in endowed chairs at your university? Have you sat in on a class? What's it like to go on a trip with a Big Brother, work on an archaeological dig, or help cancer patients?

Get out of the office and do it.

You will gather stories, quotes, feelings, insights—incomparable grist for your writing, all coming out of the program you are writing about.

Joe once wrote a case statement about an immense property in the Southwest that contained phenomenal untouched biodiversity. He knew the ranch covered 500 square miles and was rather isolated. But it wasn't until he spent a couple of days there, watching sunup without another person nearby for miles and miles around, that he understood the intimate relationship many people feel for the land and wild species.

On returning to the office, Joe understood the project far better than he would have from just reading reports and plans. He had met ranchers, had meals with them, heard them talk about things that mattered.

While working with a rehabilitation agency in New York, he used to sit in on group sessions at detox units and halfway houses throughout the city. He met counselors, addicts, administrators, and others and watched the interplay among them as they tried to restore people's lives. He spent a week with heart patients in Oakland, California, to better understand their experiences in a therapeutic program. He took the program with them—ate low-fat food, exercised, and took part in discussions.

Enter the world you are writing about. Stay overnight in the hospital. Spend a few hours manning the hotline. Go to rehearsals for a week. Then come back and tell us all about it. Write out of passion and understanding. People will listen.

READ STYLISH WRITING

We urge you to steep yourself in excellent writing. Sometimes it helps to open a book by a favorite author and read a few lines before you begin your own piece of writing. Remind yourself what language can do. Loosen up. You are not going to write the same kind of material, but that doesn't matter. You are going to use language to express thoughts. Why not remind yourself what language can do?

Listen to the opening sentences of Hemingway's *Farewell to Arms:*

> *In the late summer of that year we lived in a house in a village that looked across the river and the plain to the mountains. In the bed of the river there were pebbles and boulders, dry and white in the sun, and the water was clear and swiftly moving and blue in the channels. Troops went by the house and down the road and the dust they raised powdered the leaves of the trees. The trunks of the trees too were dusty and the leaves fell early that year and we saw the troops marching along the road and the dust rising and leaves, stirred by the breeze, falling and the soldiers marching and afterward the road bare and white except for the leaves.*

His contemporary Gertrude Stein was no slouch at the keyboard, either. Consider loosening up the words in your head with a passage from a book like *The Making of Americans:*

Sometimes in listening to a conversation which is very important to two men, to two women, to two men and women, sometimes then it is a wonderful thing to see how each one always is repeating everything they are saying and each time in repeating, what each one is saying has more meaning to each one of them and so they go on and on and on and on and on repeating and always to some one listening, repeating is a very wonderful thing. . . .

Elmore Leonard is a crime writer whose work is often read in workshops at the St. Mark's Poetry Center in New York City. Here he is in his novel *Stick*:

The effect of his medication was like swimming under water, only without any water. Floating in lights. He still moved, felt the urge, but he wasn't moving kinetically now, he was floating. He'd load up and let the mood move him along. Cock the straw boater on the side of his head and do a soft shoe on the parquet floor of the den, shuffle stiff-legged to this draggy Kool-and-the-Gang beat he'd turn on softly in his head. Just float, experiencing hundreds of thousands of colored lights popping inside his head like trip flares, only without a sound. See, Chucky said, your hearing gets so acute you have to soundproof your head, turn the decibels way down.

Keep one or two of your favorite stylists at hand and dip in before you write. You may find that words well fashioned by someone else can inspire your own writing.

GET AN EDITOR

Especially if you are a writer working in relative isolation from other editorial types, *please* find an editor.

How do you find one? They are all around you. Does your local university offer writing classes? Bring your brochure copy in as a work in progress. Is there a magazine or book publisher in town? See if someone would be willing to review your material for a fee. And don't forget the writers and editors who work in the public-relations offices of local companies. Can you work out a *pro bono* consulting arrangement through a corporate donor's firm?

Besides line editing—changing *that* to *which*, tightening sentences, and so on—an editor can help you see basic strengths and flaws in your piece. He may see a different, stronger lead. He may help you bolster your argument immensely by moving a big chunk from page 4 to page 2. Or maybe he will brighten a headline, suggest a smoother transition, or come up with a knockout ending.

Often an outsider can see things that you can't. Find an editor you can trust, who cares about good writing and your good cause, and have him review your stuff, if only your basic materials. It might make the difference between an adequate piece and one that sings.

AVOID THE MOST COMMON WRITING ERRORS

Is there anything more frightening than a stylishly written sentence with an error in it? We think not. Here are five common errors in newspaper writing, as identified by a committee of the Associated Press:

- Affect/effect. Generally, *affect* is the verb; *effect* is the noun. "The letter did not *affect* the outcome." "The letter had a significant *effect*." BUT *effect* is also a verb meaning "to bring about." Thus: "It is almost impossible to *effect* change."
- Allude/elude. You *allude* (or refer) to a book. You *elude* (or escape) a pursuer.
- Imply/infer. The speaker *implies*. The listener *infers*.
- It's/its. *It's* is the contraction of "it is." *Its* is the possessive. "*It's* the first time." "*Its* name is Maggie."
- Lay/lie. *Lay* is the action word. *Lie* is the state of being. "The prosecutor tried to *lay* the blame on him." "The body will *lie* in state."

Chapter 11

The Persuasive Argument

From Angry Letters to Ads and Editorials

I am in earnest—I will not equivocate—I will not excuse—I will not retreat a single inch—AND I WILL BE HEARD.

—William Lloyd Garrison

In classes with new fund-raising writers, we like to point out that the school of writing in which they are practicing is properly called *persuasive writing*.

A speech by a politician imploring you to give him your vote is a form of persuasive writing. So is a letter from a health club inviting you to join. Even more common are the persuasive arguments we encounter daily on television, in newspapers and magazines, and on-line.

In development writing, you are also trying to persuade. You have a strong point of view. You argue with passion and authority. You marshal facts for a purpose. And you ask the reader to succumb to the logic of your argument.

In any form of persuasive writing, you are arguing out of strength. Authoritative writing commands respect. It asserts, it gives cogent examples, and it insists on assent. That is the secret of the forceful letter, the winning ad, and the convincing editorial. Be sure you are doing the same thing for your good cause.

THE ANGRY LETTER–TELLING THEM WHAT THEY CAN DO

"Dear Sir: You are a damned fool!"

It is everyone's fantasy to write a letter expressing just how you feel about someone who is, well, a fool. You would start with the angry assertion, offer a few reasons why it's so, and conclude with a reminder that the recipient will forever be a fool.

Hmm. Write enough stuff like that and you just might grow up to be a fund-raising writer. You know:

"Smith College is great and just the place to prepare women for their new role in the world!

"It's great because of its faculty, its teaching, and its innovative approaches.

"Keep America and her women great—with Smith!"

Well, forgive the outburst (we've never written for Smith, but that venerable institution did a fund-raising campaign once tying support for it with the then-current suffragette movement), but you get the idea.

As a kid, Joe used to write letters to the editor. He lived in New York City then, in the Jackson Heights section of Queens, and grew up in the 1950s rooting for the New York Yankees and listening to radio deejay Alan Freed's show devoted to a new music called rock 'n' roll.

Freed was controversial. A trailblazer out of Cleveland, he played music by African-American singers and groups—LaVern Baker, Fats Domino, the Moonglows, the Spaniels—and presented live rock'n'roll stage shows at the Brooklyn Paramount and Brooklyn Fox theaters.

Freed and his music infuriated parents. Nick Kenny, a New York newspaper columnist, attacked the deejay and his trash music regularly. One day, deciding he'd had enough of Kenny's barbed comments on rock 'n' roll, Joe sat down and wrote his first "damn fool" letter (see box, page 180).

In all of his writing in all of the years since, Joe has never used as many exclamation points as he did in that letter to Nick Kenny! But he has made many assertions, backed them up, and drawn his conclusions.

Is there anything as satisfying as getting off an angry letter? A missive written in white heat can be a thing of great beauty. Its prose spare, its points telling, its declarations fully backed up—such a missive can cleanse the soul like a wooden spike driven fiercely into a vampire's heart.

Let's think about this. Something out there irks you. Maybe it's the way the government handles welfare. Maybe it's violence on television. Or maybe it's the way Montana is being subdivided by developers. Call it your pet peeve. What are you gonna do about it?

FROM ZOLA TO BALDWIN

The writerly impulse is to reach for words. Sometimes the resulting missive can be extraordinary. In the hands of a master craftsman, a letter can stop a nation in its tracks.

The French novelist Emile Zola (1840–1902) is best known for an open letter to the president of France that he published in a French newspaper on January 13, 1898, under the headline "J'accuse" (I accuse). Surely it is one of the most powerful letters in history.

Zola was outraged at the conviction of Alfred Dreyfus (1859–1935), a Jewish officer in the French army who was falsely charged with giving military secrets to the Germans. His letter toppled the government, freed Dreyfus, and brought honor to France.

Look at the letter. Focused, passionate, ringing with truth, and written with the staccato rhythm of righteous anger, "J'accuse" is a model of words used to persuade.

> *I accuse General Mercier of having made himself an accomplice in one of the greatest crimes of history, probably through weak-mindedness.*
>
> *I accuse General Billot of having had in his hands the decisive proofs of the innocence of Dreyfus and of having concealed them*

... out of political motives and to save the face of the General Staff.

I accuse General Boisdefere and General Gonse of being accomplices in the same crime ... I accuse General Pellieux ... of having made a scoundrelly inquest, I mean an inquest of the most monstrous partiality ...

I accuse the three handwriting experts ... of having made lying and fraudulent reports ... I accuse the War-Office of having led a vile campaign in the press ... in order to misdirect public opinion and cover up its sins.

I accuse, lastly, the first court-martial of having violated all human right in condemning a prisoner on testimony kept secret from him, and

I accuse the second court-martial of having covered up this illegality by order, committing in turn the judicial crime of acquitting a guilty man with full knowledge of his guilt.

He concluded:

I have one passion only, for light, in the name of humanity which has borne so much and has a right to happiness ... Let them dare to carry me to the court. ...

I am waiting.

Words can stir people to action. Zola's prompted a new trial and release for Dreyfus. For many it was a letter of great shock and inspiration. "I have a great desire to embrace and thank you," a poet wrote to Zola on the day that "J'accuse" appeared, "because you have so magnificently illuminated what had been hidden somewhere in the dark of our souls."

In our own time, James Baldwin's *Fire Next Time,* on the dangerous impasse of race relations in the United States, was cast as a letter to his nephew on the 100th anniversary of the Emancipation Proclamation and filled an issue of *The New Yorker* magazine. It rang out like a fire alarm in the night.

"This innocent country set you down in a ghetto in which, in fact, it intended that you should perish," Baldwin wrote. "Let me spell out precisely what I mean by that, for the heart of the matter is here, and the root of my dispute with my country."

Like Zola, Baldwin will not be denied.

There is a sense of credo about such letters. The author's belief, and his passionate expression of that belief, are communicated with visceral force.

The stakes may or may not be so great in our writing on behalf of good causes. But when you can help people see what is true and put them in touch with something greater than themselves—history, reason, justice, a noble goal—you are using words to make a better world.

As writers, we need to read such pieces and learn from them. They can be models for our own work.

PEOPLE WANT TO BE INSPIRED

Joe was once touched by a remark that someone passed on to him. A staff member in a field office of The Nature Conservancy said she had cut out the opening passages of a Conservancy fund-raising case statement and put it on the wall over her desk. "To remind me what our work is all about," she said. In retrospect, Joe would probably revise his copy a bit (see box, page 182). It reads like a hymn to nature. It is. And that is why a staff member put it over her desk.

People want to be inspired. They want to find strength to do the right thing. And they want, in a world filled with sham and sleaze, to be associated with goodness.

So remember the passion and honesty of the angry letter. The same caring and commitment must inform your writing for a good cause. The facts, the needs, the tradition of achievement, and the potential to reach new heights of success—all of these must be in your piece. But show me that your cause will allow me to act as my better self. Show me warmth, humanity, and heart. Do that and you will have worked wonders with words.

Joe's Adolescent Salvo

In 1958—the year before Buddy Holly died—rock 'n' roll was still new and under attack by adults. In New York, one of its most vociferous critics was Nick Kenny, a columnist for the *New York Daily Mirror*. One day, Joe sat down and wrote a letter that Kenny published in his Sunday column of July 27 under the headline "14-Yr.-Old Fan Defends R'N'R."

Here's part of the letter:

Dear Mr. Kenny: Although I am not an avid reader of your column, whenever I see it in the Mirror I stop to read it. For years I have respected you for your poetry, personality and column in general. Let me tell you, however, that every time you knock Rock 'N' Roll you lose at least fifty readers.

I certainly can't stop you (I don't intend to) from saying what you desire (freedom of the press, you know), but I can give you my own opinion on the subject.

I am a 14-year-old, and look at the subject through the eyes of a teen-ager. Therefore, I write through the eyes of a teen-ager.

You and all of the other anti-R 'N' Rs seem to think that R 'N' R corrupts our minds, makes us delinquents, makes us killers, murderers and thieves. Good Lord! is all I can say. They are as separate and distinct as black and white!

I will honestly never know as long as I live why adults will not let us teenagers listen to R 'N' R. I say live and let live. I don't ask parents to listen to it! I'm not twisting your arm or anyone else's! If you and the other people who are definitely against R 'N' R don't want to listen to it, don't! Who asked you to? Not me!! Listen to the music of centuries gone by! This is 1958 and I live in a fast, rapid, and swift world. I like to hear fast things with a steady beat and movement.

You people danced as fast as all heck when you were young. What can't we? Is it asking so darn much? Am I draining your blood or something?

ADVERTISING–HOW IT'S DONE ON MADISON AVENUE

We've never worked in advertising, but that hasn't stopped us from noticing that advertisers are no different in some ways than good causes. They want to:

- attract attention
- describe a product
- close a sale

Here's Paul Revere, in 1768, advertising his own brand of false teeth:

> *Whereas many Persons are so unfortunate as to lose their fore-teeth by Accident, and otherways, to their great detriment not only in looks, but speaking both in Public and Private:—This is to inform all such, that they may have them re-placed with artificial Ones that look as well as the Natural, and answers the End of Speaking to all Intents, by PAUL REVERE, Goldsmith, near the Head of Dr. Clarke's Wharf, Boston.*

He had a product to sell. He called people's attention to it by talking about their "looks" and how his artificial teeth could improve a person's appearance while speaking.

Print advertising has come a long way, to be sure. Now, ads will say—and show—most anything to sell a product. But the parts of the ad always remain the same.

There is an assertion:

"Got milk?"

"Coke is it."

Most often the assertion takes the form of a headline. Perhaps the type is wrapped around the body of an attractive woman. What's being sold? Milk? Soda? The company of attractive women?

A Passionate Plea on Behalf of Nature

Writing for a good cause often means giving voice to the voiceless. Here is the opening of The Nature Conservancy's case statement for the Campaign for Last Great Places:

In these final years of the 20th century, we have a choice. We can take from the future—from our children and grandchildren. Or we can give.

We choose to give.

We choose to do our part.

We choose to give to the future—not because we must, or because we ought, or because it is expected, but out of deep concerns made urgent by the frightening deterioration of our environment. We declare these concerns freely:

- *Our love for our families, their health and well-being.*
- *Our caring for the land, the water, and the places and animals—the bounty of our natural world.*
- *Our conviction, informed but fiercely optimistic, that we can yet preserve our natural heritage for future generations.*

These, and something more.

We choose finally to commit ourselves to the future of nature because of inescapable human needs: Our desire to nurture all that is wild and wondrous in this world; to safeguard all that brings us closer to the mystery of our innermost selves; and to touch the course of natural events, and thus, perhaps, something timeless and far larger than ourselves.

We take joy and pride in these endeavors. With Henry David Thoreau, we celebrate "the indescribable innocence and beneficence of Nature." With John Burroughs, we recognize that nature—which alone endures—is a permanent legacy:

> *Flowers bloom and flowers fade,*
> *The seasons come and the seasons go,*
> *men are born and men die,*
> *the world mourns for its saints and heroes,*
> *its poets and saviors,*
> *but Nature remains and is as young and spontaneous*
> *and inexhaustible as ever.*

The assertion grabs attention. Then the writer tells us something about the product and its benefits to us. Then he urges action: Live it! Buy it! Do it! Be it! With his product, of course.

Sometimes the advertiser doesn't even have to tell us to act. An attractive young couple, happy, smiling, enjoying each other enormously, are talking and eating. There is a bottle of Coca-Cola on the table in front of them and Coke in their glasses. "It's the real thing. Coke," says the ad. That's all. Nothing else. There is nothing else to say. You want the real thing, don't you?

When he worked at The Nature Conservancy, Joe realized that many people interested in conservation act out of deep-seated affection for place. They may appreciate the ecological need to conserve species and wild places. But they also want to act for emotional reasons. Perhaps they grew up on the land and loved the way of life there. They associate the land with home, family, and friends. It is part of their youth, and they want it to last.

Tapping into that emotion and nostalgia is crucial to persuasive writing. Here's how Joe began a case statement about conservation work on the Great Plains:

"For generations, they shaped the American experience.

They gave Native Americans the bison and a way of life.

They gave European settlers a fresh start in a new land.

They became our nation's heartland."

Not for several more paragraphs did he begin to describe the biological diversity of the Great Plains—the major reason to do conservation work there. Instead, he began with the hidden benefits of the Plains—their wondrous place in the hearts of the people (and prospective donors) who live there.

HOW A PULITZER-WINNING COLUMNIST MAKES HIS CASE

The *Washington Post* columnist and book critic Jonathan Yardley wrote his first opinion piece in the fall of 1957 in the pages of the *Daily Tar Heel,* at the University of North Carolina. He hasn't stopped since.

Yardley has been an editorial writer at the *Greensboro Daily News,* a book critic at the *Miami Herald,* and, since 1981, a kind of self-admitted curmudgeon in residence at the *Post.* As he notes in his collection of columns, *Monday Morning Quarterback* (Roman & Littlefield), "Since the world will always offer something to complain about, someone's got to do the complaining."

Over the years, his Pulitzer Prize–winning columns have covered politics, contemporary affairs, sports, the media, and literary matters.

"The National Air and Space Museum has done the right thing, but for the wrong reason," he begins one column in that book.

"Late in his long and prominent career as a television journalist David Brinkley seems to have developed what the fastidious would call an unseemly appetite for filthy lucre," starts another.

You might think Yardley mulls his columns for days before writing. Not so, he tells Joe. "I never outline, and I can never see the beginning, middle, and end of the piece beforehand," he says. "Many things simply don't occur to me until I sit down and start writing. Often I am surprised. A column will start in one place, take me to another, and bring me to yet a third without my knowing exactly how I got there."

Nonetheless, Yardley says, he is "always very conscious of making an argument" and mindful of the need to have a narrative thread. He reaches up as if pulling on a kite string and says, "There is a string that you must pull from the beginning of the piece through to the end. If the string breaks, you lose the reader."

He is adamant that "empty praise" will ruin credibility and quickly lose the audience. "If I were writing for a good cause, I would not say that 'our cause is great, give,' but rather that 'here's what your money will do.' Give me reasons to support you. There's nothing more persuasive than facts."

Judiciously used facts, he might add. "I learned the most important lesson in an early job with the *New York Times*, when I was boiling down thousands of words into 200-word week-in-review pieces," says Yardley. "I learned to tell the difference between information that was important and not important. That has stood me in good stead all these years."

EDITORIALS AND OTHER OPINION PIECES

Editorials express opinions. "An editorial, to have any rationale at all, should say something," said H. L. Mencken. "It should take a line." The same is true of columns, op-ed pieces, and reviews.

Maybe it's because people are better educated: whatever the reason, newspaper editorials these days are likely to contain more facts and less fire and brimstone. The same can probably be said for fund-raising pieces written on behalf of good causes.

Beyond that, not much has changed. "Have something to write about," advised the poet Walt Whitman, who wrote many editorials for Brooklyn newspapers. "Write short; to the point; stop when you have done. Read it over, abridge, and correct it until you get it into the shortest space possible."

The criteria for the Pulitzer Prize in editorial writing are "clearness of style, moral purpose, sound reasoning and power to influence public opinion in what the writer conceives to be the right direction." Hmm. Sounds a lot like a good standard for excellence in development writing to us.

Joseph Pulitzer's own *New York World* was noted for its crusading editorials. Here's how it kicked off a campaign to raise money for the pedestal of the Statue of Liberty:

"Money must be raised to complete the pedestal for the

Bartholdi statue. It would be an irrevocable disgrace to New York City and the American Republic to have France send us this splendid gift without our having provided even so much as a landing place for it."

Like all writers, the people who write editorials have their rituals before sitting down to the task. Susan Trausch of the *Boston Globe* has written about everything from Columbus Day to the search for Nazi war criminals. When she sits down to write, she first works with a pen and makes notes on a legal pad. By playing around and rehearsing, she orders her thoughts on a subject.

"Then I turn to the computer screen, and somewhere in that list is a lead," she says. "And then you fire away and don't stop. The trouble with writing is it is always threatening to stop, and you have got to keep pushing."

Daniel Henninger, an editorial writer at the *Wall Street Journal*, compares himself to a stand-up comic who has to grab the audience in the first few minutes of his act. "That's somewhat analogous to being an editorial writer," he told an interviewer. "You get only a very brief amount of time to capture your audience, and once you capture them you have to hold them."

Capture your reader and you have a chance at convincing him. Be direct, be forceful, and combine passion with facts. The well-made argument demands attention—and action. It can be a powerful tool for winning support for your good cause.

PART 4

Case Statements and Other Big-Money Materials

If tailored proposals are the push-comes-to-shove moments in fund raising, then the kinds of writing we want to consider now are the *nudge* moments. You want to nudge all year long. Oh, do you ever want to nudge!

You nudge with case statements, brochures, newsletters, Web sites, and other materials aimed at large audiences. These are pieces that describe your achievements and ambitions, tell your success stories, and provide news and insights aimed at cultivating Mr. Rockefeller's support. They don't ask for money. In the fullness of time, a tailored proposal will do that. No, these pieces help create the *climate* for asking for money.

These are the materials that help make prospective donors notice that you are doing something smart and that, hey, these people deserve my support.

Chapter 12

Case Statements

Striking a Noble Note

Imagine the thoughts that go through your mind when you stand for the national anthem before the start of a baseball game. We know you're conditioned to rising out of your chair and standing quietly while the music plays, but a little bit into "The Star-Spangled Banner" you inevitably begin to notice the words.

No matter how patriotic you are, you begin to think. You imagine the tattered flag over Fort McHenry. You put yourself in the place of the songwriter, stirred to words. You appreciate the fact that if it weren't for the values that the anthem celebrates, you might not be enjoying this day at the ball game.

Case statements are anthems. They are the rousing centerpieces—often elaborately produced, oversized brochures—that provide vital information not only on who you are and what you do but on the great difference you make in the quality of life. Case statements tell stories, cite achievements, provide endorsements, and carry striking images—all aimed at assuring the carefully targeted reader that *this* nonprofit is the place to wisely invest philanthropic dollars.

Indeed, a case statement is the bible, the mother brochure, of any major-gifts campaign. Most of your members or supporters will never see it. The case statement is aimed at *major* prospective donors. It tells them about your nonprofit's strengths, successes, and ambitions and suggests how *their* generosity can make the difference in the nonprofit's mission. It is sent ahead, or left behind, when your president or someone else from your group visits the prospect.

Writing a case statement is difficult, fun, and dangerous.

Difficult because you may find yourself working with a committee of 100.

Fun because the case statement allows you to argue with heart and soul on behalf of a cause you believe in.

Dangerous because *you must get the case statement right.* This is the fundamental piece in your fund-raising campaign. You may do a poor job on a fund-raising proposal and lose a battle. Do anything less than an outstanding case statement and you can lose the war.

Now, just a minute, we hear a few veterans crying out. We've done case statements and had them pile up 500 copies to a box in the hallway for years. Sure, our president or executive director uses them now and then. And we fund raisers do, too. And our board members and chief campaign volunteers seem to like them. But most of them sit in the hallway!

WHY THE CASE MATTERS

Okay, let's get this out of the way right away. Copies of case statements do sit around the office. But please do not equate the value of your case with how many copies you give away. You could decide never to print your case statement and it would still be the most valuable communications tool of your fund-raising effort.

Indeed, we won't be surprised if the day comes when the case statement is simply posted on the Web site and never printed except when someone downloads a hard copy from the site. Well, Danielle can imagine that. Joe is old-fashioned enough to think of a case statement as something that should grace the coffee table in offices of the wealthy. For him, downloading a gem onto copy paper won't cut it.

How can a case statement be valuable if it never goes to press? Because much of its work—some will tell you *most* of its work—has been done by the time it is in final draft. Indeed, there are those who believe that a case statement has done *all* of its work by the very moment before it goes to press.

"I am really convinced that the top volunteers are the only people who ever read the case statement," a development director told Joe after a particularly grueling case was completed. "As long as they are happy with it, we should be, too."

The case statement in question was a mess. It was revised many times, contained the voices of several writers, and tried to explain complex concepts to the point where the workings of the vacuum cleaner were emphasized over the benefits.

Nevertheless, from her immediate perspective, this development director was right. The men and women volunteers she worked with so closely every day—the board members, who are themselves key financial supporters and provide an entrée to others—had been thoroughly involved in the development of the case statement. They felt it was *theirs*. They had, to use the bureaucrat's cliché, taken ownership.

Joe would say they had grown bored tweaking the case statement and wanted to be done with it.

The truth probably lies somewhere in between.

There's no doubt that a superbly executed case statement serves crucial purposes before it goes to press.

It helps key constituents—officers, board members, volunteers, managers, past donors—understand where the organization has been, where it is now, and where it is headed. It lets them take stock, take pride, and take aim. In a chaotic world, this is no small thing.

A short early draft of the case—a prospectus—is generally shopped around to selected, close, prospective donors to see whether they buy the notion of the new fund-raising campaign.

Perhaps most important, a case statement that everyone in your organization is excited about becomes the basis for your fund-raising campaign. It is the sacred text from which you will draw for all your written materials. It is the persuasive argument that will lie at the heart of each of your fund-raising proposals.

The case statement informs every aspect of a fund-raising campaign. If it never went to press, in the bound and printed sense, it would be important. Once printed, it can be a valuable tool.

"The written word—the case statement—gives the campaign legitimacy," reminds Betty Marmon, a former University of Pennsylvania fund raiser who now directs development at the Philadelphia Museum of Art. "Solicitors are reluctant to go out there and raise money unless they have a piece to clutch onto. Plus the donor wants that written reinforcement of the verbal message she gets from a friend or peer."

WHY SHOULD ANYONE CARE ABOUT YOUR NONPROFIT, ANYWAY?

No, Virginia, we are not talking about case studies. The MBA programs at Harvard and Wharton publish journals filled with those. Case studies examine a topic in detail to figure out what happened. Aside from the word *case*, they have nothing to do with what we are talking about.

A case statement is a written piece that makes the case for your good cause. It tells what your cancer organization has accomplished and what it is going to do next. It explains why the museum matters, why the environmental group's work is essential, why the lives of children would be wretched were it not for your educational association.

Why the hell should I care about the American Farmland Trust?

That is the central question a case statement for that group must answer. If a case does not speak to this question, you are mired in very deep doo-doo.

You may wonder how someone can write a case statement and not talk about the essence of the organization. The answer is simple. The person sits at a personal computer and regurgitates everything she knows about the cause. She then tacks on a list of campaign needs and announces that she has written the case statement.

She has done no such thing. Nonetheless, you know what? She hires a quality design firm, and the "case statement" comes out looking pretty good! Amazing what a few striking photographs and a sharp layout will do, huh? Later, she and others may cynically remark that "nobody reads case statements."

But what if the case statement grabbed the reader with a story or a fact? What if it took the reader by the hand and said, Join me, there is something quite special going on at this institution, and I want to share it with you, I want to show you how it touches all our lives. Come, look and listen. See the children, the faculty, the artifacts, the patients, the paintings, the shelters, the whatever it is. Hear their voices. (Yes, artifacts and paintings have voices.) Share our pride in what we are doing for humanity. Consider our plans for the future. Join us!

This is the case statement you want to write. It is the one people will read. You want to write it as if your life depended on it. Your cause's life does. This is the place to link facts and passion and to show prospective donors why they should care. Sure, you may print too many copies (nobody ever knows how many copies of a case statement to print), and a few boxes may sit in storage. But when your president wants a strong send-ahead or leave-behind, the case statement stands center stage. Make it count. If it helps bring in a single major gift, if its facts and passion persuade Mr. Rockefeller to make a naming gift for an entire hospital wing, it will obviate the relatively piddling cost of design, production, and printing.

CRACKING OPEN THE EGG

When you strike a knife against an eggshell, you can make a clean cut; the eggshell splits in half, and the yolk and egg white slide splendidly into a dish. Or you can make a mess, with the shell, yolk, and egg white going every which way—through your fingers, into the dish, maybe onto the floor.

As a writer, you must make a clean cut. That goes for any kind of writing, not just case statements. But here, especially, you have got to get it just right. Ragged edges and messy goo at the beginning will not bode well for the rest of the piece. You've got to marshal your facts, think clearly, find the precise place to make your cut, and make it.

The question is: Will they let you? We refer to the aforementioned committee of 100, which consists of all those in-the-family constituents who should have a part in shaping (i.e., reviewing drafts of) the case statement. They don't always number 100. Sometimes there are 6, sometimes 16 or more. They all think they can write and that they know your good cause best; and each knows just what should be in or out of the case statement. This can reduce your role to that of a clerk who keeps track of other people's edits, which is to be avoided.

WELL, WHO *SHOULD* WRITE THE CASE?

We assume that you will be writing your nonprofit's case statement. If not, you will be deeply involved, if only as the point person for an outside writer.

An *outside* writer? Yep. Often it makes sense to go outside for a case-statement writer. In fact, some people will tell you that you should always hire a freelance writer, someone who can come in and see your organization clearly.

"It takes a very special writer to do a case statement," says management and fund-raising consultant Robert H. Forrester, who has advised dozens of nonprofits through Payne, Forrester & Olssen, in New York City. "You need a writer who is skilled and patient. A good case writer listens very, very carefully and can take in murky, sometimes contradictory information and make sense of it. She sees things differently. She captures the added value—the 'eureka' point—within something. This is how she makes the case come alive."

Another nice thing about an outsider is that she is often seen as the Lone Ranger, a highly respected pro with a reputation for saving the day. An experienced writer of case statements knows what to look for, the questions to ask, and the difference between music and static. Board members and senior staff will often confide their passions or misgivings about a cause when the writer is an outsider. They will defer to the knowledge and experience of an outsider with a ticking meter (as opposed to a salaried insider, who is nearly always without honor in her own land).

Whether insider or outsider, *one* person should write the case statement. That way, a single, strong, authoritative voice expresses the wonders of your nonprofit. A committee of 100 cannot do that. When there is such a committee, consider doing what the University of Virginia did in its latest campaign: Have one writer revise the committee's work into a coherent and polished piece. (See box "A Case in Point," page 202.)

MAKING THE CASE

The author Isaac Babel titled a book *You Must Know Everything*. That is rule number one for the writer of a case statement. Through research and interviews, she must gather all the key available information about the cause.

All?

Okay, if you are writing about a university, you may not need the minutes of university senate meetings (although with your luck, some professor probably described the institution there in words to die for). But you do want all the basic documents: institutional brochures, reports, histories, magazines, newsletters, plus access to the most articulate people in the family. That means the president, the deans; some students, alumni, and faculty; and the little old man who has worked on the campus maintenance staff for 35 years and remembers everything.

When Joe worked on a case statement for George Washington University, he was presented with a massive box filled with books, reports, and other publications—a little grist for his mill in getting acquainted with the place. In essence, he was told, this material explains who we are. Now what else do you need?

Besides a forklift to move the box, Joe asked GW's vice president for development whether he would walk around the campus with him. Not just for a tour but to create a more informal situation and elicit unofficial information not contained in the box.

It's on such a walk that you get to see the student hangouts, the contrast between old and new campus buildings, and the faces of students and faculty. This is when you hear a small remark about the rising quality of applicants or a research effort featured on network television that leads to telling anecdotes.

You can't understand an institution until you penetrate its veneer enough to learn how its key people see it. Is it a place on the move? Is it better than its reputation? Has no one yet given true voice to the very special nature of the place? As a case-statement writer, you must know everything. *Then* you can use what you need to craft the case.

A CASE-STATEMENT CHECKLIST

What goes into your case statement? Whatever will motivate the reader to make a major gift to your cause. Not one word more and not one word less.

The basic components? In no particular order, your case will explain:

— Your programs and why they are important.

What, in fact, do you guys *do*? Run a hospice? Serving how many patients and families? Providing what programs, activities?

— How society benefits.

Is your college a vehicle for minorities into the middle class? Does your drug-prevention program help keep families together? Do you save, enrich, and nurture people's lives in the region or nation? Do you generate new knowledge for your entire field?

— The philosophy behind your actions.

Do you think habitat protection is the best way to conserve the world's species diversity? Do you think an urban college must service the city? Is bread more important than bombs?

— The potential you are trying to realize.

You've come so far, built such expertise and excellence, and established credibility with everyone who matters. Are you in a position to take a quantum leap in service? Can you save more lives, train more engineers, produce more much-needed programming?

— Your vision for the future.

Precisely what is it you want to do next? Become the regional center for cancer treatment? Move from regional to national excellence in the arts? Create a residential campus to attract more graduate students nationwide? Become *the* leader in your field?

— Your financial needs.

How much will that vision cost? Include the specific price tags for all your needs, whether endowments, buildings, operating support, or whatever.

— Why the reader should care.

What is in all of this for me? Why should I give a hoot? I've got other demands for my support. What's that? You don't say? Well, I can identify with that; maybe we should talk.

The great challenge lies in how you say these things.

You must know your audience and what they care about. You must know what wins them, what moves them, what best creates a mirror in which they can see themselves.

Joe once wrote a case statement for a drug-prevention agency whose major donors were clearly most interested in preserving families. He gave great emphasis to a counseling program for recovering parents and their small children. He downplayed professional training programs for drug counselors but certainly noted the component aimed at family counseling.

Which aspect of your institution are donors most excited about? What do they identify with? Who are the people within and around the cause with whom they most like to be associated? Volunteers, celebrities, officers, graduates? Which aspect of your work most pleases them? Your noble goals, your careful management, your crackerjack staff, your measurable results? All of these? More?

In sum, you must hold out a vision that will make readers say, "I want to be part of that. I want to support that. I want to be known as someone who values that." Give your reader that and you will have helped create a climate for giving.

JOE SAVES THE FARM

Like most big-city boys, Joe has visited farms. He once milked a cow. On the whole, however, he is more at home on mean streets. So you can understand why, when American Farmland Trust (AFT) asked him to write a case statement for their first major fund-raising campaign, Joe decided to think about the project as "Joe Saves the Farm."

In fact, as one who did not grow up on a farm, he felt in a strong position to fully appreciate the passion that farmers feel about their way of life. As an outsider, he could see farming through fresh eyes. He could respond to agrarian life with the innocent awe of a newcomer.

In an ideal world, Joe might have visited farms and farmers who are associated with the work of AFT. Time and money did not allow that. Instead, Joe interviewed farmer-officers of the group, ransacked its library, and turned to the work of Wendell Berry and other authors who have worked and lived with the land.

He steeped himself in his subject.

He found himself working with powerful material. AFT has a

sharply focused mission: protecting productive farmland. It has an articulate staff and supporters. Its work has aspects that extend deeply into our country's sense of itself.

The resulting piece had seven main parts. It might have had four or eight or more. This piece had seven. Each was concise. Each had a purpose. Let's take a look:

Introduction

This was headed simply "Farmland" and opened like this:

> *For generations, the land has sustained America and its people.*
>
> *The land—farmland—drew the earliest settlers.*
>
> *The land gave birth to an agrarian nation.*
>
> *The land, fruitful and ever abiding, fueled the nation's growth and transformation into a modern urban society and world power.*
>
> *Today, from the dairy farms of New England to the vast heartland Corn Belt to the cattle ranches of the West and the valleys of California, this land is quietly vanishing.*
>
> *Each year, America loses more than two billion tons of topsoil. Each year, more and more open countryside gives way to subdivisions and malls.*
>
> *We are losing our best farmland—more than a million acres each year—and something more.*
>
> *We are losing a way of life. . . .*

In five more paragraphs, it explained that AFT is a conservation group working to protect farmland, that it had new plans for the future, and that it was conducting a comprehensive campaign called "The Campaign for America's Farmland."

Letter from the President

"My own family has been farming the same land for three generations," AFT's president said in a letter called "The Opportune Moment for AFT." The letter explained, in a personal voice, why

AFT was conducting a campaign and what it would mean for its work. "In a word," it closed, "to protect our farmland is to protect the quality of all our lives."

Program and Achievements

People give to winners. This section, called "American Farmland Trust," described the group's work: demonstration land projects, public-policy leadership, informing the public, and so on. Tight copy gave nuts-and-bolts facts: nonprofit membership group, more than 30 staff in D.C. and other offices, acres saved, leadership on farm bills, etc.

Campaign Goals

Having established its strengths and successes, the group looked to the future and the continued effectiveness that funding can ensure. The section outlined specific areas that would be strengthened to meet the challenges ahead.

Campaign Needs

A simple chart listing the dollar goals of the campaign, with a line of text about each area of need.

Letter from the Campaign Leaders

Two distinguished cochairs urged their peers to help AFT halt the tragic loss of farmland. Speaking to readers concerned with both farming and conservation, they quoted Thoreau ("I have great faith in a seed. Convince me that you have a seed there, and I am prepared to expect wonders."), then said, "Farmers and conservationists planted a splendid seed when they established American Farmland Trust. Now the philanthropic community has an opportunity to help it grow and flourish. We urge your participation. . . ."

Additional Information

There followed a historical time line of the group's achievements and then a pocket on the inside back cover for additional information on projects, or whatever. There were also a half-dozen vignettes, based on phone interviews with carefully selected and diverse farmers, that allowed the reader to hear the voices of conservation-minded people on the land.

Case closed.

TEN QUESTIONS TO ASK IN WRITING YOUR CASE

Talk to people who know the heart and soul of your cause. Which staff members live and breathe the place? Who's been around for 20 years (when they could have made a lot more money elsewhere)? Grab them, sit them down, get them talking, and yes, *listen*.

One way or another, find out the following:

1. What does this group do?
2. Why is it special?
3. What makes this place tick?
4. Why do you work here?
5. Why should anybody give money to this cause?
6. What's the most wonderful thing this place has done?
7. What's wrong with this group?
8. What are its three greatest strengths?
9. Who are some of the people who know this place best?
10. Give me a couple of examples of how this place touches people's lives.

These questions should help get your interview started. If you are talking to the right people, they will soon get excited about their work and the cause that lets them do it. They will want to be sure you understand how the group affects the lives of people. Give them a chance to tell you. When you are no longer uncovering new material from your interviews, it is probably time to sit down and write.

A Case in Point

Back then, Bill Sublette was editor of the alumni magazine at the University of Virginia (UVA), in Charlottesville, Virginia. A top-ranked public institution founded in 1817, the university was planning a major capital campaign, and Sublette watched month after month go by as a team of staff writers worked on the case statement. "I kept wondering, Why is it taking so long?" he recalls.

Since 1994, Sublette has been UVA's director of development communications, managing a staff of writers who prepare materials for a $1 billion fund-raising effort called "The Campaign for the University of Virginia." His first assignment on the job was to do the final rewrite for the case statement that had been taking so long.

Every nonprofit approaches case writing differently. At UVA, says Sublette, the case began with a vision statement prepared by the provost with the help of four staff writers. Sublette was not among them, but he knew the writers, and he watched with interest.

For two years, he says, the writing team did revisions. Drafts were circulated. "The president would send a draft ahead to 100 alumni in a city he planned to visit, asking them to bring comments to a reception. He'd bring back 100 marked-up copies, and the provost and the writing team would sit down to revise."

The case went through at least a dozen drafts, says Sublette. Most involved changes in tone and language. "Then they asked me to do the final polished draft. That was the first thing I did in my new job as development communications director. I spent about four days working it. If you think of the team of writers who had been involved as lumberjacks, I had been brought in to take the last swing of the ax.

"Let's face it, you have to have one voice in a case statement, and that's what I gave it. I refashioned the material so that it would grow out of the phrase 'We hold these truths . . . ' " Those words and the image of Thomas Jefferson, founder of UVA, appear on the cover.

"I wanted the case to reflect the soul of the organization. And here at UVA we have the advantage of having Thomas Jefferson to draw on. He had something useful to say about everything! His words formed the theme for an argument that is both rational and emotional."

HANDLING THE HANDLERS

We sometimes wonder which is the most difficult part of producing a case statement. Writing it or protecting it against the people who review it. Depending on your organization, you can run into any number of individuals whose wrongheadedness can *diminish the quality of your case statement*:

Bureaucrats who think their programs are not getting enough space.
Lawyers who think you are not using enough clauses in your sentences.
Failed novelists who need an outlet.
Board members who wonder how it will look if they do not change something.
Executives' spouses who majored in English.
Specialists who want to use jargon.
People who think it is much too long, much too short, much too understated, much too exaggerated, much too simplistic, much too complex, much too formal, much too breezy, and much more such.

Okay, how do you handle this? Here are a few suggestions:

Use an experienced case-statement writer who will not be intimidated by reviewers.

TEN TIPS ON DESIGNING THE CASE STATEMENT

The case statement must work visual wonders. Susan Walston and Jim Gray of the Concept Foundry, a Bethesda, Maryland, design firm, have designed and produced prize-winning cases for many nonprofits. Here's their advice on how to work with designers:

1. Before selecting a designer, look at her past work, ask for references, and call her clients. Interview the designer; ask about her approach to working with writers. "You want a partner, not a prima donna," warns Walston.
2. Enter into a dialogue with your designer. "The success of the piece will depend on both writing and art," says Walston. "Think about the goal of the campaign and how it can be represented visually. Brainstorm together."
3. Don't feel you must have copy ready to get the design started. Says Gray: "We love it if you have a good notion of the major sections and their length. That's a great starting place to get the designer involved." If you have a rough draft, so much the better. When you do, make sure your designer reads it. "Not all do," says Gray.
4. If you have design preferences—styles, typefaces, colors, papers, etc.—say so. "It's great when clients have sample pieces they like and when they can tell us *why* they like something," says Walston.
5. Show designs to people in-house who *must* see them. The entire committee of 100 need not be summoned. You know who has to vet them. "And remember that not everybody wants to see the design at every stage," says Gray.
6. Be specific in commenting on designs. "There's nothing worse than having a client say, 'I don't like it,' " notes Gray. What don't you like? Why? What would you rather see? "It's hard when a client offers little direction," says Walston. "Often they haven't thought hard enough about how they want their case to look."

7. Take a firm stand with in-house reviewers. "The thing that will really kill a piece is when you want *everything* to stand out, because everybody thinks their program is important," says Walston. Take charge—diplomatically, of course.
8. Avoid endless changes (or be prepared to pay extra for them). Avoid structural changes; the time for that is very early on. "If there are sections where the designer is free to be creative to bring the message out still more, let her know," says Gray. Conversely, let her know when you want things a specific way and no other.
9. Be prepared to visualize. Sample art from an illustrator is meant only to suggest the style—the look and feel—of the artist's work. Try to imagine what *your* case's original illustrations will look like in that illustrator's style. Adds Walston: "Let the illustrator help come up with ideas for you, too. Don't constrain her."
10. Never view the case statement as a competition between writing and design. "Good design engages people on the page and makes them want to read," says Gray.

Early on, have your head of development make clear to key board members and officers that the writer is being given wide latitude to write a persuasive and stylish case statement.

Have the top development officer send the case statement out for review with a cover note stipulating that comments and changes on facts and substance only, not style, are invited. In any event, the cover note should say, "We will give careful consideration to all comments and incorporate changes that strengthen the piece."

BROCHURES IN GENERAL

The case statement is the mother brochure of any capital campaign. But you may also have to produce a bevy of smaller baby brochures to reach targeted groups. These present *aspects* of your campaign in exciting ways. They are a chance to give special treatment to a key program or initiative that is only one of many in the large case statement.

Why bother? Because some prospective donors may be quite interested in your university's research program, for instance, but not in the new fine-arts center, undergraduate scholarships, or the sports complex that are also part of your capital campaign. Separate brochures allow your nonprofit to speak to the donor in terms of *his* interests, which may be quite limited.

Such brochures often describe special needs (hospital wings, libraries, endowed chairs), special relationships (with the corporate community, the high-tech community), donor groups (special giving clubs, planned gift societies), ways of giving, and so on. There are also special-occasion pieces, which can range from a small collection of relevant speeches to a campaign kick-off piece to a final campaign report.

Indeed, you may very well want to put a targeted brochure into the pocket of your case statement.

What must a writer know about preparing these other big-money materials?

- Go light on copy. Assume the reader will not take time to read each word. How are you going to communicate? Use captions, heads and subheads, call-out quotes, boxes, and other tidbits to convey information.
- Find and use designers you can rely on. Let them run with their creative juices to fashion a piece that works. When they ask you to cut copy (they will), do it.
- Polish your prose. Brochures are an opportunity to write at your most lucid, most stylish, most elegant best. Words, artwork, and design should create an informative piece that has the look, feel, and voice of your nonprofit.
- When you have a draft, go back and pretend you are the target audience. If you were a high-tech executive, what would you think about this cover? Would you read the first paragraph? Is it clear what the organization wants you to do?

In an ideal world, you will plan your case statement and accompanying brochures at the beginning of a campaign. That way, they will all be thoughtfully orchestrated. The idea is to ensure that the key themes and images of your case statement—your bible—permeate all of your other campaign materials. Do that and prospective donors will understand why your fund-raising effort is exciting, important, and worthy of strong support.

Chapter 13

Newsletters

How to Write, Edit, Design, and Print

The first time Danielle worked on a newsletter was her first day on the job at The Nature Conservancy. The editor of the corporate newsletter was on maternity leave, the stories were written but production was behind schedule, and the staff in the Brazil office hadn't read their front-page feature, much less approved it. Oh, and did we mention that the whole edition needed to be translated into Portuguese and shipped to Brasília in time for a reception in four weeks?

This is the gospel truth. Danielle has the Portuguese edition to prove it.

Later on, Danielle became editor of that same newsletter. She got started just like any other nonprofit employee: no training, no classes, no reading of books. Instead, she spent two hours with the former editor, taking notes furiously; called both the designer and the printer and told them she knew absolutely nothing; and ate immense amounts of chocolate.

She drank lots of Diet Coke and *zoomed* around the office, from her desk to others' desks to telephone to E-mail, checking constantly with colleagues who owed her a story or whom she owed some editing or answers.

In short, she was a *stress monkey*. You could say she muddled through, except muddle is too slow a word. She jittered and shook and chewed her way through.

Don't get us wrong. Newsletters can be satisfying. They are tangible objects. They have a beginning, middle, and end. Eventually every newsletter gets published, and you get to see your name on it. It's nice.

But until then the newsletter can feel like your own personal torture chamber, sent by the angry spirits of all the bugs you ever swatted. You thought we flies were annoying? We'll show you annoying, sister.

Everyone will demand a say about what goes in the newsletter, but nobody will take responsibility for the final decision. Everyone will have ideas about how to improve the newsletter, but nobody will help you act on them. Finally, the newsletter will be expensive, time-consuming, and distributed to the public. If you screw up, you will hear about it.

In the face of this bleak prediction, we now propose to help you master your newsletter in three distinct parts. The first part is the content: To whom is this newsletter going, and what do I want to tell him? The second is the writing: How do I write news and features that will grab the reader? The third is design and printing: How can I make this newsletter look as if it's worth reading?

Whose News? Figuring Out the Content

Fund-raising writers often inherit existing newsletters. Funny thing is, even though your newsletter has been around for ten years, you may be hard-pressed to find a single soul who can clearly articulate its original purpose. (Don't panic. We've seen organizations that couldn't say *who* was getting their newsletter, never mind why. Maybe the guy who made the mailing labels knew, but no one else did.)

Presumably this newsletter comes out of your development office, so raising money has some part to play. But the newsletter can't just be page after page of "Send money!" (If it is, you are writing direct mail.)

When your reader puts the newsletter down, you want him to come away with one overriding thought about your organization. Consider these possible outcomes of your newsletter, depending on the stories you include. Your reader could think:

- Oh, look, a newsletter from that agency we gave money to last year. Whaddya know—the Office Store is contributing benches to the playground. We could get our name on a bench.
- Never got fancy dorms like that when I was there. And look at all the people from the class of '72 that are giving . . . even Jim Parker, the swine. My name should be on that list.
- Just look at how happy those kids are. I am so glad we made that gift.
- I had no idea the Bright Hope Foundation had so many programs. I thought they just held walkathons for research.

And so on. The point is, you need an overall goal, and that goal does not have to be overly ambitious. We've talked to development professionals who wrote newsletters simply so corporate donors would see the good cause's name and then toss the piece.

Others write newsletters that are actually meant to inform. Mothers and Others for a Livable Planet, for example, puts out a newsletter that is filled with information about toxic substances in the food supply and home products. If the reader decides to give more money to the group as a result of the newsletter, that's great. But the primary purpose is to inform members.

Ideally, you should identify one audience for your newsletter and one overriding theme that you want to hammer home. The newsletter Danielle worked on was for corporate donors who gave $1,000 or more annually. The message: The Nature Conservancy works cooperatively and creatively with the business community.

If you can clearly identify one priority audience and message, you are in good shape. Beware those secondary audiences and messages that seize hold of your ankle and will not let go. If you must include secondary material—has there ever been a nonprofit writer given free editorial rein?—put it in the back pages. Reserve the front page for your most important story and a large, pleasing photograph.

The Usual Suspects

Whether you decide to ask for money outright or just want the reader to learn more about your organization, you are probably talking to one or two of the following groups:

- donors
- alumni
- neighbors
- potential donors
- campaign leadership
- campaign prospects
- volunteers

What are you telling them? This, too, is relatively predictable:

- Send money! You include information about your current fund-raising effort, ask for support, and include a business-reply envelope. (As we said, this looks an awful lot like direct mail.)
- Look how well the fund-raising effort is going! Campaign newsletters dominate this category. You announce major gifts and other campaign news in hopes of building excitement and making your prospects wish their names were included.
- Look at all we are achieving together! You focus on the work of the organization. The newsletter describes current activities and creates a sense of belonging among readers.
- It is time to act! You provide mission-related information to educate your audience about the issues and spur them to action.
- You guys are such good people! You prominently highlight those wonderful donors who are making it all possible. Stroke, stroke, stroke.

WRITING NEWS AND FEATURES

News stories are just news. The writer presents the basic facts, presumably about recent or current events. These are the stories on the front page of any daily newspaper.

Feature stories are more like human-interest stories. They tend to be longer and treat their subject in some depth. Feature stories often profile people or projects.

Either way, the story must grab the reader right away and lead him inexorably, paragraph by paragraph, through the story. Readers do not tolerate dilly-dallying in a news story. As a newswriter, your most important words are the headline and your first sentence, which is called the lead.

Where, oh, where, has that little lead gone? Strictly speaking, your lead may consist of more than one sentence. It may be your first few sentences or your first two paragraphs. But no matter what, the first sentence is the most critical, and the ones that follow it are pretty darn important. They hook your readers and convince them to keep reading.

Many novice writers take hours or even days trying to write a good lead. Finally, they write the rest of the story; then someone tells them their lead isn't so good, and then they cry.

Don't cry. The lead is buried somewhere in your story. In fact, it is probably at the bottom of page 3.

Read your story and look for the sentence or fact that captures your imagination. If you can't find your lead, have someone else read the story and tell you what captured his attention most. It could be that you started out talking about students using the new commons area, but the most interesting thing to the reader was that tiny bit about how students protested until they got the new vegetarian bar at the cafeteria. You could open with that and then build the story about the commons.

Which of these lead sentences do you like best?

"Located along Bolivia's border with Brazil, Noel Kempff Mercado National Park lies in a transition zone between the hot, dry Gran Chaco environment and the wet Amazonian forests."

"AEP, Pacificorp, and BP America announced that they will together contribute $7 million to add 2.2 million acres to Noel Kempff Mercado Park in Bolivia and thereby offset an estimated 14.5 million metric tons of atmospheric carbon over 30 years."

"In 1986, Bolivian naturalist Noel Kempff Mercado and two colleagues inadvertently landed their light plane on a covert airstrip used by a drug cartel in the midst of the Huanchaca National Park, in northeastern Bolivia. What was to have been an exploration of local fauna became a national tragedy when the men were gunned down by armed Brazilians tending the world's largest cocaine factory."

All of these lead sentences could open the same story about conservation efforts in a Bolivian park. Danielle chose the last one because it was the most likely to grab the reader's attention.

Why open with unsavory details about the murder of Noel Kempff Mercado? After all, development newsletters are supposed to make readers feel good, not horrify them. In this case, the story moved quickly to the more gratifying news of how the park, now named after Mercado, has become a model of innovative conservation.

The last lead, about Mercado's murder, demonstrates what journalists call a delayed lead. In other words, the writer sets the scene or describes the background before he moves on to the current story.

The second lead, about the three corporate gifts, is a summary lead. It summarizes in one sentence what the story is really about. The first lead opens by describing where the story takes place—a device that could work for almost any story, regardless of topic.

Another lead might open with a dramatic fact, quote, or question. Danielle opened a feature piece about conservation in Maine this way:

" 'What happened to the clams?'

This was a question invariably asked at early meetings of the Sustainable Cobscook Project."

The first paragraphs. Once you've got your reader by the throat with a great lead, you next assemble the answers to who, what, when, and where and line them up like soldiers.

Later on in the story you will get to the How and Why. But right up front we need the facts. (Don't worry if all the material isn't exactly where you want it to be when your first draft is done. You can always revise later.)

The trick is to place all that information up front without sounding like an automaton. Consider this example from "Artist Joins Other '02s," by Julie Sloane in Dartmouth College's alumni newsletter, *Dartmouth Life:*

> *At convocation Samuel Dahl became the only member of the class of 2002 never to have set foot in a high school classroom. Home-schooled since third grade, the eighteen-year-old from Princeton, New Jersey, has a passion for art and literature, and he says home-schooling allowed him to spend one whole day on a painting or reading a book. After receiving his first acrylic paint set at age nine, he set to work on a series of "lousy-looking landscapes" before taking private lessons and becoming the youngest member of a local artist cooperative. "I couldn't have been as good an artist without the freedom of home-schooling," he says. And he's looking forward to pursuing his art and a range of other opportunities at Dartmouth—with professors.*

Where do our key questions get answered?

In the first sentence, we learn the most basic of the basics: Samuel Dahl is who, new student is what, and we meet him at convocation, which takes place each fall on the Dartmouth campus.

But just knowing someone's name doesn't tell us much. Where is he from, how old is he, and when was he home-schooled? Sloane tells us in the second sentence without slowing the pace of her story:

"Home-schooled since third grade, the 18-year-old from Princeton, New Jersey, has a passion for art and literature." An introductory phrase covers when he was home-schooled. Rather than saying Dahl has a passion for art and literature, Sloane replaces his name with a quick description of him: The 18-year-old from Princeton has a passion for art and literature.

After these first two sentences, Sloane sets off on the how and why.

Here's another tip: Do you think this is a story about one student, Samuel Dahl? No, no. After this introduction to one member of the class of 2002, we then learn about the statistics of the entire class. How much better to start with this one interesting fellow than to begin: "Among the 1,102 students joining the class of 2002, 65.5 percent attended public schools, 30.9 percent attended private schools, and . . ."

The body. News stories hit the who, what, when, and where so quickly that often the writer must backtrack to fill in the information that explains more about those facts. Plus the writer has to fill in the how and the why. All of this appears in the middle of the written piece—what we call the body of the story.

One of the fun things about writing news and features is that you don't have to limit yourself to boring old chronological order. Readers will follow a story that moves around: from one time period to another, from one part of the world to another, from one person's viewpoint to another's. For example, look how this 1989 story from the Yale Development Newsletter starts in the present but immediately jumps back 75 years, then goes to recent history, then comes back to the present, and then ends with centuries-old history:

> *Under stormy skies, the seventy-five-year-old Boat House on the Thames River in Gales Ferry,* Connecticut, *was rededicated on June 9, 1989, the eve of the annual Yale-Harvard Race. Along with the christening of the new shells, the renovations to the Boat House over the past year were commemorated by the presentation of several plaques honoring the donors that made the restoration possible.*
>
> *Designed and built in 1914 by James Gamble Rogers, Yale 1889, 1922 M.A. (Hon.), the Boat House has traditionally housed the Freshman Crew during the weeks prior to the big race.*

Through the direction of Hans Baldauf '81, '88 M.ARCH., and Orr and Taylor Architecture & Gardens, the entire structure was reconditioned and brought up to today's standards in electrical and fire detection/suppression systems. Over 50 alumni, friends, and former members of the Crew made donations towards the renovation project.

The four-mile Yale-Harvard Race on the Thames River is the oldest intercollegiate event as well as the longest race in North America.

Although this story jumps all over the place, it hangs together.

Obviously, the body not only provides background information; it also tells the story. Good writing principles still apply: Keep it brief, use quotes, and concentrate on concrete details. Do not go rambling into fluffy words and fuzzy concepts.

Quotes are particularly useful because they break up the text and are fun to read. No offense, but we'd rather hear directly from the people than read your narrative about them.

When Amnesty International writes about abuses in Guatemala, the organization could just tell the reader what activists have been doing and suffering as a result. Instead, the Amnesty Action newsletter interviewed Dr. Carmen Valenzuela and let her tell her own story:

"I was sure they were going to kill me," she says. "Because one of them had told me, 'Now you know more about us than we know about you. You have become dangerous for us.' In fact, I did. I knew where I was. I knew who they were. I had seen some of their faces."

Quotes can also help you with those big jumps from one time period or place to the next. After introducing the decades-old murder of Noel Kempff Mercado, Danielle's article went on to explain how three corporations were joining The Nature Conservancy and its partner, FAN, in a new conservation effort. Then it was time to jump back in time again:

"The first time I visited the park I saw the need to protect it," says Hermes Justiniano, nature photographer, bush pilot, and founder of FAN. In 1986 he happened upon the three guards in charge of the park's 1.8 million acres. Two wore sandals; the third was barefoot. They were responsible for an area as large as America's Yellowstone.

Not only does the reader happily transition from current events to a description of how things used to be; he gets some terrific concrete details. Who can forget a barefoot park guard?

The end. Eventually you will have written all there is to write about your story, and it will be time to end. You could just stop. Reporters do this all time. In fact, they purposely write in "inverted pyramid" form, with the most important facts at the beginning and the least important facts at the end, so that if the newspaper editors run out of space, they can just lop off the last few paragraphs.

But if you are writing a thoughtful feature piece, it probably begs for some kind of conclusion. One time-honored way to bring closure to a piece is to echo a theme or statement made in the beginning of the story.

Perhaps your story about osteoporosis opens with the 70-year-old woman who has begun lifting weights. Come back to her in the end. Maybe she says she finds it a lot easier to get into the car these days. Or maybe she just grimaces and says, "I will take my grandkids to the beach this summer, and I will carry the toys." Echoing the beginning helps bring closure to the end.

You might also want to end the story with a moving quote or description. Perhaps you close with a donor watching three homeless children play dodgeball with a volunteer. He says, "If my gift can make one kid feel safer, it will be worth it." The end.

The headline. If you're lucky, once you have your story written, your headline will be obvious. Like the lead, the headline must grab the reader's attention and at least hint at what the story is about.

As usual, writing a newsletter for fund-raising purposes complicates things. The *New York Times* headline can simply say, "NATO Launches Daytime Strike: Milosevic Resisting Fiercely; Two Serb Jets Are Shot Down." The news in and of itself rivets your attention. Your news, on the other hand, may need just a bit of sprucing up.

"Whitaker Foundation Makes $10.5 Million Grant" lacks punch. *Virginia Engineering* instead chose to title its piece "Biomedical's Healthy Future" and run a photo of the chair of the biomedical engineering department with an enormous grin on his face.

Writers seem to either love or hate creating catchy headlines. If you're stumped, here are some strategies to get you started:

- Alliteration. Alliteration is the repetition of the consonant or vowel sounds at the beginning of a series of words, such as "The Power of PDRs" or "Media Meisters Massage Messages."
- Assonance. Assonance is the repetition of vowel sounds within words, such as "Legal Eagles Spin to Win," or "The Rites and Kites of Spring."
- Literary or Other Cultural References. One environmental organization titled a piece about river conservation "Water Music," a reference to the famous work by composer George Frideric Handel.
- Puns, Plays on Words, and Unexpected Amusements. "Catching a Break (or Three)" is the title of an *Outside* magazine story about surfing. "Columbia Heights: Looking Up" is a *Washington Post* story about a neighborhood. "A $33 Trillion Dividend" is the title of a Nature Conservancy piece about the value of the goods and services that nature provides. All of these are just a little funny or unexpected.

EDITING OTHERS

If you are the editor of your newsletter, you have a lot more to worry about than writing. There is the obvious goal of consistency: eliminating redundancy or conflicting information; putting all your numbers into the same style. There is the matter of shortening someone's story to make it fit. And then there is that very sticky matter of editing a colleague's story to make it better.

If you are going to make significant changes to someone's text, you may have to explain why or at least show the person what you've done. Here are a few tips to help you do so without ruining your work relationships:

- Know exactly why you make each change. If you tinker with punctuation, make sure you know the rule of grammar that applies in each case. (In fact, look it up just to be sure.) There is nothing more embarrassing—or damaging to your credibility—than being challenged on a correction and finding out you are wrong.
- Open your discussion on a positive note. For example: "I really liked the way you described Peter and his work with the police. I did have some concerns about the lead, though, so I'd like to show you my suggestions on how to get to the Peter section more quickly."
- Call your changes "suggestions," "questions," or "concerns" rather than corrections or edits.
- Don't make your edits in red ink. Red reminds people of their meanest English teacher; some 30 or more years later, they still have a visceral reaction to it. An erasable pencil works well as long as you don't write so lightly that your edits might be missed.
- Ask the writer to send the copy to you in electronic form. Make your edits in the electronic file and send a clean, hard copy back to the author. One former magazine editor told us she does this all the time because people often don't remember exactly how their copy read, so they don't recognize all the changes made. They simply see the revised article and think, Gee, I did a pretty good job.

DEALING WITH DESIGN

Now that we've made you manic about writing killer leads and headlines, we must admit that it may all be for naught. If you plop your fantastic writing into a lousy newsletter design, nobody will read it. Period.

Regardless of whether you design the newsletter yourself or

have someone else do it, you must consider the overall "look" or impression of your newsletter. Even the seemingly smallest choices, such as fonts, make a big visual impression. (See Glossary of Design and Printing Terms, 321.)

The look you want. The same two questions that dictated the content of your newsletter also dictate its design: Who will read the newsletter? What do we want them to think when they see it?

Do you want your corporate newsletter to look fun and hip? Do you want your newsletter for teenage volunteers to look like a conservative business report? Of course not. You want just the opposite. Knowing that, you can make educated choices about the physical characteristics of the newsletter.

— Paper

Do you want newsprint paper or a normal paper stock (like the stuff that comes out of your photocopying machine) or a heavy, textured paper that says: Keep me forever? Light paper is more economical; heavier paper costs more and looks more important.

Do you want plain or coated paper? Coated paper is slick, like magazine paper (although you can get it in a dull matte finish). Coated paper makes colors stand out from the page. (That's why magazines use it.)

— Photos and Artwork

Will you include photographs, illustrations, or clip art (images made by computers)? Photos and illustrations tell the reader as much or more than an entire written story. On the downside, scanning photos adds time and expense to your newsletter; commissioning illustrations can be quite expensive as well.

— Color

What color will your paper be? Bright white is fine for most newsletters. A cream-colored stock looks elegant. Gray paper looks businesslike; light brown papers look more natural. Pinks and blues and such look cute.

And speaking of color, will you use color in the artwork or photos? You generally have three choices:

1. black and white
2. black plus a single accent color (called two-color art)
3. full-color photos and accents (called four-color art, like what you see in magazines)

Can you do a three-color newsletter? Certainly. But the cost of three colors will be close to that of four colors, so why not get the top of the line?

Danielle's corporate newsletter at The Nature Conservancy was two-color, using black type, black-and-white photos, and a green accent for the logo, artwork, boxes, and lines. It was printed on a coated, cream-colored stock. It looked tasteful. A school for the arts might choose a four-color newsletter with large photos of students' work. An advocacy organization might choose simple black and white so that the newsletter could be photocopied and shared with neighbors. (Color can muddy up photocopies.)

— Fonts

The best advice of even the most chic designers is this: Don't go crazy with fonts. Choose one for the body copy, choose another for headlines, captions, and other thingamadoodles. Keep your use of fonts absolutely consistent throughout the newsletter. Don't use one font for the headline on the cover story and another for the headlines on the back cover.

Usually, one puts the body copy—that is, the text of the actual story, as opposed to the headlines and captions—in a serif font. Serif fonts have little lines at the edges of each individual letter. If you look closely at the font in this sentence, you will see those little lines on each letter. People find it easier to read serif fonts in print than sans-serif fonts, which don't have those little lines.

Sans-serif fonts work well as a secondary font, for headlines and captions. (Sans-serif fonts are recommended for on-line materials such as the text on your Web site. More on that in chapter 14, "Writing for the Electronic Age.")

Aside from that basic choice, you may want to use a special font for the nameplate (the name of your newsletter; also called the banner). A newsletter for a summer camp might want a nameplate that says Camp Wachuka News. But you would not want The Springfield Business Advocate to use the same font. It looks too silly.

— Format and Size

Newsletter formats can range from tabloid style—like that of the *New York Post*—to magazine style to just an 11-inch-by-17-inch paper folded in half so it is a four-page letter 8.5 inches by 11 inches. If you plan to print the newsletter in-house, then you may want to use a bunch of 8.5-inch-by-11-inch pages stapled together in one corner. The larger the dimensions of the newsletter and the more pages, the more it will cost. An irregular size (something a far cry from 8.5 inches by 11 inches or 11 inches by 17 inches) will also cost more.

— Distribution

How will you distribute the newsletter? If you plan to mail it, you must decide if the newsletter will be a self-mailer (folded, stapled, and mailed as is) or mailed in an envelope. If you are considering using the nonprofit bulk mailing rate, the requirements for the design of your newsletter will be even more stringent. Plan to spend time poring over postal-service regulations.

— Miscellany

Does the design go well with your organization's logo? Does it look like other newsletters your group puts out? Does it need to?

The Wide World of Photography

Whereas strong photos can tell a story and make your programs real to the reader on an emotional level, most clip art merely looks nice. The problem, of course, is that good photographs usually cost money. Depending on your needs, you may get photos from three sources: professionals you hire, stock agencies that sell existing professional photos for a fee, or amateurs like yourself and your volunteers.

— Hiring professionals

If you need a series of photographs to illustrate a story or you hope to take photos that may later be used in important documents, like a case statement, then hiring a freelance professional photographer makes sense.

As with most things, the best way to find a photographer is to ask colleagues for recommendations. You could also look at publications similar to your own and see who is taking the photos. Photography directories that list the stock files of photographers and photo agencies are another option: AG Edition's Green Book, for example, lists photographers specializing in natural history, while their Blue Book lists photographers geographically. Ask your other vendors—designers and printers, for instance—for recommendations as well.

Before you hire anyone, however, review the photographer's portfolio; many photographers now post their portfolios on the World Wide Web. Keep in mind that photographers specialize. Do not hire a landscape photographer to take pictures of your board members at a meeting. Specialization aside, make sure the portfolio demonstrates different approaches to photos, from close-ups to scenics to portraits.

Ask for references as well. Just as important as the quality of the work is the quality of the person. Does this photographer meet deadlines? Does he deliver what you ask for?

FINDING A LOOK YOU CAN AFFORD

Coming up with a fabulous design is all well and good, but the reality check usually comes when you talk to the printer. For advice on cutting printing costs, we turned to Bill Spencer, a sales representative with District Lithograph Company Incorporated in Forest Hills, Maryland. In his more than 25 years in the printing business, Spencer has helped more than a few nonprofits put out a newsletter.

"The more prepared a newsletter is and the less the printer has to do, the cheaper it will be," he says. "If we have to load the fonts or strip in artwork at the last minute, that will cost you money. If we can just stick your disk in the machine and spit out the job at the other end, it will be a whole lot cheaper."

Spencer's other suggestions for cutting down the cost of your newsletter:

- Decrease the number of colors. You may be pleasantly surprised at how polished a newsletter with black body type and a single accent color can look.
- Decrease the number of pages.
- Decrease the level of complexity. In other words, avoid designs with overlapping colors and other fancy effects that require the printer to spend lots of time making sure the ink is going exactly where it needs to go and in the exactly right proportion.

HOT TIP: Always print extra copies. The printer charges you mostly for the time and labor involved to set up the presses to print your newsletter. The paper is comparatively inexpensive. Two hundred extra copies cost nothing compared to the price of going back to the printer in a few months and setting up the press all over again.

- Choose a different paper stock. If you print just a couple thousand newsletters, the price difference between the most expensive and least expensive papers won't amount to much. But if you print 500,000 newsletters, paper choice makes a big difference.

Once you've chosen a photographer, it is wise to get a signed contract. The contract should include information about the subject matter (you want photos of people at the walkathon); the format requirements (35 mm, color, etc.); how you plan to use the photos (for the cover of your newsletter and related stories on your Web site); and an itemized list of the images you want. If you want close-ups of children, specify that. If you want a mix of young and old, say so.

Usually, you will buy "onetime rights" to the photographer's work, meaning that you will use the photos one time in one publication. Photographers generally charge a day rate plus expenses for travel, film developing, etc. A member of the American Society of Media Photographers (ASMP) might charge $1,000 or more per day plus expenses. But this can be negotiable. (See our box "Getting Good Photography for Cheap" on page 226.)

— Buying Stock Photography

Stock photos are photos that already exist. There are thousands of stock agencies and stock houses that sell professional photographs for you to use. Their fees will depend on several factors:

Whether you want the photo for editorial or commercial use. Commercial use includes things like advertising, putting the image on posters that you plan to sell, and so on.

The size, color, and placement of the photo. A four-color photo on the cover of your membership magazine will cost significantly more than a black-and-white quarter-page photo on the inside of your newsletter.

The circulation of the publication. A stock image in a newsletter that goes to 1,500 people costs less than the same image in a newsletter with a circulation of 100,000.

GETTING GOOD PHOTOGRAPHY FOR CHEAP

Connie Gelb of Washington, D.C., worked as a media photographer and a wire-service photo editor before she became the photo editor of *Nature Conservancy* magazine in 1993. We talked with her about how nonprofits can secure good photography on a tight budget.

"These days, imagery is important for all organizations," says Gelb. "If you have the budget to pay for a professional freelance photographer, do it. I don't recommend trying to talk professional photographers out of their fees unless you absolutely have to. They work incredibly hard and are worth the money."

But if paying full price is not an option, as is so often the case for nonprofits, Gelb recommends several strategies for the cash-strapped organization in search of photos:

- Hold a photo contest. Offer prizes in several categories and specify in the rules that your organization will acquire all rights to the submissions. "The photographers can still use the original in any way they want, while you get nonexclusive rights to use all the submissions," says Gelb.
- Hire a local photographer. "Look at the masthead of your daily newspaper or state magazine. There's usually a roster of professional photographers who don't charge as much as a stock photographer," says Gelb. "The photo editors themselves are usually photographers and may be eager to get out on a new kind of assignment. You might end up paying only a $300-to-$400 day rate."
- Look on the Web. "Several on-line stock houses have Web sites offering inexpensive royalty-free photos that you can purchase for multiple uses. Corbis, Mira, and Picturequest all do that," says Gelb. "Also try using an on-line search engine. When I needed a photo of a rare fish, I typed in the name of the species and pulled up the Web site for the American Fisheries Association. They charged me only $25 to use one of their images."

- Offer something in return. "I often ask photographers to donate images for the Web site," says Gelb. "In exchange we post their names, E-mail and Web addresses, portfolios of their work, and brief biographies in our 'About the Photographers' section. We spend the money to get the photos digitized, prepared, and posted to the Web. Many photographers think this is a fair deal and don't worry about their photos getting 'stolen' because we post them at a low resolution."
- Build relationships with professional photographers. "Some photographers believe in the Nature Conservancy's mission so strongly that they forgive their creative fees," says Gelb. "But there is also a payoff for them, because we send photographers to exotic places where they can build up their own stock of wildlife and scenic images. If your organization can offer something in return—access to a special place or event—you might be able to convince them to go for free or for a reduced fee."
- Piggyback on other photo shoots. "One photographer called us because *Life* magazine was sending him down to Central America for a month and he wondered if we wanted anything from that region. We ended up hiring him to shoot one of our projects nearby, so we paid for his short side trip rather than paying to fly him all the way to Central America."

— Amateur photos

Clearly, if all else fails, you can take your own photographs. Indeed, it is probably worth some time and effort to teach yourself and other staff members how to take decent photos. Encourage your volunteers, some of whom may be talented amateurs, to take photos on your behalf. If you plan to use the photos in black and white or on a Web page, the photo quality does not have to be spectacular. Merely decent will suffice.

Ten Tips for Better Photography

Connie Gelb offers these tips to amateurs who want to improve their photographs.

1. Shoot slide film (also called chromes or transparencies).
2. Use ASA 25-, 50-, or 100-speed films for highest reproduction quality.
3. Avoid noonday, overhead sun; it creates high contrast and "blocked" shadows.
4. Shoot in the morning, late afternoon, or on overcast days for the best natural lighting.
5. Use a tripod and cable release to produce the sharpest photos without "camera shake."
6. "Bracket" your exposures; shoot above and below what your light meter indicates.
7. Avoid "bull's-eye" (center-weighted) compositions.
8. Move closer to your subject and shoot both horizontals and verticals.
9. When shooting plants or animals, use a large aperture to make the subject "pop."
10. Try using a telephoto lens from a distance to isolate your subject.

Show the people in your photographs doing something. Rather than just taking a picture of the speaker at the podium, take a shot that shows the speaker and the audience listening. Or show people working together around a table or your president with her shirtsleeves up, holding a shovel. Indeed, try to photograph your subjects outside in natural lighting conditions as much as possible.

— Writing Captions

Most people who get your newsletter will look at photos and read only headlines and captions. They will rarely read the text.

HOT TIP: Try to avoid "the Suits." This is the standard picture of your top donors all standing together and looking at the camera. It makes us wonder, Is that all they do–stand around and smile? Another no-no: "the Check," in which beaming officials and donor hold a six-foot-long check representing the big gift.

Knowing this, be sure to engage the reader by writing lively captions. Don't merely identify what's in the photograph; also summarize the main points of your story. The caption for a photo of grandmother and grandchild in the park could say, "Mrs. Smith and her granddaughter Evina enjoy a day in the park." But the wise writer, knowing the reader may never get to the story, will write, "Mrs. Smith and her granddaughter Evina enjoy Mercer Park's new playground equipment, purchased with a $5,000 gift from the Acme Corporation."

A wise writer also never forgets to credit the photographer. (You are legally obligated to do so.) Even if you took the picture, credit yourself or your organization: © Good Hope Agency.

HOT TIP: When you design your newsletter, make sure you leave enough room for captions. Even with ample space, you should write captions as tightly as possible.

Working well with an outside designer. Life is too short to work with a designer who makes you miserable. In addition to looking at samples to ensure that the designer has talent, ask for references from other clients. Did they like working with this firm? Was the designer open to changes and feedback? Was the designer cost-conscious? The answer to all three should be yes.

Once you have chosen a designer, it's your job to establish a good working relationship from the start. If you are collaborating with a designer to create a newsletter, bring samples of publications you like, suggests Lynn Komai, co-owner of the Watermark Design Office in Alexandria, Virginia. "It helps if you have already figured out a pithy name for the newsletter. If you're wedded to certain color combinations or type styles, tell the designer about that also," she says. "The more of those details you can decide, the better."

When Komai first meets with a client about a newsletter, she will ask about the importance of each element in the newsletter. Do you want just a single story on the front cover or a story and a box? If you are planning to list donors, how prominently do you want to display that list? Should it go in the front, the middle, or the back?

"I also suggest that people talk to a printer before they are too far along in the design process," says Komai. "You need to find out if what you want is what you can really afford."

Once you have agreed on a basic newsletter template, you write the copy, collect photographs, and give some kind of intelligible package to the designer. Despite what you may think, designers are not in the clairvoyance business. Make your desires clear to the designer:

- Create a dummy copy of the newsletter. For a twelve-page, magazine-like newsletter, take three blank pieces of paper and fold them in half. Then scribble the name of each article on the page where you want it to appear. If there will be two articles and a box, put the name of article number one on the top and that of article number two on the bottom. Draw a box so that the designer knows you want a box on that page.
- Mark up the text of the hard copy. Print out all the text for the newsletter and then mark the headlines and subheads and sub-subheads. This can be as simple as writing "Head A" next to the headline, "Head B" next to the subheads, and so on.

- Key the photographs to the hard copy. In the margin next to the story about toxic waste, simply write "photos 1–4." Then use tape (designers have this great tape that sticks and unsticks easily, without leaving residue) or sticky notes to mark the slides one through four.
- Send everything at once. (Alas, we have broken this rule many times; at least make an attempt.) "We look at a newsletter like a puzzle," says Komai. "We have to fit everything into a designated space, so it is very helpful to know what all the pieces are."

Now the onus is back on the designer to make things look good, which may be impossible. If your designer tells you there is too much text, do not tell him to shrink the photos and headlines. You, dear writer, must cut the copy. Eliminate an example or a quote. Get rid of extraneous words.

For a couple of really tough editing cases, Danielle had to read each sentence of her feature story, one by one, to see if there was a way to delete a word. We are talking desperate measures here: *The fields of rice* became "rice fields." *Bill Duncan, a field biologist in Utah*, became "Utah Field Biologist Bill Duncan."

When the initial design is finished, it will come back to you for proofreading. This is called the page-proof stage. Make sure the design works, everything is where it should be (pictures in the right place, headlines correct, captions correct), and your own text is clean. And guess what? The latter invariably poses the biggest problem.

We don't know what it is about text that has been laid out in newletter format, but it seems to highlight mistakes that you just didn't see in the pure text version. You will find hilarious (or hair-raising) mistakes in the copy. You will see that you said there were 300 attendees in the cover article but only 200 in the box on page 6. The title of the article on the back page won't match its listing in the contents. The president's message will have his first name misspelled. Whoops.

Now is the time to get anal. Begin by reading just the text of every article. Then go through the whole newsletter again, this time just reading the peripherals: the headers, the footers, the captions, the key to the map. Read a third time to check numbers and names. Mark all your corrections, make a copy of the marked-up proof, and send the original back to the designer.

After that, you may look at one more proof or five, depending on how many changes you make. After a while, this gets to the point of diminishing returns. (See the box "Top-Ten Things Designers Hate," page 234). Once you think the proof is perfect, the designer will send a disk and your photos to the printer.

What is good design? We are not professional designers, but we have worked with good designers. And you know what? They walk on water. No kidding. They copy one sentence out of the middle of your story, make it into a pull quote in large type off to the side, and voila! It reads like poetry. Who knew you were so talented?

So how do you, a writer, figure out what good design looks like? You'll know it when you see it, or you don't see it, as the case may be. "Most of us don't pay much attention to a design if it's a good one," says Thomas H. Bivins in his book *Fundamentals of Successful Newsletters*. "We only tend to notice a design when it is either badly executed or when it is so overdone that it shouts down the content."

Take an objective look and trust your eye. Does the copy look too crowded on the page? Do the elements on the page look balanced? How about the emphasis? Your designer may put the first sentence of your story in large type. Designwise, it looks fabulous. But as the writer, you know the headline is far more important than the first sentence. (After all, you're using a delayed lead, and the first sentence isn't really the heart of the story.) Tell the designer to emphasize the headline more than the first sentence.

Finally, take a look at consistency. Certain elements should be consistent throughout the newsletter, such as the size of the lines that separate one article from the next and the way you treat subheads and the placement of the byline.

Printing

Okay, the newsletter is written, edited, and designed. It's time to print!

It is fine to print your Little League's newsletter on a color printer at home. It is not fine to print Oberlin College's alumni news at home.

Working well with an outside printer. Your printer doesn't ask a whole lot of you besides clear instructions and help with collecting the materials he needs to get the job done. If you're handing over a disk, make sure the fonts are loaded on it. Provide all the photos at once, if possible. If you have changes to make, do them yourself instead of asking the printer to do it. (It'll save you money, too.)

Ironically, the trickiest part about printing your wonderful fundraising piece is trying to communicate with the printer himself. Printers use some of the most incredible jargon on the planet, but they don't want you to use it unless you know what you're talking about. (See Printing Terms, page 323.)

"If you start using those technical terms, I will assume you understand our language and know exactly what you want," says Bill Spencer. "You are much better off asking me a question in plain, simple English." The printer will have questions for you as well:

- What kind of paper do you want to use?
- How many pages is the newsletter?
- How many copies of the newsletter do you need?
- How will this be folded and bound?
- When do you need to see the blueline?
- When do you need the finished piece to be ready?

As you go through those questions, the jargon will be *flying*. For example: Do you want a four-panel single fold or a six-panel letter fold? Just keep asking questions until you both understand what you're talking about.

TOP-TEN THINGS DESIGNERS HATE

Writers and designers usually get along pretty well, both being overworked and underpaid humanities-type people. When we talked with Lynn Komai, Susan Walston, and Jim Gray, all designers in the Washington, D.C., area, they did admit there were just a few things writers do that can raise their hackles.

As of this writing, most professional graphics designers use a Macintosh system, while most nonprofits use Windows-based computers to write the content of the newsletter. This can lead to some technological headaches. Here are some of the pesky things that slow designers down:

1. Putting hard returns at the end of every line. "There is no easy way for us to delete all those hard returns," says Komai. "We want you to just type, type, type, and only use hard returns to create a line of space between paragraphs. In fact, don't even indent your paragraphs. Just leave them flush left, with a blank line to separate them."
2. Writing headlines in all caps. "Again, there is no easy way for us to convert those caps to regular type," says Komai. "We have to retype the words."
3. Using the quotations key on your keyboard. "It is much easier for us if you use the "smart quotes" feature in Microsoft Word and WordPerfect, which makes opening quotes slant one way and closing quotes slant the other," says Komai. "If you don't, we have to go in and manually correct the quotation marks to make them look right."
4. Using two spaces after periods. "If you put double spaces after each period, we either take one out or we go through and make sure the spacing is consistent in the whole document."
5. Sending a disk with no hard copy. "Always send a printed-out version of the newsletter. Sometimes there will be problems with the conversion to Macintosh, and it really helps if we can see what the text was supposed to look like."

Then there are the run-of-the-mill bad habits (and bad manners) that drive designers insane:

6. Vague criticism. "It is not helpful to say you just don't like the design," says Walston. "Be specific. What don't you like? Try to put it into words."
7. Bad photos. "So many organizations send us 'grip-'n'-grin' photos," says Komai. "They are terrible. Do everything in your power to get quality photographs."
8. Never-say-die attitude. "Some people change, change, change, all the time, so there is never an end moment. It's never over," says Komai.
9. Disrespect for design. "I've had people ask me, 'Did you really go to school for this?' " says Walston. "Have some respect for what the designer does. Or at least pretend you do."
10. Design by committee. "Design by committee is a lot tougher than just working with one or two people," says Gray. "The worst is when the writer actively solicits other people's opinions. Just by asking people, you make them feel like they have to criticize. If you'd never asked, they might have liked the design."

At this stage, Spencer also highly recommends that you get a written purchase order. The purchase order sets out in writing exactly what paper, colors, and so forth you want. Its purpose, again, is to ensure everybody is on the same page (so to speak).

So let's assume that everybody now understands how the newsletter should look. You give the printer the disk and the photos and sit back and wait.

The next thing you know, the printer has delivered a package with a big blue proof of your newsletter, called the blueline. This proof is an actual photographic representation of your newsletter. For example, a blueline for a two-color newsletter using green as an accent will come in two parts: One shows everything that will be black (or shades of black), and the other shows everything that will be green (or shades of green). Except in both cases all the lines and text show up as blue. Just have faith; in the end, everything on the black version will be black, and everything on the green version will be green.

You will probably also get a little notice with your blueline stating that you are responsible for catching any mistakes at this point. Once you sign off on the blueline, the printer accepts no responsibility for any errors that you missed even if the error was the printer's fault. In real life, most printers will try to make some kind of accommodation if you find a mistake that was the printer's fault after the fact. But once you sign the little proof form, no printer is obligated to do that.

So now that the stakes are sufficiently high, what should you check on the blueline? Spencer recommends the following checks, at the least.

- Check your own writing—again. "This is your last chance to catch any terrible errors," says Spencer. "It costs more to fix an error at this stage, but it's still cheaper than reprinting the whole job." This bears repeating: It costs more to fix mistakes at this stage. You still should look for them, but correct only disastrous errors.
- Check the photographs. Are they in the right place? Have they been reproduced clearly?
- Look at the relation of other elements on the page. Are they in the right place? Are the colors correct? Look at the relation of colors to other colors. Are those correct?
- Are the pages in the right order? Is the newsletter trimmed to the right size? (Keep in mind that most bluelines are trimmed by hand, so there may be some irregularities.)

Once you've convinced yourself that the blueline looks right, you just sign the little form, send it back, and bask in the glory of being done.

Chapter 14

Writing for the Electronic Age

E-mail and the World Wide Web

In 1999, Memorial Sloan-Kettering Cancer Center in New York raised more than $800,000 from world-famous actors, businessmen, and politicians. Boy, were the fund raisers unhappy.

The money came from a chain E-mail letter sent without the center's permission by a well-meaning volunteer nurse. The letter simply asked recipients for $10—and no more—to support the life-saving work of the world's oldest and largest private cancer center. It also asked them to send the E-mail to friends.

The story made national headlines as the E-mail became a status symbol, with ever-more famous people joining the list of donors and forwarding it to others. Meanwhile, Sloan-Kettering found itself awash in $10 checks from the likes of Dustin Hoffman and Danielle Steel.

"Our sense is that if somebody was willing to give $10, they would have given more and we missed an opportunity," a Sloan-Kettering spokeswoman told one reporter. "We're grateful for the money, but please, if you have one of these letters, just throw it out."

Welcome to the world of electronic fund raising. The control freaks among you will find the following material disturbing. Those of you who enjoy a little confusion and ambiguity will have a ball.

IT'S AN E-WORLD, AFTER ALL

E-mail is standard in most offices in the United States, and even the truly antitechnology holdouts are slowly shuffling aboard the E-mail train. Case in point: In March 1999, Danielle's mother finally got an E-mail account and began to systematically demonstrate the value of electronic communication.

- It's cheap! Danielle usually sends her mother, who lives in Jerusalem, E-mail about four times a week. This costs her a mere $19.95 per month.
- You control the content and duration of the communication. Danielle doesn't have to worry about being interrupted or dragged into an interminable conversation.
- You send your message when it is convenient for you. Danielle's E-mail can go out at 9:00 P.M. local time and be waiting for her mother when she wakes up.

Reading this, you might think that E-mail is simply a faster form of a letter. But there are key differences, and this is where the fun begins.

First, there is the writing. Technology geeks—those friends of yours addicted to acronyms and ever-faster ways of doing things—invented E-mail. Today everybody uses E-mail with the same speedy verve. As a result, there are some spectacularly bad E-mails out there that often do more harm than good. What you think is a pithy joke your mother finds abrupt and hostile.

Realizing the potential for misunderstanding, the geniuses in the high-tech world introduced "emoticons" to indicate emotion. The emoticons consist of punctuation marks and letters that together look like little sideways smiley faces, frowning faces, or winking faces, like so ;-).

In the old days, if you sent your mother a letter that caused a misunderstanding, you would have been compelled to improve your writing the next time. Today you slap a smiley face on that nasty sentence and your mother must concede you meant it in good humor. Alas, this does not do much for the cause of writing well.

Perhaps a bigger disadvantage to E-mail, as demonstrated by Memorial Sloan-Kettering, is that you have no control over what happens to the message once you send it. If Danielle's mother wants to send Danielle's E-mail to the rest of the family, she can do that—easily. No photocopying, no collecting of envelopes, no licking of stamps. What's worse, if she wants to tamper with Danielle's E-mail—make the message just a bit more flattering to herself, let's say—she can do that, too. (Luckily, Danielle's mother wouldn't do that.)

SO WHAT'S E-MAIL GOT TO DO WITH FUND RAISING?

For decades, the mantra of raising big money has been personal relationships. You take Mrs. Jackson to lunch, you invite her to the gala, you send her clips about the new cancer ward, you inquire after her granddaughter. After a year or two of this, you ask her for $5 million. Badda-bing, badda-boom.

Could it all be done by E-mail instead?

Thus far, no. As Sloan-Kettering sadly noted, if Dustin Hoffman will give $10, wouldn't he just as easily give $10,000? Yes, but he won't send $10,000 in response to an E-mail.

But how about *cultivating* a major donor? You bet. Here are just two examples we've heard of:

- A director of information systems at an East Coast nonprofit begins courting the chairman of a technology firm in California. Although they meet in person from time to time, much of the cultivation between visits occurs by E-mail. Over time, the executive donates equipment, then free consulting services, and eventually cash.

- A director of development in Anchorage, Alaska, gets a call from a former donor who just visited a project site and loves it. The development director talks with the donor about the plans for the project and mentions that they are on a fund-raising drive. A flurry of E-mail ensues over the next few weeks, including sending an electronic draft of a proposal to the prospect, who sends back comments and instructs the organization to fax the proposal to a foundation on whose board he sits. A few days later, the director of development logs into his E-mail from a remote Alaskan lodge to find another message from the donor, this one saying a check for $50,000 is on its way.

Writing E-mail to donors and prospects. Allow us to point out that major donors tend to be people who have accomplished much in their lives. They are treated with deference at the office, at the country club, at the Four Seasons Hotel. An off-the-cuff E-mail from a pipsqueak like you may not be well received.

Follow the prospect's lead. If Mrs. Jackson gives you her E-mail address and suggests that you E-mail her, then do so. Otherwise, stick to a good old-fashioned letter on bond paper.

E-PEEVES

Think we're being a little stodgy about using proper English in E-mail? We're in good company. *New York Times* book-review editor Patricia T. O'Connor dedicated an entire page in her book *Woe Is I: The Grammarphobe's Guide to Good English in Plain English*, to complaints about bad writing in the electronic age. Hers is sage advice, especially when communicating with donors:

Let's clean up cyberspace, gang. You wouldn't use *pls* for "please," *yr* for "your," or *thnx* for "thanks" in a courteous letter. So why do it on the Net? You don't shout or whisper on the telephone. So why use all capital or all lowercase letters in your E-mail? Making yourself hard to read is bad "netiquette."

And another thing. IMHO (in my humble opinion), those abbreviations like CUL (see you later) and BTW (by the way) are overused. You're too busy for full sentences? So what are you doing with the time you're saving by using cute shortcuts? Volunteering at your local hospital? Sure. I'm ROFL (rolling on the floor laughing).

Even if the prospect does suggest E-mail, be conservative. Old friends are allowed to shoot off E-mails with emoticons smiling, ALL CAPS bellowing, and other *fun* things popping off the screen. You and your organization—well, you guys have your hat in your hand. A little decorum is called for.

In the beginning, write the E-mail as you would a formal letter, however, don't include items that will appear in the header, such as the date, the enclosure notations, and carbon-copy notations. For example:

```
Mrs. Jackson, It was a pleasure talking with you at
the luncheon yesterday. As promised, I am
forwarding a copy of our communications plan
for the opening of the new children's oncology
wing. We would very much appreciate your thoughts
on media outreach for the event.
```

Note that this E-mail is utterly devoid of acronyms, shorthand words, and informal language. If the prospect sends you an informal reply by E-mail and addresses you by your first name, you may follow suit:

```
Barbara, Thanks so much for your note! I spoke with
the president, and he would be thrilled to
```

talk with your friend at CBS. Perhaps you could ask her to come to lunch with all three of us? I will call you this afternoon to discuss. Again, many thanks. You are wonderful! —Juanita

WORLD WIDE WEB OR WORLD WIDE WAIT?

Anyone who was listening to certain high-tech executives (or Al Gore, for that matter) in the late 1990s would have thought the World Wide Web was about to make Renaissance men of us all. Need to know how to build an igloo? Look on the Web. Want the latest on human rights in East Timor? The Web's for you. Want to send an audio recording of flatulence to your little brother? Web.

Hop on the World Wide Web for 15 minutes, however, and you will see why so many people are still calling it the World Wide Wait. Regardless, both the World Wide Web and the number of people using it are growing fast. The Pew Research Center for the People & the Press reported in 1998 that 41 percent of Americans went on-line, up from only 14 percent in 1995. Certainly nonprofit organizations have leaped into the fray like so many lemmings, trying to catch their share of the market.

Don't get us wrong. There are many eagles among nonprofit Web sites. But it is surprisingly easy to be a lemming. And you know what? All those Web surfers out there really, really hate lemmings.

What the World Wide Web can do for nonprofits. Why would any sane person get involved in the World Wide Web? You do it either because you believe in the amazing potential of the Web or because your clients and/or competition are forcing you to. If all the other environmental groups in the state have Web pages, you're going to have to build one also.

Before you go leaping, however, try to get the tiniest grasp on the way this new medium works. The World Wide Web goes way beyond text. It contains all media, from text to graphics to sound to video. Best of all, it has links; anything underlined or in a bright color on a Web page instantly connects you to another Web page. And that Web page might be totally different from the one you were on.

Here's how Bud Smith describes the World Wide Web in *Creating Web Pages for Dummies:*

> *How to picture the Web? Imagine that a single copy of every magazine in the world was laid on the floor of a huge building. Imagine that pieces of string connected specific locations in each magazine to relevant information in other magazines. The result would be a giant web of text and graphics. That's pretty much what the Web is like.*

Web-site links can also take you to an E-mail form, a comment form, or an order form that you can fill out and send back to the organization that hosts the Web site.

Whoa, there. You mean the reader can talk back?

Yes, indeed. It is standard practice these days to give your Web-site readers—all those potential supporters out there—a way to talk back to you about anything their hearts desire. What a blessing! Now you can learn more about your audience, find out what they like, and court them even better than before. What a curse! Every cranky old fart on the planet is going to correct your grammatical mistakes. It's true. The people will not be ignored. If they don't like something on your Web site, you're gonna hear about it.

Once you're committed to creating (or improving) your Web site, consider the following things that the Web site could do for your organization.

- *Inform the world that you exist.* This was the original reason everyone jumped on the Web and started looking like lemmings. Of course, your Web site should prominently display your name, your mission, and how people can contact you. These days, however, your Web site should do more than merely proclaim your existence.

- *Build appreciation for your organization.* A good Web site will highlight your organization's strengths and describe recent accomplishments—to a point. As Mary S. Morris and Randy J. Hinrichs note in their book *Web Page Design*, people do not appreciate an on-line pep rally. Instead, they say, "Content reigns supreme at a Web site."

  If you want repeat visitors, provide them with useful information. For example:

  —The University of Wisconsin-Madison's National Institute for Science Education created a series of Web pages called the Why Files, which explain the science behind the news.

  —The Environmental Defense Fund offers a Scorecard feature where you can type in your zip code to find out what pollutants are being released into your community and who is responsible.

  —The March of Dimes' Web site offers a Health Library where you will find information about birth defects, having a healthy baby, and more.

- *Promote activism.* If your organization engages in advocacy, the Web can spread the word about issues and provide people with the means to act. For example:

  —Amnesty International posts information about victims of human-rights violations and where to send a letter of protest.

  —The Web site of the National Congress of American Indians tells visitors how to contact the Senate Committee on Indian Affairs, the House Resources Committee, and the Native American Caucus.

- *Attract volunteers and donors.* Many organizations report that a Web page brings in lots of inquiries and even some money from donors.

—As of this writing, the American Red Cross' Web site had raised more than $1 million for Kosovo relief efforts through its Web site—far more than most other nonprofit Web efforts.

—According to *CASE Currents* magazine, Brown University raised almost $10,000 on-line in 1998. More important, most of those gifts were made on December 29, 30, and 31, when the development office was closed.

- *Announce news and upcoming events.* Most Web sites have a news section that contains the latest press releases or even an on-line newsletter.

  —Girl Scouts of America's home page includes news stories such as "Colorado to Kosovo: What Can Girl Scouts Do?" and "GirlSports 2000 Update."

  —California Voter Foundation's Web site offers archives of its on-line newsletter about voter education, money in politics, and political disclosure.

- *Recognize major donors.* Some donors may appreciate a special recognition of their gift on your Web site. (Always check with the donor first, however.)

  —Click on the corporate logos on the Special Olympics Web site—Coca-Cola swirl, for example—and you will jump to the corporations' own Web sites.

- *Link to related sites.* You can link people to government Web pages that contain more information related to your cause, to partner organizations, or even to donors. Some organizations offer a Web-site link as a benefit for a certain level of campaign gift.

  —The NAACP maintains a page of links with some 30 like-minded organizations, ranging from the American Association for Affirmative Action to the Sierra Club Legal Defense Fund.

- *Make your case.* Campaign case statements, because they rely so heavily on graphics, often make a terrific presentation on the Web.

  —WHYY, a public television and radio station in Philadelphia, posted its case statement on the Web, including a 3-D digital tour of the new technology facility the campaign would make possible.

- *Build relationships with your donors.* If your Web site includes any kind of interactive capability—even just a place to send an E-mail back to you—then you have the opportunity to cultivate your donors. A quick answer to a prospect's on-line inquiry builds considerable good-will.

HOT TIP: The converse is true! Make sure you have staff dedicated to responding to donors. Being ignored is no fun.

What the Web hasn't done for nonprofits (yet). The Web has not replaced print communications. Not everyone has access to the World Wide Web, and even those who do might not have time or the interest to find you. The computer itself ties people down. They can't take it with them to the beach or hand it to a friend. They can print stuff from your Web page, but then it lacks that "I am printed on good paper therefore I am worth reading" quality.

Finally, the Web has not yet raised truly major gifts of the six- and seven-figure variety. It has, however, blown through the five-figure barrier. In reaction to world crises, such as Hurricane Mitch and the war in Kosovo, some donors have sent charities completely random gifts of $10,000 or more, based on what they see on a Web site. We have even heard of a family foundation donating $30,000 out of the blue through an organization's Web site.

But when it comes to the really big gifts—what fund-raising expert Bill Sturtevant calls the "stop and think" gifts—people still rely largely on their emotions and their affinity for the person who is asking. It remains to be seen if people will ever be so moved by their computer screens that they are willing to write a huge check on the spot. Joe is betting against; Danielle thinks it could happen. Time will tell.

WRITING FOR GOOD CAUSES ON THE WEB

So you and your colleagues want to create some kind of magic Web site, the content of which will instantly attract zillions of donors and dollars, like so many flies to fly paper. The task is exciting, beguiling, and above all, utterly confusing. As you embark on your task, keep in mind this golden rule:

Writing is just one piece of the puzzle. In some ways, the writer is the flea on the toe of the elephant that is fording a raging river. You don't count for much.

A good Web site uses design, not just text, to convey information. A good Web site combines text, design, and the flow of information to guide a visitor toward some action, but unlike a book or brochure, you cannot dictate the path the visitor will take. You entice; you suggest. On top of all this, a sophisticated Web site will include E-mail forms, searchable databases, and all kinds of technological wizardry.

Writing to avoid lemming city. To whom are you talking? A discussion of who surfs the Web often characterizes people somewhere along a continuum: On one end you have people who get on the Web for entertainment, and on the other end you have folks who doggedly search for one piece of information and nothing else.

We guess that most nonprofit Web-site visitors fall on the searcher side of the scale. Adults looking for entertainment can easily go to Dilbert.com, Scrabble.com, and Playboy.com. Your cause is entertaining, but not *that* entertaining.

So, you are speaking to searchers. At first, that may be all you can say about your Web visitors. Once the site is up, you can ask people to register or put themselves on an E-mail list, which will give you more information. If this Web site is a serious undertaking, your organization may decide to spend money studying whom exactly you want to reach and what they would like to see. If nothing else, check with your membership department to see if it has done any surveys or research on your donors. You can always begin by targeting them.

So what will you put on the Web? Whatever will lead visitors to take the action you want them to take. Here are some pointers to get you started:

— Make Content King.

If most of your readers come in search of information, give the people what they want: solid, helpful information. In other words, put your assets on-line. Share pictures of artwork, testimonials from survivors, back issues of your classroom materials. Do you have experts on staff? Organize an on-line chat session or a regular question-and-answer column so that members and donors can talk to them.

Every day, the staff at *www.netscape.com* select a few Web sites to feature on Netcenter's "What's Cool" page. How do they decide what's cool?

"Content is by far the most important barometer," declares the site's editorial policy. In addition to personality, relevance, and links, the editorial staff looks at *utility*: "Believe it or not, cool sites need to impart some worthwhile information. If readers can't figure out what they are doing at a Web site by the time they say to themselves, What am I doing at this Web site? then the site does not effectively communicate its objective."

By the way, if you want to see if your site cuts the cool mustard, Netcenter takes submissions. See the "What's Cool" page for instructions.

— Think Like a Surfer.

Yes, you can recycle some (not all) of your written material on your Web site. But you must rearrange it and supplement it with new material, for the following reasons:

—People do not read Web sites for very long.

—People do not read Web sites in a linear fashion, from beginning to end.

—People cannot see your entire document. They can only see what is on the screen and often don't know whether they are in the beginning, middle, or end.

Good Web-site text is both skimmable and immediately understandable. Most people skim Web sites until they find the information they are looking for (or until something else catches their eye). In fact, they will often just read the links—those words that you have underlined or put in bright colors to indicate that they go to another page—before reading anything else. People expect the links to indicate where they lead to; they expect the buttons to do the same.

WRITING LINKS

When you write Web-site material, you must think about which words and phrases will become the links to other pages. Sun Microsystem's style guide (*www.sun.com/styleguide*) suggests that you write about your subject as if there were no links in the text at all. In other words, say: "*Writing for a Good Cause* offers several tips on how to incorporate already existing text into your Web site." On screen, the underlining alone indicates that you can link to a Web site about the book (which you can, by the way, at *www.writingforagoodcause.com*). You do not need to write: "*Writing for a Good Cause*, which has a Web site, offers several tips . . ."

Make sure that whatever words used as links are big enough to be seen easily. One measly *word* is pretty easy to miss; *a longer phrase* is more likely to be seen.

You can put the text from your old brochure on-line, but you must cut the copy into little chunks. Use subheads, graphics, and links to help the reader skip to exactly what she wants or entice her in the direction you wish she would go.

— Make It Quick.

The biggest turnoff for any Web reader is to go to a home page (that's the opening page of your Web site) and wait for 30 seconds or more for some fancy logo to load. Surfer's reaction? I'm outta here.

WRITER BEWARE! You might think that making text skimmable means keeping it all short and light. Not necessarily so. Some people will come to your site in search of in-depth information because they already read your printed brochure and want to know more. For those people, the Web site must offer detailed information. As a general rule of thumb, put the short, skimmable stuff up front. Use links for people who want to dig down to that meatier text.

Make sure your home page loads quickly and clearly indicates where to go next for information. Typical buttons on a home page might include:

contact information
program information
how to get involved
news
background on the organization

HOT TIP: To make life easy on your visitors, consider including a diagram of your Web site or a site index. A complex Web site should include a SEARCH feature.

— Three Clicks and You're Out.

Most Web gurus recommend you follow the three-clicks rule: The visitor must be able to get to what she is looking for within three clicks. Again, you must organize your information so that it is easy to find.

WORKING OUT THE KINKS

Once you get your Web site up, you will immediately find things that need fixing. Such fixes range from the benign to the horrifying, so leave yourself time to deal with them.

When the Consumer Federation of America first put up its Web site, it was "very serviceable and very plain," says state and local development director Nancy Register. "We created it in-house, and it just opened with a title bar and some buttons. The first button was GRANTS, but that was password-protected. When visitors found they couldn't open the first button they tried, they left."

Easy enough to fix. More upsetting was the experience of another development officer who signed up four new members the first week her organization's membership form went on-line. Unfortunately, when she downloaded the forms, she got nothing but weird symbols and nonsensical text, then the name Charles, then more nonsense, some numbers that might be a street address, then more nonsense. Fortunately, she was able to discern telephone numbers to call the members and get their information.

Try putting a list of topics and links right at the top of each page. For example, if the reader clicks on the PROGRAMS button, immediately show her the links to all your different programs. If the entire text under "Programs" is just one long page, make the links take the visitor to the section she wants. In other words, if text about housing assistance is five paragraphs down, the "Housing" link should take the reader directly to that fifth paragraph.

— Write for the Screen.

At least in the first few pages of your Web site, break your text up into chunks that fit on a screen. (Most screens show about half of one 8.5-inch-by-11-inch page—a short horizontal slice.) Short sentences, short sections, and clearly demarcated subheads rule the day.

NMP, INC.: MAKING THE WEB WORK FOR NONPROFITS

NMP, Inc., a division of AppNet, is an award-winning Internet and Web solutions provider. With clients ranging from St. Jude Children's Research Hospital to the American Civil Liberties Union, NMP has helped many nonprofits create Web sites that communicate effectively *and* raise money. NMP chairman Jeff Hallett and Stephen Love, director of creative services, shared their advice on creating successful Web sites and making the writer a key part of the Web team.

- Know what you want. "If you are serious about your Web site, the best thing you can do is to examine who you're talking to," says Hallett. "Really understand your message. You should also define what you want visitors to do once they get to your site. We ask our clients for a quantifiable goal so that down the road they can turn to their management and say, 'This was a success.' "
- Involve the right players. "We've run into trouble when we work with just one department of an organization,"

says Love. "Then, when the rest of the organization sees the Web site, they insist, 'That's not our message!' On the other hand, we've also worked with organizations that asked us to structure the Web site just like the organizational chart. You are not going to reach your objectives that way."

- Work on content and design together. "Ideally, you should have a content person, an information architect, and a designer all working together," says Love. "The architect and the designer can tell the writer how the information will fit into the architecture and tell her if it's too much or too little."
- Change your writing to match the Web environment. "A writer should be open to the fact that this is a new medium," says Hallett. "You could have a photo go with your text, or you could have 40 pages of graphs and charts go with it. How will you write differently knowing those materials will be there?"
- Use your skills to improve the Web site. "A Web site needs an information collector, a traffic cop, and an editor all in one," says Love. "It needs someone to make sure the organization is speaking with one voice. A writer's skills can really help with that."

HOT TIP: Do not refer back to previous text or other parts of the Web page. Yes, you may try to entice visitors to take one or two paths through the site, and your writing from one page to the next should build toward the ultimate conclusion (to join, to act, etc.). Each page's text must be able to stand alone, however, because the visitor may jump in three layers down from the home page and never see what came before.

— Write for a Worldly Audience.

Indicate that budget figures are in U.S. dollars. Specify which time zone you're talking about. Use metric measurements.

— Keep it Current.

There is nothing more amateurish than to have January's volunteer activities still posted in May. Take that stuff down! If you know you won't be able to update the Web site as often as you'd like, keep time-sensitive material off it. At the very least, eliminate dates.

Being a Successful Cog in the Giant Web Wheel. "Who would knowingly go to a place that's going to ask them for money?" asked Southwest Missouri State University's Kelly Gillespie of *CASE Currents* magazine in March 1997. Who indeed? Only true-blue supporters will intentionally seek out your campaign fund-raising pages.

Gillespie decided to link her pledge forms to the pages of the university's more than 40 academic departments. That way, when visitors swelled with pride about the chemistry department's accomplishments, they could immediately make a gift.

As the development writer, you may gently insert yourself all over the organization's Web site. Make sure the membership page indicates that gifts larger than $500 are entirely appropriate either through a line of text or a special link for those who want to do more. Offer to edit program descriptions to make them even more winning and upbeat. Keep yourself in the loop on new technologies for the Web site; communicating with potential donors should be at the top of the Web site's agenda.

No matter what kind of writing you end up doing for the Web site, the most important advice we can give is this: Look at the copy once it's on-line. The copy that sang on the page may now be split up over two different screens and make no sense at all. Your written description of the new building would look so much better as captions for the architectural drawings; of course, no one told you all the drawings would be there, but don't take it personally. Just fix it.

The second most important advice we can give is to improve the Web site regularly. If your organization doesn't have time or the money to hire professionals, then devote the time and talents of one staff member toward making the Web site great. Look at what the best of the best are doing:

- HotWired.com's webmonkey section contains on-line tutorials about designing an effective Web site.
- Highfive.com profiles a new well-designed Web site each week.
- Webbies.com lists the prestigious Webby Award winners, chosen by judges at the International Academy of Digital Arts and Sciences.

Visit the Web sites of other nonprofits in your field. Visit premier institutions. If Stanford University can't put together an effective Web site, then who can? Visit the sites of corporations that make their living from the Web: Sun Microsystems, Cisco Systems, Netscape, Dell Computer. Certainly check out the Web sites of local Web design firms as well.

PART 5

So Now You're All Set, Right?

By now you must feel fully empowered. Maybe our "Down-and-Dirty Proposal Kit" (page 275) has already helped save your life. (Did it? Write and tell us, will ya? Thanks!) Maybe you have a better sense of this curious branch of writing you find yourself in. And maybe you've picked up some useful pointers on writing and development materials.

Wow, you *are* all set, aren't you?

Ha! That's what the top-flight specialists down in the boiler room on the *Titanic* thought. Great ship, cutting-edge equipment, historic journey, who wouldn't sign on? Can you imagine how thrilled they were to be on staff? The ship was running beautifully—thanks to those very specialists—until some guy upstairs steered into an iceberg! And where did the water come pouring in first? The boiler room!

Now, we're not saying higher-ups will steer your good cause's boat that far astray. But stuff happens. When it does, we hope you will find our advice in this section useful. Here's our take on how to survive in the wacky world of fund raising, how to flourish as a writer, and how to find the good life working for your good cause.

Chapter 15

The Fund-Raising Writer's Survival Kit

What to Do When Stuff Happens

Breathing in, I calm my body.
Breathing out, I smile.
Dwelling in the present moment,
I know this is a wonderful moment!
—Thich Nhat Hanh

One Saturday several years ago, Joe and Danielle and their writer-friend Beth got up early, packed light vegetarian lunches, blankets, and cushions (as instructed), and drove to a nearby university campus, where they quickly chose places together on the floor near the back of the gymnasium. There, with several hundred others of all ages, they spent the day meditating with the Vietnamese Zen master Thich Nhat Hanh and the monks of Plum Village in France.

They sat quietly while Thich recited mindfulness meditations.

They practiced yoga positions.

They walked silently through the halls of the university library.

"Peace is present right here and now, in ourselves and in everything we do and see," writes Thich Nhat Hanh in his popular *Peace*

Is Every Step. "The question is whether or not we are in touch with it. We don't have to travel far away to enjoy the blue sky. We don't have to leave our city or even our neighborhood to enjoy the eyes of a beautiful child. Even the air we breathe can be a source of joy."

Words like those filled our day. They relaxed us, helped us let go and clear our minds of the clutter of daily life. It was a lovely few hours, a refreshing retreat from weekday concerns.

We're not suggesting you take up meditation. Your favorite stress reliever may be knitting, running, reading thriller novels, snowboarding, or entertaining. Whatever it is, be sure to do it regularly.

Fund raising is stressful work, and fund-raising writing is more stressful. Why? For many reasons:

- High stakes—your cause depends on the money you raise.
- Big players—your president, your board, your donors.
- Much ambiguity—nothing fixed in stone.
- Fast turnaround—ASAP, if you please.

On leaving one fund-raising job, Joe was asked to write the classified ad that would be used to recruit his successor as director of development communications. Joe wrote that the ideal candidate must be able to handle "nuanced situations under pressure."

The same might be said of most any job in fund raising. But the writer—the guy or girl who puts black on white—has to try to say it just right in a way that will please everyone.

As we all know, it is not possible to please everyone. Ergo: stress!

TRY TO KEEP SOME PERSPECTIVE

You and your colleagues—all bright and well intentioned—may trip over each other's feet now and then. You're human, and anytime two or more humans get together, well—can the water cooler, the gossiping, and the jockeying for position be far behind?

Why here at the heart association? Here at the opera society? Yes, *especially* there, where the stakes—the money stakes—are sufficiently low compared to elsewhere that politicking sometimes runs rampant. There's simply less to fight over.

There isn't much you can do about human nature except remember that life goes on. Besides, think of all the places you are not working. You are not writing instruction manuals for weapons systems, you are not writing press releases for clear-cutters, and you are not writing ads for cigarettes. There's no need to get self-righteous about it—hey, you still put your pants on one leg at a time in the morning. But you can look at yourself in the mirror and know you'll make a difference when you get to the office. Many people can't.

So, you feel good about your cause. Now, how do you survive the everyday bureaucratic nonsense and get your job done?

THIS AIN'T NO PARTY

Let us take a wild guess: The two things you hate about your job most are (drumroll, please) last-minute assignments and the meddling of other people. Right? Clairvoyant we are, yes.

We hate to say it, but both are simply facts of development life. Do not take them personally or give up, because clearly your organization is going to hell in a handbasket. (*You* may be going to hell in a handbasket; the organization is fine.)

In truth, the last-minute assignment allows you to prove your mettle. (For instructions on how to conquer the last-minute assignment, see our "Down-and-Dirty Proposal Kit," page 275.) If you can crank out a decent proposal in four hours, your development colleagues will not soon forget it. They will kiss your delightful, efficient fingers. If it weren't for you, they would be stuck writing the stuff themselves.

Ironically, emergency assignments make you suffer most before and after they happen. Before, when you learn about the assignment, you go into an instant panic laced with anger. How could they have forgotten to tell me about this deadline? How am I going to get this done? Of course, this falls on my plate today, of all days! But once you sit down to do the work, the heartburn goes away.

When the emergency ends, you fall apart. Only then does your brain have time to fog up and turn to mush. Only then do you have time to get steamed about the incompetent so-and-so who made this happen. Or you feel so, so tired. The day after, you get nothing done. In fact, plan on it. Do some filing that day and just let the adrenaline drain out of your system.

Reading this, one might think the key to happiness in an uncertain world is to ignore your thoughts and just do the work. Thich Nhat Hanh would certainly agree.

The other bane of a writer's existence, excessive meddling by others, drives you crazy because it seems as if you should be able to control the situation. Take it from us—you cannot. You cannot because it is absolutely impossible to control what other people do. Moreover, what you write, and what then gets funded, shapes the destiny of your organization. For that very reason, anyone with the least bit of turf to protect will be on your case. As Joe likes to say, beware of the bureaucrat with an agenda.

It is the development writer's fate to be stuck in the middle. The president orders you to emphasize community outreach in the case statement when your organization has *always* emphasized research. Yikes! Just pray that old salts in the research department have an inkling that this change is coming before they see your draft.

Although you cannot control what meddlers say and do, you can control yourself. In your own mind, decide who are the real decision-makers and listen to those few people. Nod politely and listen carefully to everyone, but do what the decision-makers want. In the end, if the president and the board chair aren't happy, a whole army of satisfied researchers won't save you. You'll be rewriting.

THE WORRYING LIFE

Now that we've told you to go to the gym on your lunch hour, plan some fun weekends, and catch a *Monty Python* episode, we have to unveil a dirty little secret: Worriers—people who respond excessively to stress—make great development writers.

Worriers remember every single comment from the committee of 100 and carefully weigh a response to each. Worriers grind their teeth at night dreaming about a better headline for the newsletter. Worriers read the blueline six times. Joe once told Danielle that he would hire only people who obsess about stray commas, for those people get the job done and done right.

Unfortunately, lots of people die from stress, whereas no one has ever died from a stray comma. But for a chronic worrier, it *feels* as if that lurking typo might just do you in.

Danielle runs, eats right, practices yoga. She still worries. And we won't even get into Joe's ability to brood for hours at a time.

For the professional worrier, we can suggest a surprisingly effective stress reducer that Danielle's father (an accomplished worrier himself) taught her: Explore the worst-case scenario.

Think about the project you're stressed about and methodically imagine everything going wrong. Imagine it to the extreme: You can't finish the proposal on time, so you cut corners. The president hates the proposal but sends it out, anyway. Then the foundation turns you down, and everyone says it's your fault. Then the president berates you in a staff meeting and fires you on the spot. All of your colleagues erupt in shouts and cheers as you slink out of the room.

Pretty silly, right? The worst that can happen is that you lose your job—a totally survivable, highly unlikely outcome.

If that doesn't help, go volunteer for an organization that helps people less fortunate than you, such as a homeless shelter or a children's hospital. It will take your mind off work and make you grateful.

YOU CAN DO IT, CHAMP

You really can. We have. Joe has been writing fund-raising material since the 1970s, for God's sake. We have found many ways to not merely survive but prevail on the job. Here are some of them:

- Get good at your work. Get *very* good. That will earn you the respect of colleagues. You'll be surprised what they will let you get away with.

HOW TO CIRCULATE COPY FOR APPROVAL

Carefully. Very carefully.

Set ground rules so that colleagues will understand the spirit in which you want them to read your draft work. You want them to be kind, collegial, and caring. You want them to help make your copy better *so that we can all get the job done*.

Here are some tips:

- Write a pleasant cover note indicating that you would like the person to review the copy "to help ensure there are no factual errors." Make clear you welcome comments or suggestions and will take them all under advisement.
- Get a rubber stamp that says DRAFT in capital letters and use it on the cover page. You might even use it on each inside page. They will get the idea.
- If three or four people in a single department have to see your copy, try to get one of them appointed to coordinate the responses of all. That way, you can deal with one person instead of four.
- Give reviewers a firm deadline. "Please let me have your comments as soon as possible—by [date] at the latest. If I have not heard from you by then, I will assume this copy is okay. Thanks!"
- Make sure your draft is clean—no typos, no cross-outs, no nothing. Send it by E-mail if that makes sense. (Be sure the recipient can handle the copy as an attachment.) Consider sending a hard copy, too, just to be safe.
- Leave sufficient time for review. When setting deadlines, allow at least a week for people to look at your copy. Set the due date for a couple of days before you really need their comments back.
- The day before the piece is due back from a reviewer, send a pleasant-reminder E-mail to those from whom you have not heard. People don't mind a tickle.

- When the copy comes back, *don't simply start entering all the changes*. Other people's changes or comments should be viewed critically. Whose suggestions matter the most? Whose make sense? Where are people contradicting each other in the changes they've suggested? Read, think, and use your best judgment. Your goal is to produce an effective fund-raising piece. Don't take the edge out of something you have written because a reviewer thinks its might offend someone. The president of one nonprofit once told Joe, "Don't let them water it down." He knew that innocuous often means useless.
- You will develop your own successful techniques for circulating copy. In a bureaucracy, they are every bit as important as knowing how to write a bright lead.

- Treat others with respect. No more or less respect than you expect for yourself. They will return the favor.
- Be a diplomat. Sure, you're right and they're wrong. We know that. But you don't have to hit them over the head with it. Ask whether they've thought about doing it the other way. Be gently persuasive.
- Be on time—or early. Promise copy for Friday and deliver on Wednesday. Nobody will complain.
- Keep everybody informed. There *is* a proverbial loop, clichéd though that phrase may be, and you had better keep everybody in it (that's why there's a "cc:" on your E-mail) or you may find the loop around your neck. Nobody likes surprises. Repeat after Joe: Nobody likes surprises.
- Ask questions. The only time you will look dumb is when you *don't* ask questions. Your questions will help other people think. They will signal possible problems. They will prompt discussion and help shed light. Now and then ask, "Am I understanding you correctly?" and repeat what you have just heard said.
- Listen. Have we said that before? If so, it is because your job

is to help give voice to the passion of your cause and the facts of your program. Listen and learn. Then you can give voice.
- Wear a Snoopy tie now and then. Show that you can smile at yourself and other people will lighten up, too.

MAKING IT AS A BEGINNER

The only thing more stressful than being a development writer is being an inexperienced development writer. When Danielle started her career, she had all the usual troubles with deadlines and mastering new material, but even worse were the troubles in her own head: *Am I good enough? I won't ask that question because he'll think I'm an idiot. I don't even know how to write a newsletter feature. As soon as they see this draft, they'll fire me.* And so on.

Thank goodness she worked with people who were willing to talk her through the assignments, edit her attempts, and let her try again. And thank goodness she learned not to take each critique as commentary about her worth as a person.

As a beginner, all you can do is look for a mentor and dedicate yourself to learning the ropes. A good mentor is someone who:

- knows how to write well, first and foremost. At the very least, the person should know good writing when he sees it.
- makes time to read drafts carefully and gives you thoughtful comments
- helps you revise and make things right
- wants you to succeed and pushes you to try new things

Sometimes you find several mentors, each willing to do one of these tasks. Your immediate supervisor makes time to comment on your drafts, while a program director pushes you to try new things. Perhaps the woman in the next cubicle helps you with the multiple revisions. It doesn't matter. Just make sure you are working with people who want you to succeed and who are helping you do so.

WRITER BEWARE! At every single job she has interviewed for since college, someone has told Danielle that he or she would be willing to mentor her. She doesn't know why this is–perhaps she *looks* like a person in need?–but more important, she has found that the help rarely materializes. If someone promises you he'll teach you the ropes, ask him how that will work: Weekly meetings? Formal training sessions? Outside classes? Mentoring can be as simple as talking to you before you write an assignment and sitting down with you afterward to go over it. If your prospective mentor doesn't indicate that he will regularly spend time with you, be suspicious.

As for you, you must be willing to learn. If you are haunted by doubts about your abilities, don't let them defeat you. Perfectionism is so destructive, as if you alone among all human beings should know how to walk, talk, write, and build rockets as soon as you leave the womb. You don't need training. You don't need experience. You should be an ace naturally.

Perhaps someone told you such thinking is a good thing, that it means you are motivated and have high standards. Don't kid yourself. It is just the voice of fear robbing you of your ability to focus. It is the mental equivalent of the playground bully pushing you around for no reason, calling you names, making you eat dirt.

For once, pretend you are the wonderful big brother you never had. Give yourself permission to learn, like other mortals. Read successful proposals. Write the lousy drafts. Listen to what your mentors tell you about your leads, your examples, your concluding paragraphs. You are learning; you are trying. That's all that matters. Repeat after Danielle: Trying is all that matters.

Even after you've mastered writing a proposal, there is a world of material still to learn. When Danielle first started working in development, she wrote donor letters. When she mastered letters, she wrote proposals. Then she mastered proposals, so she moved on to newsletter articles. And so on. She wrote magazine pieces, case statements, advertisements for planned giving, even a business plan for a publishing program. All of it was new, and all of it made it worthwhile to stay in that job.

If you are in a situation in which you like your cause and you are working with good people, we suggest you stay there and suck every last bit of knowledge and experience out of that organization. Even when you've mastered the writing, there is a lot more to learn.

- Get involved in design and production. Try your hand at designing a fact sheet. Oversee the printing of the newsletter. Offer to proof the blueline for the annual report.
- Try different communication forms. Help with the campaign video. Take a crack at a direct-mail letter. Go on fund-raising visits and talk with the donors.
- Explore your subject matter. You may be an expert on your organization's after-school program, but don't let that keep you from learning about the parent counseling sessions, the support group for grandparents, the effort to build a new art room. Seize the opportunity to write about new things.
- Help others improve their writing. Learn to be a constructive editor and you will never want for friends.

YOUR SECRET WRITING LIFE

Most salaried writers we know have some other kind of writing that gives them great personal satisfaction: fiction, criticism, poetry, magazine articles. The fact is, you will never be writing independently—just for yourself—as a writer for a good cause.

If you feel the need for other outlets, we are here to tell you to go for it. You will not be the first writer working in a corporate setting to seek a voice of your own. Kurt Vonnegut used to work in public relations at General Electric, Joseph Heller wrote ad copy for New York magazines, and the young Ernest Hemingway turned out trade-magazine stuff in Chicago.

MY FIRST PROPOSAL

"Every aspect was completely terrifying," says Beth Duris, a writer and editor at The Nature Conservancy, about her first proposal. "I didn't know what a good proposal looked like. I had no confidence I could put two sentences together. And I wanted to impress my supervisor and the program people I was writing about.

"It was my first taste of how people all have an opinion on what you write," she recalls. "They give you the vaguest of criticism and expect you to fix things. The worst is frustrated writers. One person replaced a sentence of mine with 20 lines of text. I kept thinking, This is not *War and Peace;* it's the science program!

"But I never said that. When you're beginning, you think everyone's advice has equal weight. You don't even know the program you're writing about, so you can't judge who to listen to.

"At first if feels like there is so much on the line. You feel like you're just exposing yourself by writing. You're giving everyone a complete window on exactly how smart you are.

"I guess the moral of the story is to just take a crack at it and realize that no one else has any better sense of how to do this than you do. If you're struggling because the material seems complicated, it's because it *is* complicated. Everything comes down to confidence in yourself. No one is taking it as seriously as you are. They just want a first draft."

Does outside writing interfere with your good-cause job?

On the contrary, it can get you through the crazy times at work. Accomplishments that win the praise of editors and other wordsmith professionals can sustain you through the bureaucratic machinations that often affect your copy at work. Besides, anything that contributes to your growth as a writer helps you on the job.

MOONLIGHTING

Everybody does it, but nobody talks about it. If you are any good, sooner or later someone from another nonprofit is going to ask if you're available to take on a freelance writing assignment.

Well, er . . . yeah, you reply. Then you begin wondering whether anybody at your present job will complain.

Unless you are under some legal obligation to refuse any offers of outside fund-raising writing, you are free to take on assignments. We know writers who discuss the matter with their bosses when they are hired. Many people working on nonprofit staffs have to supplement their incomes with outside work.

A few tips:

- Work on your own time. Lunch hours, evenings, weekends, vacation days; there's plenty of time available to handle freelance assignments.
- Be a professional. Set the rates you will charge. Use your own computer. Bill on your own letterhead. Have people you are working with on the project call you at home (where you have an answering machine). There is no need whatsoever to have the assignment interfere with your regular job.
- Don't go out of your way to call attention to freelancing of this sort. It's easy for someone to accuse you of doing the work on office time. Why let it become an issue?
- Avoid working for a competitor of your own good cause. Ironically, if you work for a cancer-related group, it's other cancer organizations that will find you attractive. You presumably know something about the disease. Use good judgment.

Joe and Danielle worked together writing campaign case statements for all the schools and colleges of a major university while they were on staff elsewhere in full-time jobs. Easy? No. But it can be done. It's a way to earn extra money and, who knows, maybe find a better or more interesting job or get a taste of the consulting life.

Depending on your job, there are many ways in which your two lives as a writer can play off one another nicely. For example, you might do the following:

- Take an evening class in fiction or magazine writing. Either can help you sharpen skills needed for the job. And your cause may cover the tuition.
- Review books or write articles related to the work of your good cause. While working at NYU years ago, Joe became a columnist for *Change*, the magazine of higher education, and a contributor of features to the *Chronicle of Higher Education*. There are probably many publications that cover the issues addressed by your health, cultural, policy, or other organization. As long as your writing does not occasion any conflict of interest, you should be able to freelance without any problem.
- Join a writer's group. Every town has one, and big cities have many. Or consider joining a book group. You will find writers there. And don't overlook the Internet.
- Set aside writing time that is all your own. Get up an hour early weekdays or spend Saturday morning or Sunday evening on your book idea.

Maybe you're hoping for an eventual career as an author or journalist. That's great. Charles Monaghan felt the same way when he worked as a writer years ago at NYU, and he went on to become editor of *Washington Post Book World* and then *Travel & Leisure* magazine.

We've seen people go on to all kinds of interesting fates:

- Other writing jobs at the same organization. If you're good and you've learned the ropes, you could move over to the

membership magazine, the media-relations staff, the publications office, and so on.
- Other fund-raising writing jobs in the same field. If you proved useful in one hospital's development office, another might well be interested in having you on staff.
- Other fund-raising or management jobs. Writing is a wonderful skill for any position in a nonprofit organization. We have known development writers who became development officers, communications directors, even executive directors.
- Independent consulting jobs for all kinds of good causes. Some writers decide to work as communications consultants for their former employers and others. (That's what we did.) Consultants can control their schedules a little bit more to make time for the other writing they love—you know, like poetry, magazine pieces, and how-to books.

Whatever your goals on or off the job, write with all your heart, grow—and reach your full potential.

IT'S ALL WORTH IT

Writing is such solitary work, it's easy to feel unappreciated. No one can truly know how hard you worked to create that wonderful proposal. They can surmise from your exhausted expression, but they can't really know unless they've been there. If you're wondering whether all this effort is worth it, consider what development people told us about their own experiences and the writers they've worked with. Perhaps you are appreciated, after all.

> *Writers do the hard part. It's easy to be friendly with foundation people. I love talking with program people. But I don't want to write those proposals.*
>
> —A DEVELOPMENT DIRECTOR

There is power in being a grant writer. You are the mouthpiece, yet you have power to shape and make it happen. You connect people to resources to ideas.

—A CHIEF EXECUTIVE OFFICER
AND FORMER DEVELOPMENT WRITER

Writing is not a natural thing for most people. I am very grateful for the people who can take my idea and make sense of what I've said on paper. It's a wonderful gift.

—A DIRECTOR OF DEVELOPMENT AND PROGRAMS

As a writer, I can affect the mission and put money in the hands of people doing the work. This is the gift I have to offer. If I can convey how wonderful your work really is, then the person giving money feels great and the person getting money feels great.

—A DEVELOPMENT WRITER

I think it's harder to be a writer than a good talker. It's easier to fill a room with your personality than it is to convey something from the written page.

—A DEVELOPMENT WRITER

And here's our favorite. You, too, will have this experience, and we hope you relish it just as much:

The worst proposal experience I ever had was also the most successful. I spent six months writing one proposal. I must have interviewed at least ten staff members and probably had about that many people reviewing parts of each draft. But I have never been so excited as when I was standing at a phone booth at a friend's wedding in Rhode Island and got the message that that proposal was funded. It was so neat.

—A DEVELOPMENT WRITER

The Gotta-Get-It-Out-Right-Now, How-Late-Is-FedEx-Open? Down-and-Dirty Proposal Kit

It happens like this: Your board chair has been cultivating Ms. Cantankerous, the famous art dealer, for well over a year now with little success. On Thursday afternoon you get a call because he got a call. Ms. C has decided to allow a short visit on Tuesday afternoon. This situation calls for a proposal!

"Something on the small-grants program for student artists," the vice president muses aloud. "Make sure we offer an endowment for the program-director position. I know she's in thick with the Chicago Art Institute. . . . Isn't there something in Chicago we can use? Call Derek Jones and ask if we could extend the intern program to students in Chicago. Don't tell him why, though, because I don't want him lobbying me for money. Oh, and make sure you include naming opportunities, because Ms. C will want her name all over everything. . . .

"Could you get me a draft before I leave for New York tomorrow?"

Or maybe it happens like this: You finally take a day to go through the piles on your desk, only to find the Smith Foundation's proposal guidelines. There on top, the kiss of death: Submissions due June 15. The day after tomorrow. You are counting on the Smith Foundation for a seed grant.

Just in case you're wondering, there *is* a place where donors tell you well in advance when they would like to make a gift. There is a place where fund raisers have a well-conceived project in mind for every request they make. And there is a place where foundation deadlines naturally hover in your mind, giving you plenty of warning as they approach.

That place is called the World of Make Believe. For those of us who live in the real world, the Ms. Cantankerous and Smith Foundation scenarios are all too familiar. In fact, Ms. Cantankerous happened to Danielle in 1998. When Ms. Cantankerous happens to you, turn to this emergency proposal kit for tools to get the job done.

A Philanthropist Is on Line 1

This Situation Calls for a Proposal

In emergency cases, time is the enemy. Sure, if you had weeks, you could sift through the background material, work out a compromise among rival program managers, and spin some beautiful prose. But there is no time.

You have but one choice. In the military, they call it taking no prisoners. In writing, we call it the white heat. You just go as fast as you can, and you do not look back. Here are the rules of the road:

- *Take control.* This is not the time to be polite. Get organized. Tell people how they can help. Turn your office into command central.
- *Go straight to the source.* Get a few minutes of undivided attention from the key player—the person who talked with the prospect and/or generated the proposal request. If it was you, great. If it was someone else, corral that person immediately. The key player must tell you who the proposal is going to and what that person wants to see. Ask the key player the Ten Key Questions on page 279.

- *Set a schedule.* This is the most important part of the emergency effort. Decide how much time you can spend on each step of the writing process. Take two minutes to set the following deadlines, beginning with when you must finish and working backward:
  — When the final product must be done and out the door.
  — When you will stop revising and begin proofreading/packaging.
  — When you will give a draft to reviewers and when you will get their comments back.
  — When you will finish your first draft (for your eyes only).
  — When you will finish your research.

If time is really tight, some of these stages may overlap. For example, you can begin revising the introduction while you wait for a program director to comment on the description of his project.

- *Steal from existing material.* Borrowing is a virtue when writing for a good cause! Perhaps the president just reviewed the final draft of the annual report, which has a quick program summary. Get the draft. Go through old proposals to cull background material. Ask your colleagues for their latest information.
- *Get help.* Delegate tasks. Have someone else put together the budget. Ask an assistant to collect the background pieces on your organization. Have someone proofread the pages as they come off the printer.
- *And one last thing—keep your chin up!* Hey, if you think this is bad, imagine how reporters or political speechwriters feel—now there's some crazy-making deadlines for you. Grab a cup of coffee, a Diet Coke, green tea, whatever, and get moving.

THE TEN KEY QUESTIONS

Be sure to answer these ten questions before you start writing. (For more information on each of these areas, see Part 2: Writing the Perfect Proposal.)

1. Who is this proposal to and who is it from (i.e., who will sign the cover letter)?
2. How much are we asking for, and what program(s) will the money be used for?
3. What is our ultimate goal for the project/program?
4. What attachments do we need to include? (501(c)(3) statements, audited financial reports, news clips?)
5. Who on staff must review a draft?
6. When must reviewers get the draft, and when can they return their comments?
7. When must the recipient get the proposal and in what form? (fax, hard copy, bound proposal with architectural drawings?)
8. How will the final product be delivered to the recipient? (U.S. Mail, FedEx, courier?)
9. What written materials do we already have that I can steal from?
10. Who else can help me with this task?

Obviously, you may want to ask other questions, such as, What appeals to the donor about this program? Should I include a lot of detail about evaluation, or would the donor rather I didn't? And so on.

A REAL-WORLD EMERGENCY

Let's see how the emergency approach and the Ten Key Questions worked when Danielle was assigned to write a proposal for Ms. Cantankerous.

Take control: Taking control comes down to attitude. Danielle assured her development director that she could finish a first draft by Friday afternoon, especially if some of the program directors could provide written summaries of their programs. Then she started on the Ten Key Questions.

Go straight to the source. Danielle and the development director, who knew Ms. Cantankerous well, brainstormed the content of the proposal together. They decided to take a menu approach: five short summaries of programs where Ms. C could make a big difference. Once they had ideas together, they got the board chair on the phone to run the ideas by him and clarify the schedule for reviewing and finalizing the draft.

Steal from existing material: Danielle was able to cull three program descriptions from old proposals. That left two programs with no information and a tricky introduction about how Ms. C's gift would build on her already formidable record of philanthropic leadership. Danielle checked Ms. C's file and found the script written when Ms. C received an award in 1994. It was complete with a history of accomplishments, shameless hyperbole, and inspiring quotes. Perfect fodder for the introduction.

Get help: The development director asked the remaining two program managers to write a first draft of their summaries while Danielle worked on the introduction.

Set a schedule: Danielle knew that a laser-printed proposal had to arrive at the board chair's house by Tuesday morning. The chair would then deliver it during his visit with Ms. C. That meant the proposal had to be finished and walked to the FedEx office before it closed at 8:00 P.M. Monday night. Thus, the schedule looked like this:

— 5 P.M. Thursday: Finish research. Danielle checked the files, skimmed the background material, and scribbled down a preliminary outline to use the next morning.

— 1:00 P.M. Friday: Finish first draft. Danielle wrote like a madwoman all morning to finish a first draft. Afterward, she took a walk around the block, brought lunch back to her desk, and began revising.

— 4:00 P.M. Friday: Draft to reviewers. The development director took a draft with her on the shuttle to New York. That weekend, she faxed comments back so that Danielle could revise first thing on Monday. The president also read the draft over the weekend.

— 9 A.M. Monday: Meet with reviewers. Danielle sat down with the president and the development director on speaker phone to discuss their changes. They decided to turn the proposal into a concept paper by taking out the request for a specific amount and instead describing generally the opportunities for giving.

— 11 A.M. Monday: Revised draft to board chair. Danielle faxed a second draft, which incorporated the development director's and president's comments, to the board chair and walked a copy to the president's office as well.

— 3 P.M. Monday: Comments back. Luckily, the board chair was pleased with what he saw and had few changes. The president said if the chair was happy, he was happy.

— 4 P.M. Monday: Begin proofing/packaging. Danielle and a colleague read the proposal out loud to each other to check for any typos and inconsistencies. Danielle then printed the proposal on bond paper, wrote a cover note to the board chair, and put both in a FedEx envelope.

— 6:30 P.M. Monday: Final product walked to FedEx. Danielle dropped the package at FedEx, went home, put her feet up, and asked her husband to bring her a beer.

Figuring Out What to Include

From Notes to Outline

Everything that can be delegated has been delegated. You've talked to the key player, gotten your notes together, and now you're— Well, now you're on your own. Time to face the wilderness and blaze a trail.

We suggest that you start with an outline. Don't go cursing our names just yet—as if you have time to write an outline in the midst of this crisis—because we've written a basic one for you already. Just decide which sections you need and plug your information in.

But wait! Before we reveal the secrets of the Great All-Purpose Outline, we give you the single most important tip of your career as a proposal writer: *Follow the donor's guidelines.*

The donor is always right. If an individual tells you she wants two pages of narrative and a budget, then give her what she wants. If a foundation publishes a specific format for a proposal, follow it exactly. In fact, take the headings from the foundation guidelines and just type them right into your document. There's your outline.

Make like cousin Vinnie. Fund raisers hate to admit it, but a proposal is merely a formal way of saying what your cousin Vinnie says when he wants to fix up your car.

"Hey, you know that pieceacrap car of yours needs fixing. Just look at the engine; it needs this piece here, turn that like so, run it a little while, and it'll work great. Of course I know what I'm talking about. What, I look like some chump standing here? Gimme 20 bucks and I'll get the parts right now."

The outline below is the polite, soup-to-nuts version of what Vinnie just said. Instead of fixing the grantmaker's car, you want to fix the world she lives in. It is that simple.

As you review the outline, you may decide to change the order or merge a couple of sections together. That's fine. Just be sure to answer the logical questions anyone would ask before they shelled out their cash.

I. COVER LETTER (REQUIRED)

The cover letter answers these questions:

- What is this proposal about?
- Why are you sending it to me and not some other guy?
- Why should I bother reading it?

Length: ideally no more than one page; definitely no more than two.

All proposals must have a cover letter, usually signed by a senior-ranking official in your organization, such as your president or a board member. At minimum, the cover letter tells the recipient how much you are requesting and what you want the money for. It closes by thanking the recipient for her time and indicating when you, the sender, will follow up.

WRITER BEWARE! Never write "To Whom It May Concern." Address your letter to a specific person. Call the recipient if necessary to locate the right person and get the correct spelling of her name.

Grantmakers almost always read the cover letter before they read anything else, so this is your opportunity to shine. Focus on the information that will pique the reader's interest: maybe your board member knows her board member, or maybe you just recruited a researcher for whom she has great respect. Remember, however, that many foundations will separate the cover letter from the proposal when they circulate it for review, so don't put vital information in the cover letter without also including it somewhere in the proposal.

HOT TIP: Try to link your request to current events or other activities going on in your community. Mention a recent study, media reports, or the latest city budget and explain how that makes your cause more important and timely than ever.

II. COVER SHEET (OPTIONAL)

The cover sheet answers these questions:

- What is this document about?
- Who sent it to me?
- When did you send it?

Length: one page.

HOT TIP: Consider including all of your basic facts on the cover sheet. You might include a contact name, contact phone number, the specific amount of the grant request, and a one-paragraph summary of the proposal. That way, you make it very easy for a busy program officer to find your proposal and pick up the phone to call you.

The cover sheet is just the cover of the proposal. Cover sheets usually contain the name of the organization to which the proposal is being sent, the name of your organization, the title of the project for which you want funding, and a date. For shorter proposals or letter proposals, you can put all this information at the top of the first page rather than dedicate an entire cover sheet to it.

WRITER BEWARE! Make sure your title conveys what your proposal is about. A proposal entitled only "Reaching New Heights" could be about helping disabled veterans, tutoring schoolchildren, conducting research in the Himalayas–you name it.

III. TABLE OF CONTENTS (OPTIONAL)

The table of contents answers these questions:

- What the heck is inside this monster?
- Where is that section on . . . ?

Length: If the table of contents exceeds one page in an emergency situation, you are in deep weeds, friend, very deep weeds.

Include a table of contents if your proposal exceeds seven pages or has lots of appendices. Most word-processing programs will create a table of contents for you automatically *if* you use consistent formatting for each heading. Figure out how the table-of-contents feature works before you start typing or you'll end up going back to redo your headings.

HOT TIP: Number your pages even if you don't have a table of contents. You would be amazed at how many people forget to do that and how frustrating it can be to the reader.

WRITER BEWARE! When you proofread the proposal, check the table of contents against the actual page numbers. You may discover you have two page 5s or that the conclusion slipped onto page 8 when you made that last edit.

IV. EXECUTIVE SUMMARY (REQUIRED)

The executive summary answers these questions:

- What's this proposal *really* about?
- How much money do you want?
- Do I still think this thing is worth reading?

Length: no more than one page.

The executive summary does just that: It summarizes your proposal with one or two sentences about each section. It acts as a "cheat sheet" for busy proposal reviewers who want to get a general feel for the proposal and decide whether they should read further. State your request—the amount of money you want and the project it will be used for—in the first paragraph.

WRITER BEWARE! Many grantmakers will judge your entire proposal by the cover letter and executive summary. Make your words count.

HOT TIP: Most people write the executive summary after they've finished the proposal because then they can lift a sentence or two from each section and massage them to form a cohesive executive summary. Some proposal writers, however, always write the executive summary first because it forces them to define the most important points to make.

V. INTRODUCTION (REQUIRED)

The introduction answers these questions:

- Who are you?
- Why should I trust you to get the job done?
- Can you really handle this type of project?

Length: usually no more than one page.

The introduction spells out the basics: when your organization was established, the mission, how many employees, how many clients, the annual budget. More important, the introduction highlights your accomplishments in dealing with the problem or opportunity presented in this proposal. Cite your partnerships with like-minded organizations and reference any letters of support, newspaper articles, or other attachments you are including in the appendix. All of these supplemental things help establish your credibility.

HOT TIP: Make your organization look as if it has been destined since the beginning of time to address this special challenge at this moment in history. Perhaps your staff are experts in the field, you've done similar work before, or there is no one else around with the facilities and equipment that you have. When the reader gets to your description of the challenge at hand, she should nod her head and think, Of course they're the ones to do the job.

If the grantmaker knows your organization well, then you may focus on why your organization is the best qualified to take on this project rather than offering all those basic facts. In other cases, you may find it natural to describe the background of the project you're talking about as well as your organization's background. If it makes sense, do it.

WRITER BEWARE! A common pitfall in the introduction is to describe your organization's entire history, complete with a lengthy list of programs. Don't merely list programs and expect that to explain your organization. Stick to pertinent strengths and accomplishments.

VI. PROBLEM STATEMENT (REQUIRED)

The problem statement, or needs statement, as it is sometimes called, answers these questions:

- What problem or opportunity do you plan to tackle?
- Is this an issue I care about?
- Could you even make a dent in this problem?

Length: anywhere from half a page to two pages.

The problem statement talks about the specific condition that you want to address. Your description of this problem should be detailed enough to demonstrate that your organization thoroughly understands the issues involved.

HOT TIP: Shorter is better in the problem statement. Devote more time to writing about solutions.

The problem statement always talks about the need in society you seek to address, not your organization's needs. We know you need money—*everyone* needs money—but grantmakers award funds on the basis of merit, not on the basis of need. Describe the need in society that you seek to address, whether it is protecting rare species, improving literacy, or providing top-notch education to tomorrow's leaders.

WRITER BEWARE! Be sure that the problem does not seem insurmountable. A problem statement that is too broad or complex will seem too complicated and expensive to tackle. Also, cite local statistics if you are addressing a local problem. A general trend in society doesn't necessarily mean that your community has the same problem.

VII. PROGRAM/PROJECT DESCRIPTION (REQUIRED)

There are actually four parts to a program description, and you may tackle them in any order that makes sense: goals and objectives, methods, evaluation, and future funding.

A. Statement of Goals/Objectives (required)

Goals and objectives answer the following questions:

- What do you plan to do about this problem?
- What will you consider a successful outcome?
- Are you being realistic?

Length: usually not more than a page.

The goal is often one sentence that describes how things will be different if the project is successful and how you plan to get to that successful outcome. Indeed, the goal statement could simply be the inverse of the problem statement. For example, if the problem is a lack of access to health care for single mothers and their infants, an organization's goal statement might read like this: "Merrimack

Family Services will improve the health of newborn babies and their single mothers over two years by creating a free in-home visiting-nurse program in the Good Hope neighborhood."

Once you state your overall goal, the next question is how you plan to get there: What incremental goals must be achieved to reach your overall vision of success? Those incremental goals are your objectives. You can list them or put them in narrative form. Merrimack Family Services' objectives might include a 50 percent reduction in the number of new-mother visits to the emergency room, for example.

HOT TIP: Objectives that include hard numbers (reach 300 people, decrease by 25 percent, etc.) make your organization sound as if it really means business.

WRITER BEWARE! Don't get too confused trying to figure out what's a goal and what's an objective. Who cares? Just make sure the reader knows what you're trying to accomplish.

B. Methods (required)

The methods section answers the following questions:

- How are you going to reach those goals and objectives?
- Who is going to do the work?
- When will the work be done?
- Why are you doing it that way?

Length: as long as it needs to be.

Think of your methods as the logical reaction to the problem statement. If you knew there were more than 100 new single mothers in your neighborhood who had few resources and nobody to tell them whether their baby had colic or a deadly disease, what would you do? You'd send help, right? How about a visiting nurse to provide free help and advice?

If we told you to pick up a pencil and write down how that visiting-nurse program would work, you could do it in five minutes. You might suggest working with the local hospital to make new mothers aware of your program; equipping the nurse with some basic medical supplies; and printing some leave-behind brochures about baby ailments and how to handle them. Or, after thinking for a minute or two, you might decide what they really need is a hotline for mothers to call.

When you write a methods sections, you simply tell the donor everything she needs to know to visualize how your program will work: how many visits the nurse will make, who will write and produce the brochures, what hours the hotline will be staffed, and so on. The more concrete your description, the more the grantmaker will believe you know what you're doing.

WRITER BEWARE! Make sure your description of what you plan to do matches your budget. If you say you plan to print brochures, put that expense in the budget or include a sentence explaining how the brochures will be paid for.

HOT TIP: If you have a long-term or complex project, you may want to include a formal work plan in the methods section or as an attachment. Set up a chart with columns for tasks and indicate who will do the tasks and when the tasks will be done.

C. *Evaluation (sometimes optional but worth having)*

The evaluation answers the following questions:

- How will I know you were successful in this project?
- Who will evaluate the success of the project?

Length: from as little as one paragraph to as much as a page.

Most foundations require you to describe how you will evaluate your success. But unless specifically asked, some organizations skip this section altogether, especially if they are asking for general operating support. We recommend that you make some attempt to explain how you will know the project—or your organization as a whole—has succeeded.

In discussing evaluation, look not only at the outcome (whether you in fact achieved your objectives) but also at the process (how the program was conducted, which activities were most effective, and so forth).

For especially large or complex projects, you may suggest hiring an outside firm to evaluate your success. If so, explain who will do the evaluation and what they will provide: a final report, interim feedback, survey results, etc. Be sure to include the expense for hiring an outside firm in your project budget.

HOT TIP: If seeking general operating support, you might find some evaluation criteria in your organization's strategic plan. For example, if the plan is to expand by 30 percent over the next five years, then perhaps your two-year goal is to expand by 12 percent.

WRITER BEWARE! In a crunch, you may be tempted to go lightly on evaluation, but realize there are risks. You may be asked to provide this information later. Worse, the funder may decide to evaluate your project in terms that you never prepared for.

D. Future Funding (optional)

A discussion of future funding answers the following questions:

- What will happen after you use up the money I give you?
- How serious are you about this program?

- Do other people think this program is worth supporting?

Length: usually no more than a paragraph or two.

If you are asking a foundation for an operating grant, it is only logical that the foundation will wonder what's going to happen after the money runs out. Describe where future funding will come from: new donors, graduates of the program, businesses that benefit from your services, or perhaps all three.

HOT TIP: In some cases, it may make more sense to put information about other funders or future funding in the budget section of the proposal.

WRITER BEWARE! Many foundations will not give more than one operating grant to an organization, and some won't give them at all. Make sure you read the guidelines carefully before you blithely state that you will come back to this foundation and others for operating money.

VIII. CONCLUSION

The conclusion answers the following questions:

- How much money do you want?
- What difference will my gift make?

Length: anywhere from one paragraph to a few paragraphs.

The conclusion is where you ask for the money (or "make the ask," as fund raisers like to call it) and close on a high note. Ask clearly for the amount of money you want and the time period in which you want it. Describe recognition of the donor if there is to be any. Then end with a noble sentence or two about the big picture: how this project and the grantmaker's involvement will improve people's lives, leave a legacy for future generations, or change the face of America.

HOT TIP: Conclusions can be difficult to muster, especially after you've been writing hard for several hours. Keep a file of conclusions that you have liked and adapt them for your own purposes. One of our favorites is the "not only . . . but also" approach, as in: "The foundation will not only ensure maximum access to the arts in this city but also set a national example for others to follow." Another good one is the "to do this is really to do that" approach, as in: "To establish an endowment for sciences at this time is to ensure the continued leadership of students and scholars for decades to come."

WRITER BEWARE! Ask for a specific amount of money. Under no circumstances should you ask for "whatever you can spare."

IX. BUDGET (REQUIRED)

The budget answers the following questions:

- What will you spend my money on, specifically?
- What other sources of income do you have for this project?
- It sounds good, but do the numbers add up?

Length: usually one page.

The budget should include an itemization of wages, benefits, contract services, consultation fees, materials, equipment, printing, and overhead (rent, utilities, etc.) involved in completing the project. If you are not asking the grantmaker to cover the whole cost, be sure to indicate what portion the grantmaker will cover. (In most instances, that means telling the grantmaker that she will pay $30,000 of the $100,000 total budget. Do not tie yourself down to specific line items—for example, the XYZ Fund will cover the cost of building materials but not labor—unless you absolutely have to.)

Also indicate who else is being asked to help cover the costs and/or the other funds that have already been secured. (Even if you discussed this in the future funding section, make sure it appears in the budget as well.)

HOT TIP: Make your budget easy to read. Copy a budget format that you find pleasing to the eye.

WRITER BEWARE: Proofread carefully! Get your calculator out and add all the numbers one last time. Go back to your source materials and make sure the supplies figure really is $21,000, not $12,000.

X. APPENDICES (OPTIONAL)

Appendices answer any questions that have not been answered in the text, such as:

- Who is on your board?
- Have you had an audit lately?
- What methodologies will you be using in your survey?

Length: as long as necessary.

THE GREAT ALL-PURPOSE OUTLINE FOR A FORMAL PROPOSAL

I. Cover Letter (required)
II. Cover Sheet (optional)
III. Table of Contents (optional)
IV. Executive Summary (required)
V. Introduction (required)
VI. Problem Statement (required)
VII. Program/Project Description
  A. Statement of Goals/Objectives (required)
  B. Methods (required)
  C. Evaluation (sometimes optional, but worth having)
  D. Future Funding (optional)
VIII. Conclusion (required)
IX. Budget (required)
X. Appendices
  A. Longer Background Narrative (optional)
  B. Credentials of Key Leaders (optional)
  C. List of Trustees and Their Affiliations (optional)
  D. Strategic Plan, Press Coverage, Letters of Support (optional)
  E. 501(c)(3) Tax-Exemption Notification (optional)
  F. Audited Financial Statements and/or Annual report (optional)
  G. Maps, Photographs, or Charts (optional)

Many grantmakers will ask for certain appendices as a matter of routine: your audited financial statements, a list of board members, a letter from the IRS confirming that you are indeed a nonprofit organization. The appendix also is a good place for letters of support, media clips, and other tidbits that bolster your case.

HOT TIP: If you must include lots of detail on something–for example, if you want to describe the scientific methods you will use in your research project–put that wealth of detail in an appendix. That way your proposal text continues to be easy to read and those who want more detail can find it.

If you are still squirming uncomfortably because you limited your introduction to one page—even though there is so much more good stuff to say about your organization—then the appendix is the place to unburden yourself. The appendix is the place for a longer background narrative or whatever other *pertinent* information you want to include.

WRITER BEWARE! There is a difference between providing useful supplemental information and needlessly jamming more facts and articles and campaign case statements into the appendices. More is not necessarily better. Indeed, some foundation executives complain bitterly when they receive entire annual reports, videos, and whatnot along with proposals.

A list of common appendix materials appears below. Your organization may think of still more that could be useful for a proposal:

- longer background narrative
- credentials of key leaders (if relevant to your proposal)
- list of trustees and their affiliations (if grantmaker is unfamiliar with your organization)
- strategic plans
- press coverage

- letters of support
- 501(c)(3)tax-exemption notification (if necessary)
- audited financial statements and/or annual report (if necessary)
- maps
- photographs
- charts

Writing It Right

From Introduction to Reprise

Your research is done and you have your outline. It is time to write! Even if you are feeling shaky about your material, your best strategy is to just start writing.

Ha! you think. Easy for you to say. Nothing like a crisis to bring out the writer's block.

Yes, it is far easier to tell you to write than it is to actually have to write. To stare at a mass of notes and a blank computer screen, with the clock ticking loudly on your wall, is hell. We know it's hell because we wrote this whole book and it was hell. And to think this book is something we both *wanted* to write!

A PAIR OF CRUTCHES FOR YOU

Accept the inevitable. Writing on deadline is like marching through chest-deep swamp water. You just slog through. You don't think about the snakes, you don't look at what is twirling around your ankles, you don't worry about whether you're on exactly the right course. You just keep moving in one general direction, knowing solid ground is out there somewhere.

To help you move through that swamp with gusto, we offer you two crutches.

The first crutch is the law of revision: Revising is always faster and easier than writing from scratch. This is an immutable law of the universe, up there with $E = mc^2$. Quickly write a terrible, embarrassing, stinking-to-the-high-heavens draft and you are in great shape. Once the words are on paper, you—or if worse comes to worst, a helpful colleague—will see which paragraphs should go where, which need fixing up, which read pretty well, and which are totally unnecessary. Trust in the law of revision and let your first draft fly.

The second crutch is the short assignment. Forget the whole godawful swamp in front of you. Just resolve to spend the next 15 minutes getting to that stump over there. Set your watch timer to 15 minutes and write the problem statement without thinking, without editing. That's all. When 15 minutes are up, stretch, go get another cup of coffee, come back, sit down, and spend 15 minutes on your goals and objectives. Just take it in bite-sized chunks.

HAVING TROUBLE GETTING STARTED?

If you still feel stuck, you probably have fallen victim to one of two notorious conditions: Too Much Information or Too Little Information.

In either case, read through the notes and background material you have and decide where each piece of information fits into the Great All-Purpose Outline.

If you have too much information: Look at your outline to see which sections look overloaded and whittle those down. Which pieces of information don't seem to fit in anywhere? Throw those away. Keep asking yourself, What's the main point? What's most important?

If you have too little information: Look at your outline to see what's missing or which sections look thin. Maybe you don't have a clear sense of who will conduct the program or how it will be done. Regardless, you have three choices:

- Go back and get that info! Call the program people again, leave one last message for the president, be shameless in your pursuit of more.
- Fill in the sketchy parts using words with wiggle room. Conduct, implement, develop, create, improve, advance—all these verbs have a certain amount of fudge factor to them. Do the best you can to sound convincing.
- Skip the sketchy parts completely and hope no one notices (not likely, but it could happen). Or insert a sentence in your conclusion saying additional information is available upon request. Unfortunately, that calls attention to the fact that you're missing certain elements. Neither approach is very good, but when you're desperate, you're desperate.

In the final analysis, sending half-baked proposals undermines your credibility and wastes everyone's time. Once this emergency is over, talk with your colleagues to make sure it doesn't happen again.

BEYOND THE FIRST DRAFT: REVISING

Earlier we talked about the content of your proposal. But what about its tone? What about the writing itself? When you have a first draft done and you are going back to revise, keep these principles of good proposal writing in mind.

Tell the human story. People are interested in people. They want to know what happens to others and what those stories mean about themselves. Even the meanest, most disagreeable person you know is more interested in how little Jimmy recovered from his terrible burns than in a discussion of burn research at your hospital.

Take No Prisoners

Sometimes it is hard to get going, and at other times it is hard to keep going. Here are a few tricks to turn off that editor in your head who keeps slowing you down.

1. To get yourself in the right frame of mind to write your proposal, read something that will have key words or inspirational messages having to do with the program. When Danielle wrote an emergency proposal for a donor who was known to be status-conscisous, she flipped through magazine advertisements and copied down words that conveyed the tone she wanted: distinguished, achievement, standard of excellence, tradition, legacy. With those words taped to the side of her computer, she began writing.
2. Eliminate distractions. Turn off your phone, close your office door, wear headphones with soft music, or go home and write in a dark room. If you find yourself retyping sentences because you think they're no good, turn down the brightness on your computer screen so you can't see the words. That will force you to keep moving.
3. If you're stuck on a particular section, go look at somebody else's old proposal. How did they do it? Would that approach work for you? Try it and see.
4. Really stuck on a particular paragraph or section? Leave it blank and move on. You can even type xxxxx or (to come) in the text so that people who review your draft will know that you will fill that piece in later. Once other sections of the proposal are in place, the sticky parts will be a little easier to deal with.
5. Absolutely, positively, 100 percent stuck on something? Take a quick break and do something physical. Danielle likes to walk around the block. Joe walks up the street to get a grande latte. Danielle's father, a lawyer, keeps yo-yos and juggling balls in his office to get the old mental wheels

turning. Playing darts, stretching, moving boxes of files, all help break the block.

And one last piece of advice: Always take a break between drafts. In emergency situations you may only have time to get a drink of water before sitting back down to revise. But do take a break—it is amazing what a short walk will do to help you see your own writing with clarity.

- Before you describe your research program, mention little Jimmy's story. We are not saying you should get out your violin and play the heart-wrenching story of Jimmy; rather, mention him as an example of the advances made possible by your new laboratory and its groundbreaking research.
- If your cause lacks human stories, talk about the human efforts behind your cause. Maybe a fifth-grade class in Pennsylvania started a campaign to build a tunnel under Route 113 so that endangered salamanders could pass in safety to get to their breeding grounds each spring. Now you're raising money to purchase 40 acres of salamander habitat in the Smithfield township, and your proposal is off and running.
- But, you say, there are no humans behind my cause, either! Danielle once wrote a proposal asking a corporation to donate land in Texas to protect habitat for the endangered Attwater prairie chicken. Take it from us, prairie chickens do not elicit an immediate sympathetic response from your average corporate executive. But Danielle was able to dig up this amusing tidbit: During World War II, Attwater prairie chickens were so numerous that air-force pilots at a nearby base had to chase the roosting chickens out of their planes each morning and shoo them off the runway before they could take off. Today there are only a few hundred Attwater prairie chickens left, and they are struggling to survive. These details made for an interesting introduction.

Be passionate and assertive. Get yourself "up" for writing. You want to talk about your organization's accomplishments, the significance of your mission, the tremendous impact your programs have on people's lives. Don't worry about creating powerful rhetoric; if you care, the passion will come through naturally.

- Go back and read your organization's mission statement. Think back to when you first got this job and how excited you were. Read your organization's magazine, chat with one of the people your organization serves, talk with a colleague on the front lines. This is what matters now. Get excited about it. Get passionate. You care. You're loaded for bear.
- Choose powerful verbs. Don't undertake the rehabilitation of a historic building; rehabilitate it. Don't say the program is active in rural communities; say it empowers rural communities. Rather than saying your program *would* reach out to new audiences, say it *will* reach out. Rather than saying it is *demonstrating* a successful approach, say it *demonstrates* a successful approach.
- Remember that you are offering the donor the opportunity to make a difference and feel good about it. There's no need to make apologies or strain your arguments.

Simplify. Oh, if only you could be a foundation officer for one day, with a stack of 40 proposals on your desk. Oh, how your writing would change. You would just get to the point.

Write with the harried and overworked reader in mind. When you have time, please turn to Part 3, The Writer's Craft. But for now, here are the basics:

- Use concrete detail. If someone tells you his new program will devote 50 percent of its resources to organizational capacity building in Central America, you'd better lift an eyebrow. What the heck does that mean? If it means a trainer will travel to Honduras over the next two years to help the local community group put together a list of fund-raising prospects, then say so. Enough with the capacity building.

WHERE TO FOCUS YOUR EFFORTS

If you don't have time to polish your draft, then focus your efforts on your cover letter, the executive summary, and the budget. Your readers are most likely to look at these sections first and decide whether to continue based on what they see.

The cover letter hooks the reader. Make sure it flows well and includes timely information that will interest the reader. A good cover letter convinces the reader to glance at the executive summary.

The executive summary gives a thumbnail sketch. It should be clear and concise enough to pass the elevator test: If the reader finished your executive summary and then stepped into an elevator with a friend, he could tell the friend what your proposal is about before the elevator doors opened again.

The budget proves you know what you're doing. The figures should be reasonable, and they should add up. The budget line items should be easy to understand. If they are not, then include a few words of explanation. A well-done budget alone will give the reader a good sense of what your whole proposal is about.

- Eliminate jargon. You could talk about hydrologic alteration, or you could simply say dams and water diversions. If you must use technical words, define them. Don't assume that the reader will understand your lingo even if he has known your organization for a long time. For all you know, your proposal will go to the foundation officer's sister for one last opinion. Better make sure she can understand your proposal, too.
- Don't throw in words just because they sound good. "Unique" is terribly overused. "Collaboration" is so ubiqui-

tous that some foundation officers instantly question what an organization really means by it—true problem solving or just a conversation?

- Eliminate unnecessary words. Get rid of adverbs and adjectives. You could say, "This grant will make possible critically important research into the debilitating effects of multiple sclerosis." Or you could say, "This grant will help our researchers find a cure for multiple sclerosis." Which sentence hits harder?
- Create white space. Use short sentences, keep your paragraphs to seven lines or fewer, use headings and subheadings to break up the text. Danielle has even made her left margins three inches wide so the text would appear more like a column and therefore look more inviting to read.
- Be brief. Make your point and move on. If you want to provide lots of detail about how your program will work or how your organization was founded, put it in an appendix.

HOT TIP: After a few months on the job, you may not recognize your own jargon. If you have time, ask a friend outside the field to read your draft. He'll spot the jargon instantly.

How Late Did You Say They're Open?

Proof, Package, and Out the Door

Danielle's grandmother used to whisper to her in restaurants, pointing out people who were not displaying proper table manners. To this day, Danielle imagines that each proposal she writes is going to someone with that same critical eye, noting every error with quiet alarm.

This is not such a far-fetched fear. Corporate and foundation officers are deluged with proposals for funding. How are they going to sift through them all? You'd better believe that typos, grammatical mistakes, and poor writing will count against you.

Emergency or not, your proposal must be neat, clean, and easy to read, with no typos.

SPELL CHECKER IS NOT ENOUGH

Never trust the spell checker alone. A good proofreader uses an eight-step process to weed out lurking mistakes:

- Spell check the document.
- Print it out.

- Proofread the document.
- Make corrections.
- Spell check again.
- Print again.
- Check the corrections.
- Print the final copy.

Why can't you use the spell checker alone? Because it won't cash a mistake like this. The spell checker would *cach* this mistake, but it would suggest *cache* as the best replacement. If you unthinkingly click okay, cache it will be.

The best way to proofread: After you use the spell checker, have two people read the text aloud to each other. While one reads, the other follows along on paper. Look for misspellings, grammatical errors, and inconsistencies. Did you write 10 in one place and ten in another? Are some subheadings indented five spaces and others flush with the margin? Do the numbers in your budget match the numbers cited in your text? Both readers should stop when a mistake or an inconsistency appears and mark the correction.

HOT TIP: The writer can be one of the people proofreading, but try to find a proofreading partner who has never seen the document before.

After the two of you have finished reading to each other, go back and make the changes in your draft. Then print out a new copy and compare the new against the old in every place where you made a change. Check to make sure you didn't accidentally delete a word, cause one line of a paragraph to appear alone at the bottom or top of a page, or make a noun change that now requires a plural verb. Also check to make sure you did indeed make all the corrections you were supposed to make.

Once you have compared the two versions and ensured that all the changes were made correctly, go back and print your final copy. If you did find a couple of problems, fix them, use spell checker again, and print again to be sure everything is in place before you print the final copy.

HOT TIP: After proofreading, if you make any change to your document–even just changing "a" to "an"–use the spell checker again before printing your final document. It will save you untold moments of embarrassment.

The second-best way to proofread: Give your final document to someone who has not seen it before and ask her to read it carefully by herself.

The third-best way to proofread: The least desirable way to proof is to read your own work by yourself. If you must proof your own work, try to take a break before you begin; anything that will take your mind off the document for even a few minutes will give you clarity. For more tips on proofreading, see chapter 6.

HOT TIP: Check the math in your budget. Even if your chief financial officer gave you the budget for your proposal, do a quick check of the addition to make sure it totals correctly. Mistakes with numbers are all too common.

HOW TO PACKAGE WHILE MAINTAINING YOUR SANITY

It's a fact: Office machinery will detect human panic and immediately initiate bewildering new behaviors. Printing sideways, adding dingbats in front of apostrophes, photocopying two pages at once—you've been there; we know you have. The experts call this user error, but don't you believe them. It's the machine.

Plan accordingly. You need more than ten minutes to print and send your proposal. Really. (We know this is true: Danielle was late in getting a draft of this section to Joe because her printer decided it would only print three pages at a time.) Leave an hour for printing and final proofing, if possible.

Figure out the logistics first. Figure out how the proposal will be delivered to the recipient *before you begin writing*. Will it be sent via overnight mail or couriered? If it will be couriered, do you have the courier's phone number? If it will be overnighted, do you know where all the forms are? Do you have the right envelopes?

WRITER BEWARE! Some foundations detest receiving proposals via Federal Express or other costly express-mail options. They consider it a strike against you from the start. If so, they usually will state their preference in the proposal guidelines.

Decide what form your proposal will take. Will you simply laser-print and staple, or will you be wrestling with the plastic binder gizmo and transparent covers? Do you have the binder gizmos and transparent covers in stock?

Package to please. Determine how fancy your proposal should look by considering who will receive it. A longtime donor might well enjoy pictures of your program in action; if so, include color copies of photos in your proposal and use a plastic-toothed binding with a nice, heavy paper cover. On the other hand, most foundations—which must copy and distribute your proposal to several evaluators—hate those plastic-toothed binder things because they have to take them apart to make copies. Foundations definitely prefer a proposal with a single staple in the corner.

Reflect your image. No one expects to receive an expensive-looking proposal from an organization that feeds the homeless. On the other hand, one might well expect a handsome piece from the Metropolitan Museum of Art in New York.

OUT THE DOOR!

Ah, the end is nigh! You've held up your end of the bargain; the proposal is written, proofed, and ready to go. Now all you have to do is make sure it gets to the recipient on time. Alas, even this stage can be fraught with peril.

Couriers. Especially if you are delivering the proposal in a city, give your package to the courier early enough so that it doesn't get stuck in rush-hour traffic. It never hurts to call the recipient to tell her to be on the lookout for the courier or to call later on to ensure that the package arrived.

Express mail. Most express-mail service providers can track a package for you if it gets lost. If you're feeling nervous, choose a service that also requires the recipient's signature. It's good insurance for those few occasions when the recipient claims never to have gotten the package.

Personal delivery. If you're the worrying type, there is no substitute for taking the proposal to the recipient yourself. If one of your colleagues is taking it for you, make sure you know when she is leaving the office. And keep an extra copy ready just in case you get a frantic phone call about a stolen briefcase.

THE CHECKLIST

Before you send out your proposal, run through this checklist to be sure you've got everything you need.

Proposal Contents

- Check donor guidelines for desired format, questions to answer, special attachments.
- Cover letter includes a bit of special information to grab the reader's interest.
- Cover sheet has a title, the name of recipient, the name of your organization, and a date.
- Executive summary clearly states how much money you want and what you will use it for.
- Introduction highlights your strengths and accomplishments in addressing the problem.
- Problem statement focuses on a need in society (not your organization's needs).
- Goals and objectives are clearly stated and include measurable outcomes if possible.
- Methods section answers who will do the work, when the work will be done, how the work will be done, and why it will be done this particular way.
- Evaluation section matches the goals and objectives you set out.
- Future funding does not rely solely on operating grants from foundations.
- Conclusion asks for a specific amount of money and tells how this gift will make a difference.
- Budget line items match the text of your proposal.
- All necessary appendices have been attached (501(c)(3) letter, audited financials, etc.).

Writing Style

- Include human stories or human examples of how your program makes a difference.
- Use active verbs. Weed out forms of "to be."
- Change "would" and "could" to "will" and "can."
- Use concrete detail rather than abstract descriptions.

- Eliminate jargon. Ask someone else to read and circle words she doesn't understand.
- Eliminate clichés and unnecessary words (such as adjectives and adverbs).

Overall Appearance

- Pages are numbered.
- Pages are in the right order.
- Headings treated consistently in terms of font, spacing, italics, etc.
- Numbers treated consistently (10 versus ten, etc.).
- Program names treated consistently. (Is it an initiative or a program?)
- Acronyms are spelled out at first mention; for example, National Endowment for the Humanities (NEH).
- Cover letter is signed.
- Cover letter is addressed to the right person, and name is spelled correctly. (Check if unsure.)
- Table of Contents uses the same headings as the text.
- Table of Contents corresponds to the correct page numbers.
- Budget figures add up correctly.
- No paragraphs longer than seven lines.
- Plenty of white space.

APPENDIX

Resources

Nothing is lost on a writer. Everything you see and hear counts. Your knowledge of our society in all its facets will serve you well no matter what good cause you write for.

Joe assumes you read the *New York Times* each day as well as your major local newspaper. He urges you to read magazines with an ear to the ground, such as *Harper's*, *Atlantic Monthly*, and *Utne Reader* as well as the *New Yorker* and *Vanity Fair*. Look at *Fortune* and *Business Week*, but also pick up a quarterly now and then, such as the *American Scholar*, *Granta*, the *Wilson Quarterly*, or the *Paris Review*. On-line, he likes *Salon* and *Slate*.

Danielle seeks out magazines known for great writing: *Outside* and *Preservation* are two award-winners that regularly attract accomplished authors. She admits, reluctantly, that catalogs and mailings can also be a great lesson in persuasive writing. (Her credit-card bills prove that White Flower Farm, for example, puts out one persuasive garden catalog.) She suggests you read your direct-mail solicitations and give each piece a grade: A+ if you act as a result (sucker!), B if you were tempted even for an instant. (By the way, Danielle does not read the *New York Times*. The *Washington Post* will do, thank you very much.)

BOOKS

Fund Raising

There are many books on fund raising; most are academic, long-winded, and boring. These titles are nicely done and worth dipping into.

Cutlip, Scott M. *Fund Raising in the United States: Its Role in America's Philanthropy.* New Brunswick, NJ: Transaction Publishers. 1990. This is a readable and scholarly history of fund raising through World War II. Author Cutlip, a reporter, writer, and dean emeritus of the University of Georgia's School of Journalism, captures the diverse forces and colorful characters that shaped the field.

Golden, Susan L. *Secrets of Successful Grantsmanship: A Guerilla Guide to Raising Money.* San Francisco: Jossey-Bass Publishers. 1997. This refreshing and well-written guide includes advice on the intangible keys to fund-raising success, like how to call a foundation and how to prepare for your first meeting.

Kelly, Kathleen S. *Effective Fund-Raising Management.* Mahwah, NJ: Lawrence Erlbaum Associates, Inc. 1998. Kelly's textbook takes an authoritative look at how fund raising is done today and explains the rise of today's major campaigns.

Writing

There are excellent books on aspects of the craft. Here are a few that we highly recommend.

Goldberg, Natalie. *Writing Down the Bones: Freeing the Writer Within.* Boston: Shambhala. 1998. Let go and write!

That is Goldberg's view in this neat compilation of short, zen-like takes on the craft. This "pocket classic" edition from Shambhala is great to keep handy.

Lamott, Anne. *Bird By Bird: Some Instructions on Writing and Life*. New York and San Francisco: Pantheon Books. 1994. A delightful collection of short pieces that brim with warm advice for writers.

Noonan, Peggy. *On Speaking Well*. New York: HarperPerennial. 1998. A speechwriter for presidents and corporate CEOs, Noonan offers a bright, nonthreatening guide to writing words meant to be spoken. Much of what she says applies to writing of any kind.

O'Connor, Patricia T. *Woe Is I: The Grammarphobe's Guide to Better English in Plain English*. New York: A Grosset/Putnam Book. 1996. Put this wonderful volume in the bathroom; each cheerful lesson takes about that much time.

Strunk, William Jr., and E. B. White. *The Elements of Style*. 3rd ed. New York: Macmillan. 1979. Anyone who writes for a living must read this book, preferably once each year. This is the bright, tight mother lode on writing.

Zinsser, William. *On Writing Well*. 6th ed. New York: HarperPerennial. 1998. A contemporary classic on nonfiction writing by a seasoned professional. "Clutter is the disease of American writing," says Zinsser. How can a book on writing be this much fun to read?

Proposals

Most books on proposal writing are written by nonwriters. They are tightly focused on specific kinds of proposals—for government, for business, and so on. Here are titles with something of value to anyone who writes any kind of fund-raising proposal.

Geever, Jane C., and Patricia McNeill. *The Foundation Center's Guide to Proposal Writing.* New York: Foundation Center. 1993. A fund-raising consultant's step-by-step manual on writing the proposal.

Gooch, Judith Mirick. *Writing Winning Proposals.* Washington, DC: Council for Advancement and Support of Education. 1987. A lucid explanation of how to write proposals aimed at foundations and corporations. Includes a good section on creating a complex program budget.

Robinson, Andy. *Grassroots Grants: An Activist's Guide to Proposal Writing.* Berkeley, CA: Chardon Press. 1996. The best of all the books we've seen on writing proposals to foundations. Sympathetic, sound advice written for social-change organizations but helpful for everyone.

ORGANIZATIONS

These are key national organizations that serve the needs of fund raisers. Each has resources of use to writers. The membership groups offer some services and discounts to members only; check to see whether your nonprofit belongs or whether you can participate as a nonmember.

Association for Healthcare Philanthropy (AHP), 313 Park Avenue, Suite 400, Falls Church, VA 22046; (703) 532-6243; *www.ahp@go-ahp.org*. Created in 1967, AHP is a professional group consisting of more than 2,700 fund raisers from hospitals and health-care organizations. Its wide-ranging education and publications programs are tailored to the health field.

Council for Advancement and Support of Education (CASE), 1307 New York Avenue NW, Suite 1000, Washington, DC 20005; (202) 328-2273; *www.case.org*. CASE's more than 26,000 members work in advancement—alumni relations, communications, and fund raising—at educational institutions, mainly colleges and universities. Since colleges are the major players in fund raising, CASE's resources are considerable; they range from educational and publishing programs to reports and updates on current issues—all centered on education.

The Foundation Center, 79 Fifth Avenue, New York, NY 10003 (national headquarters); (212) 620-4230; *www.fdncenter.org*. The Foundation Center has served as a clearinghouse for information on foundations and related subjects since 1956. Its offices in five cities (see Web site) have libraries—open to the public—with directories, books, and periodicals on grantmaking, philanthropy, and the nonprofit sector.

The Grantsmanship Center, 1125 W. Sixth Street, Fifth Floor, P.O. Box 17220, Los Angeles, CA 90017; (213) 482-9860; *www.tgci.com*. Noted for its workshops and materials on proposal writing, the Grantsmanship Center was founded in 1972 to offer training and publications to nonprofit groups and government agencies.

National Society of Fund Raising Executives (NSFRE), 1101 King Street, Suite 700, Alexandria, VA 22314; (703) 684-0410; *www.nsfre.org*. Founded in 1960, the NSFRE serves the broad professional needs of fund-raising executives who work for all types of nonprofits. The group has more than 10,000 members in 100 chapters across the country, publishes a journal, and offers many courses. Its chapter meetings are occasions for networking. Its library in Alexandria is a treasure trove of the field.

PERIODICALS: FUND RAISING AND NONPROFITS

These are selected trade publications with news, features, trends, and how-to from the worlds of philanthropy and the nonprofit sector.

Advancing Philanthropy
Journal of the National Society of Fund Raising Executives
1101 King Street
Suite 700
Alexandria, VA 22314
(800) 666-3863
www.nsfre.org

The Chronicle of Philanthropy
1255 23rd Street, N.W.
Washington, DC 20037
(202) 466-1200
www.philanthropy.com

The Chronicle of Higher Education
1255 23rd Street, N.W.
Washington, DC 20037
(202) 466-1000
www.chronicle.com

Currents
Magazine of the Council for the Advancement and Support of Education
1307 New York Avenue, N.W.
Suite 1000
Washington, DC 20005-4701
(202) 328-2273
www.case.org

Fund Raising Management
224 Seventh Street

Garden City, NY 11530
(800) 229-6700

The NonProfit Times
240 Cedar Knolls Road
Suite 318
Cedar Knolls, NJ 07927
(973) 734-1700
www.nptimes.com

Philanthropy Journal Online
Philanthropy News Network
5 West Hargett Street
Suite 805
Raleigh, NC 27601
(919) 832-2325
www.pj.org

A Glossary of Design and Printing Terms

DESIGN TERMS

It can be tough when you are trying to describe over the telephone what you want changed in a newsletter design. What the heck is that thing called? Here are some of the common terms you will run across:

Banner or Nameplate: The name of your newsletter and any design that goes with it. This tends to be located at the top of the first page.

Bleed: Artwork that goes right to the edge of the page. Most magazine covers are full bleeds: the photograph or image goes to the edge of the page on all four sides. Bleeds increase the cost of your newsletter because a printing press always leaves a little bit of white space at the edge of the page. To get the bleed effect, the printer prints on a larger piece of paper and trims the white edges off.

Crop: To cut off a portion of a photograph. Designers often crop photographs to make them look better.

Gutter: The white space between two facing pages in a newsletter or between columns on the same page.

Heads: Short for headlines and subheads.

Initial Cap or Drop Cap: An initial cap is the first letter of a line set in larger type than the rest of the letters. A drop cap is also set in larger type, but the character begins at the same height as the rest of the line and drops below it (often alongside a couple of lines below).

Jump or Jump Line: When an article continues from one page onto another, it is a jump. A jump line informs the reader that the story is continued on page 3 (or on page 3, the jump line says, "Continued from page 1").

Justification: The alignment of your text. Left-justified type means that the first letter of each line is aligned directly below the first letter in the line above it (but the right side will be ragged, or not aligned). Full justification means both sides of the column are perfectly straight. The first letter and last letter in each line are aligned with all the other lines.

Kerning: The amount of space between individual characters.

Leading: The amount of space between lines of type.

Masthead: The small box or column where you give the name of the editor and publisher of your newsletter and any additional information, such as your organization's mission, address, and statement of tax exemption.

Pull-quote: A quote that is set in large type in a box or sidebar. The pull-quote serves as a design element and helps draw the reader into the story. Usually the pull-quote is taken directly from the text of the story, although it may be edited down for ease of reading.

Reverse: White characters printed on a solid dark background.

Rule: A line between sections, columns, etc.

Scan: To turn a photograph into information readable by computer programs. If you scan a photo, you can then electronically paste it into your newsletter.

Sink: White space at the top of a page.

TIFF, EPS, BMP, JPEG, etc.: Extensions that refer to different computer-file formats that can contain graphics.

Tint Block: A tinted screen behind a boxed item.

Up Style or Down Style: The manner in which headlines are capitalized. An Up Style Capitalizes All the Major Words in a Headline. A down style capitalizes only the first word and proper nouns, like London and Russian.

PRINTING TERMS

And you thought talking to designers was bad; just wait until you get a load of what's coming out of the printer's mouth. The glossary below will get you through the basics. If you're looking for more, go to the Web sites of printing companies for helpful tips and glossaries. We got help with this glossary from Balmar, Inc., which maintains an impressive glossary on its Web site (*www.balmar.com*; go to the resource room).

20 lb., 24 lb.: These refer to the weight of a paper stock. Standard photocopy paper is 20 lb. If you are printing in color, a 20-lb. page might not be opaque enough to hide the color on the page behind it. In that case, you might shift up to a 24-lb. paper, which is slightly more opaque.

Blueline: A photographic proof made before you go to press so that you can check and make sure all the photos are where they should be, all the type is correct, and no dead flies are in the middle of the president's message. It is called a blueline because all colors appear as a blue image on white paper.

Camera-ready: A page, photograph, or artwork that is ready for the printer to take a picture of and thereby create a negative that will be used to print the final product. If someone asks you whether the artwork is camera-ready, she wants to know if it is absolutely final and cleanly printed so that a good negative can be made.

Coated stock: Paper with a surface coating, which can vary from matte to glossy. The coating helps make colors stand out to the eye.

Folds: This term refers to how you will fold the paper. There are all kinds of folds to choose from: four-panel single fold (that would be a piece of paper folded in half so that there are four panels), six-panel letter fold, eight-panel gate fold, and so on. Ask your printer what these will look like or go to *www.balmar.com*'s resource room to find a folding glossary.

Four-color: Anything printed in full color. It is called four-color because printers create all colors by mixing four basic colors: yellow, red, blue, and black. Four-color printing costs more because the printer has to lay down each color separately, exactly on top of the last one. It takes time and skill.

Halftone: This term is often a shorthand way to refer to photographs that will be printed. The printer will convert the photo you give him (which consists of continuous tones) into a series of dots. Thus, the halftone.

Matte stock: A coated paper that has a dull finish to it—not glossy like magazine paper.

Offset printing: In the old days, you put the little metal letters into the printing press, loaded it up with ink, and then pressed the letters directly onto the paper. Today offset printing uses an intermediate cylinder, so the image goes from the letters (or, more correctly, the image carrier) to the intermediate cylinder, and then the cylinder transfers the image to the paper.

PMS (Pantone Color Matching): This is a color-matching standard used to consistently create any color you want. If you tell a printer to use PMS 348 as your green accent color, you will get exactly that color. (There are other color-matching standards, so make sure you and your printer are talking about the same one.)

Saddle stitch: A way of binding sheets together by stapling them where they fold at the spine. Think of a magazine held together by staples instead of glue; that's saddle stitching.

Screen: An area where the printer uses just a percentage of the full color. A 10 percent screen of Kelly green appears as a very light green. A 50 percent screen of red looks pink.

Two-color: Anything printed in black and one accent color. Usually the type is black, and the design elements—shading, lines, dingbats—are colored.

INDEX

ABOUT THE AUTHORS

Joseph Barbato is president of Barbato Associates, a consulting firm that gives distinctive voice to the achievements and programs of nonprofit clients. His company provides writing, design, and printing services. Since 1979 he has managed editorial projects for clients ranging from colleges, hospitals, and community agencies to the Special Olympics and the United Nations Foundation.

A native New Yorker, Barbato earned B.A. and M.A. degrees at New York University, where he worked for more than 10 years as a writer, editor, and communications director. He has also been a public-information director at the City University of New York and an editorial director at The Nature Conservancy. He was a founder and editor of the *Remington Review*, a little magazine, and directed publicity for the New York Book Fair (1974–87), an annual event that won new recognition for small presses in American publishing.

Barbato is also a contributing editor of *Publishers Weekly* and has written for publications from *Smithsonian* and the *Progressive* to the *New York Times* and *Washington Post Book World*. He is coauthor/editor of several books, including *You Are What You Drink*, a report on alcohol and health, and the literary anthologies *Heart of the Land* and *Patchwork of Dreams*. He is a member of the National Book Critics Circle.

He and his wife, Dusty, a high school teacher, live in Alexandria, Virginia and have two children. He can be reached at his E-mail address: *jabarbato@aol.com*.

Danielle S. Furlich is an independent writer and consultant. A native of New Hampshire, she earned her B.A. in English and creative writing at Dartmouth College, where she taught writing to first-year students. She has produced a wide range of fund-raising materials as a writer and editor at both the Wilderness Society and The Nature Conservancy and served as director of development communications at the National Trust for Historic Preservation in Washington, DC.

Furlich has worked closely with Barbato for many years and continues to do so. She writes proposals, case statements, newsletters, and other fund-raising pieces for good causes ranging from George Washington University to Children's Express. She also creates Web-site and marketing materials for business clients.

She and her husband, Brandon, live in northern Virginia with two cats, both of which closely supervised the writing of this book. She can be reached at her E-mail address: *dsfurlich@mindspring.com*.

For examples of fund-raising materials, visit the authors' Web site: *www.writingforagoodcause.com*